ASIAN CHALLENGE

John Andrews

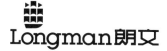

Longman 朗文

© John Charles Andrews 1991
First published 1991

Published by
Longman Group (Far East) Ltd
18/F, Cornwall House
Tong Chong Street
Quarry Bay
Hong Kong
and associated companies throughout the world

ISBN 962 359 580 8

Printed in Hong Kong

To Hilary, my wife and greatest support

About the Author

John Andrews was born in England in 1946 and read classical and modern Arabic at Cambridge. After teaching at the University of Libya and the American University of Beirut, he became a journalist in Lebanon in 1973. Until 1976 he worked for NBC News in the Middle East and then spent six years in London on *The Guardian*, the last three as energy correspondent. He joined *The Economist* in 1982 as industrial editor before being posted to Asia in 1986, first in Singapore and then in Hong Kong. In May 1991 he returned to London to be *The Economist*'s Asia editor. He is married, with one grown-up son.

Preface

To quote the American wit, Wilson Mizner, 'When you steal from one author, it's plagiarism; if you steal from many, it's research.' This book bears my name but has more ancestors than I can easily acknowledge. Its conception came during a bibulous lunch in Hong Kong with Longman's Lesley Pausey and Stephen Troth. Why not write a book about Asia? Why not write a snappy and controversial book — Stephen had just been enthused by John Naisbitt's and Patricia Aburdene's *Megatrends 2000* — about Asia's future? Why not, indeed? We shook hands, drained our glasses, and staggered off to reality.

The consequence of that lunch is not the brand of futurology Stephen had in mind. On reflection, I realised that Asia's present is almost as unknown to most people as its future. Most of us assume that Asia will soon be the world's most important continent — if it is not already. We point to the economic might of Japan, the huge populations of China and India; and some muse sadly (if, perhaps, prematurely) at the relative decline of the West. Yet our knowledge of Asia is remarkably limited. How many educated adults can name Asia's leaders and political systems, or appreciate the challenges they face? Or even spot Asia's countries on the map (I once received a letter from a French bank addressed to me in 'Hong Kong, Japon', and a letter from England reached me in 'Singapore, China')? The truth is that in any country we learn about ourselves before we learn about others, so why should an American know about Malaysia, or a Japanese about India?

Add this general ignorance of Asia to the obvious fact that the unknown can be predicted only on the basis of the known, and the result is this book: an attempt to inform the intelligent layman without insulting the expert. The attempt, as explained in Chapter 10, does not embrace the geographical definition of Asia; nor does it delve far into Asia's past. Instead, it seeks to analyse present trends in an arc that sweeps from the Indian subcontinent to the coastline of the Pacific, and then to discern how those trends will develop over the next decade — a time-span imminent enough to be useful.

That, of course, is more easily said than done. Clearly some countries are more 'important' than others (Laos, for example, is fascinating to anthropologists but, compared with Japan, is of underwhelming interest to bankers, businessmen, politicians, and military strategists). It is equally clear that what is significant in one country is not necessarily so in another: achieving literacy is a daunting challenge in India but is taken for granted in the Philippines. This book's chapters, therefore, go from issue to issue, not from country to country. Each chapter begins with a few lines to show how an issue could — and I deliberately do not say 'will' — develop; the rest of the chapter is meant to show why and how such developments may happen.

If I have failed, the blame is, of course, mine. But, if I have succeeded, I should not forget the wise words of Mr Mizner (he also said, 'Be nice to people on your way up, because you'll meet 'em on your way down.'). I wrote this book towards the end of five years in Asia, first as *The Economist*'s South-east Asia correspondent, based in Singapore, and then as the China correspondent based in Hong Kong. I had visited the Asia covered by this book several times before, beginning with a trip to Pakistan in 1973. But to reside is more revealing than to visit, and I am grateful to *The Economist*'s editor, Rupert Pennant-Rea, for agreeing (with customary good humour) to prolong my stay away from London beyond the normal three years' escape from British taxation.

My greatest debt as an author, however, is owed to my fellow journalists. We all read each other and learn from each other — which makes it hard to apportion credit fairly. I would, however, have learned remarkably little were it not for the excellent journalists of the *Far Eastern Economic Review* (who are lucky to have as their librarian the charming and resourceful Jan Bradley). Similar thanks are due to *Asiaweek* and to several colleagues on *The Economist*, especially Bill Emmott (author of the prescient *The Sun Also Sets*), Paul Maidment, Nick Valery, Chris Wood, and Jim Rohwer (my predecessor as Asia Editor in London).

Most of the Asian proverbs I quote are shamelessly borrowed from the entertaining and erudite *The Dragon's Almanac*, by Justin Wintle (published by Graham Brash, Singapore). Most of the figures come from the World Bank, the Asian Development Bank, or government institutions (money, unless otherwise stated, is in American dollars and my billions are American ones — ie, a billion is 1,000 million). That does not, of course, guarantee their accuracy; statistics can be dubious everywhere, especially in Asia's developing nations. But they are the best available. Daniel Burstein's *Yen!* (Ballantine Books) was a very useful source on the tensions attending America's relations with Japan, as was Tokyo's International Institute for

Global Peace. Ranjan Pal was unfailingly willing to provide insights into India's politics and economics (and thereby prove himself to be a better economist than squash player!). Morale-boosting encouragement flowed freely from my wife; from my editor, Hope Steele; from all at Longman, especially Lesley Pausey and her successor, Kim Silver; and from the many good people who have become my friends in the past five years. I am grateful.

London
May 1991

Contents

Map of Asia featuring the countries mentioned in *The Asian Challenge*

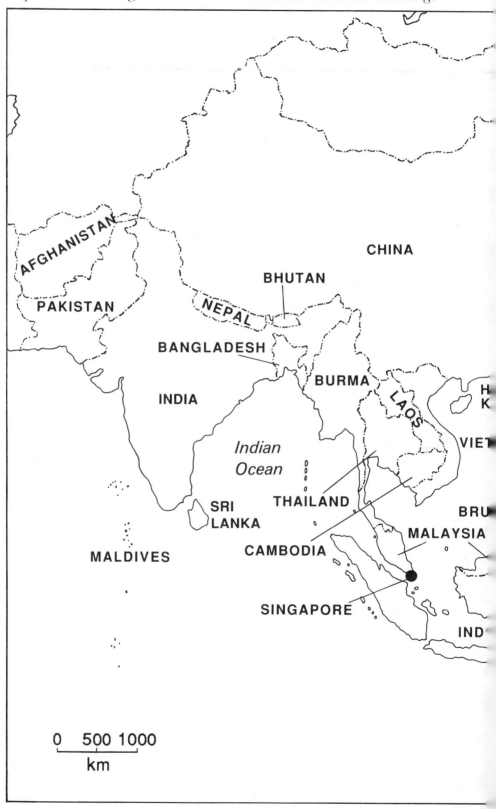

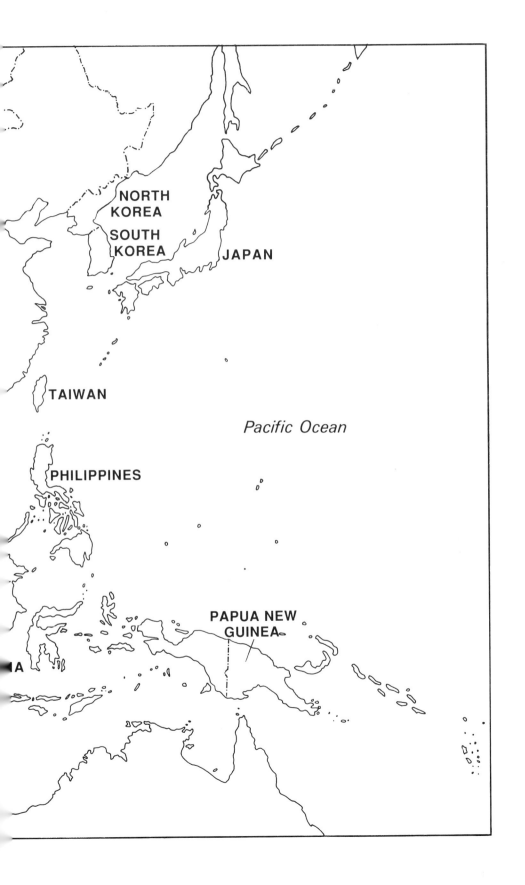

AFGHANISTAN

Population 18 million/per capita GNP $150/communist republic

Straddling the high mountains between the Soviet Union and the Indian subcontinent, Afghanistan was invaded twice by Britain in the 19th century to stop the encroaching Russian empire. Its independence was recognised by Britain and Russia in 1921. King Zahir Shah was ousted in 1973 and a left-wing republic proclaimed under General Muhammad Daud. In 1978 a pro-Moscow military coup led to chaos and a succession of leaders. At the end of 1979, Soviet forces invaded, supposedly in support of Hafizullah Amin, who was killed and replaced by the pro-Soviet Babrak Karmal. The Soviet troops were then harried by the *mujahideen* guerrillas, Muslim tribesmen supported by American arms and money. The Soviet troops eventually withdrew in 1988–89, leaving Major-General Najibullah, leader since 1986, to survive as best he could in a continuing civil war.

BANGLADESH

Population 115 million/per capita GNP $180/republic

Formed from the bloody civil war in Pakistan in 1971, Bangladesh — formerly East Pakistan — has known only poverty and unstable politics. Its first leader was Sheikh Mujibur Rahman. His Awami League had won enough votes in the Pakistan elections of December 1970 that Sheikh Mujib should have become the prime minister of all Pakistan. But he refused to abandon his demand for regional autonomy, hence the civil war which, with India's help, led to East Pakistan's succession. In 1973 Mujib abandoned parliamentary democracy in favour of one-party presidential rule. He was assassinated in a military coup in 1975. After two years of instability, Major-General Ziaur Rahman took power until he, too, was assassinated in 1981. He was succeeded by Abdus Sattar, who was soon deposed — this time in a bloodless coup — by

Lieutenant-General Hossain Mohammad Ershad in 1982. Ershad was forced to resign, and was then arrested, in February 1991, when free elections brought to power Ziaur Rahman's widow, Begum Khalida Zia. At least as harmful as the country's political problems is its exposure to flooding during the cyclone season. In April 1991, tidal waves and storm-swollen rivers killed more than 100,000 people. Discussions with India on flood-control schemes have consistently been dogged by mutual mistrust.

BHUTAN

Population 1.5 million/per capita GNP $190/constitutional monarchy

A landlocked Buddhist kingdom in the eastern Himalayas, Bhutan signed treaties with British India in 1774, 1865, and 1910. Their effect, confirmed in a 1949 treaty with independent India, was internal autonomy for Bhutan but subservience in foreign policy to India. The country relies on aid from India and other foreign donors; most of its people live by subsistence farming. The rule of King Jigme Singye Wangchuck, head of state and government since 1972, has recently been marked by ethnic resentment between the Bhutanese in north of the country and Nepali immigrants in the south. In 1989, when the King emphasised the 'preservation and promotion of the national identity', Bhutan's schools stopped teaching Nepali as an optional language.

BRUNEI

Population 200,000/per capita GNP $17,000/absolute monarchy

The tiny sultanate, split into two enclaves on the north coast of Borneo, is all that remains of a Malay empire that once stretched as far as the Philippines. Britain made Brunei a protectorate in 1888 and in 1906 posted a resident to govern the state. Internal self-government came in 1959, and the British assumed Brunei would want to join the Malaysian federation on its formation in 1963. However, Sultan Sir Omar Ali Saifuddin decided to keep Brunei separate lest the federation take the revenues from the growing oil and gas production (oil was first found by Shell in 1929). The year before, the country's first election had been won by a socialist party on an anti-Malaysia and anti-British platform. The Sultan, however, refused to let the party take power and used British troops to put down a rebellion. After full independence on 1 January 1984, Sultan Hassanal Bolkiah — reputed to be the richest man in the world because of Brunei's petroleum revenues — maintained the tradition of his father's autocratic rule, softened by a cradle-to-grave welfare state. Political parties were banned in 1988. In any case, government employees, two-thirds of the work force, were always banned from political activity. The small business community is dominated by Chinese, who find it very hard to acquire citizenship, not least because the Sultan in 1990 began promoting the concept of Melayu Islam Beraja, or 'Malay Muslim Monarchy'.

Rangoon

BURMA

Population 42 million/per capita GNP $280/military-run republic

Blessed with the resources of rice, teak, and gems, Burma was annexed by Britain and made a province of British India in 1895. However, after a series of peasant revolts in the 1930s, Britain gave Burma self-government — only to see it occupied by Japan during World War II. In 1945 the Union of Burma declared itself an independent republic outside the British Commonwealth. But the country's parliamentary democracy under Prime Minister U Nu was ended in 1962 by a military coup led by General Ne Win. By the start of the 1990s his 'Burmese Way to Socialism' had made Burma (which in 1990 renamed itself Myanmar) one of the poorest, most isolated, and most corrupt countries in the world. In 1988, amid mounting protest at one-party rule by the Burma Socialist Programme Party, Ne Win, the party's chairman, officially retired (although he was believed to wield dictatorial power from behind the scenes). A general election held on 27 May 1990 brought a landslide victory for the opposition National League for Democracy. The military ignored the result, refused to allow parliament to convene, and imprisoned virtually all NLD leaders. Meanwhile, insurrections by Burma's ethnic minorities continued to defy the regime.

CAMBODIA

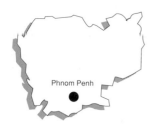

Population 8 million/per capita GNP $110/republic

The former centre of the large Angkor empire, Cambodia by the 18th century had become a buffer state wedged between Thailand and Vietnam. In 1864, the country became a French protectorate, a status that lasted until the 'gentle kingdom' was given independence in 1953. In 1955 King Norodom Sihanouk abdicated in order to enter politics. His efforts to keep Cambodia immune from the war in Vietnam and Laos in the late 1960s ultimately failed: in 1970 he was ousted by the coup of the pro-American Marshall Lon Nol. Sihanouk (now called 'Prince') then formed an alliance with the communist Khmers Rouges, led by Pol Pot. In April 1975, the Khmers Rouges captured the Cambodian capital, Phnom Penh. Their rule, in which Sihanouk was kept a virtual prisoner, was a nightmare of extremism: in an attempt to form a new agrarian society, the cities were emptied of their people; about a million of the 6–7 million Cambodians died of hunger, disease, overwork, or torture. In December 1978, Vietnam invaded and installed Heng Samrin as head of a government of Khmer Rouge defectors and pro-Vietnamese communists. This led to protracted civil war, with Sihanouk as the nominal head of a resistance coalition of the China-backed Khmers Rouges and two non-communist groups. In September 1989, Vietnam announced the withdrawal of its troops. The following year, the United Nations withdrew recognition of the resistance as the legal representative of Cambodia in favour of a Supreme National Council charged with reaching a settlement. The council was headed by Sihanouk and formed from the government in Phnom Penh and the three resistance groups.

CHINA

Population 1.1 billion/per capita GNP $325/communist republic

Home to a fifth of the world's people, China traces its history back for at least 4,000 years and lays claim to possessing the world's oldest continuous civilisation. This heritage shows in a sense of cultural superiority and of China as the 'Middle Kingdom', surrounded by barbarians and placed between heaven and earth. In fact, China's civilisation has had to endure constant episodes of instability. In 1912 Sun Yat-sen's Kuomintang (Nationalist) forces swept away the Qing dynasty and established a republic. But the republic was prey to corruption and unrest among regional warlords. The Kuomintang and their military commander, Chiang Kai-shek, were weakened by the effort of fighting both the Japanese invaders in the 1930s and the communists of Mao Zedong. Eventually, the Maoists were victorious and on 1 October 1949 declared the 'People's Republic of China'. Mao's rule was marred by the disastrous economic policy of the Great Leap Forward (which led to famine) at the end of the 1950s, and by the Cultural Revolution begun in 1976, which destroyed all education for another decade. After Mao's death in 1976, Deng Xiaoping emerged as China's leader. His economic reforms moved China away from Marxist dogma and multiplied incomes, first in the countryside and then the cities. The image of the Deng era, however, was tarnished when the regime ruthlessly repressed pro-democracy demonstrations in the heart of Beijing in 1989.

HONG KONG

Population 5.9 million/per capita GNP $12,000/British colony

Acquired from China between 1841 and 1898 by imperial Britain, Hong Kong will revert to China's sovereignty in 1997. This transfer was agreed in a Sino-British Joint Declaration of 1984, with the British conceding that when the 99-year lease on the New Territories expired in 1997, the rest of Hong Kong, which had been given to Britain in perpetuity, would no longer be economically viable if separate from China. Under British rule Hong Kong became the world's 13th biggest trader and the richest part of Asia apart from Brunei and Japan. Most of this miracle occurred after mainland China fell to the communists in 1949. Hong Kong was flooded with refugees: their cheap labour and entrepreneurial skills, flourishing under the laissez-faire policies of an efficient British administration, made the colony a world leader in textiles and light manufacturing. Since the 1980s and the 'open door' economic policy of China, Hong Kong has increasingly become an entrepôt for China. The two economies are now inextricably entwined, but few Hong Kong Chinese (who comprise 98 per cent of the population) relish the 1997 transfer. In theory, they have nothing to fear: the Joint Declaration says that Hong Kong will become a 'Special Administrative Region' of China, with its pre-1997 practices and life-style unchanged for 50 years.

INDIA

Population 843 million/per capita GNP $350/federal republic

The world's largest democracy, India achieved independence in 1947 after almost two centuries under the British Raj (first under the control of the East India Company, and from 1870 as part of the British Empire). Secular by constitution, the Hindu-dominated country is nonetheless racked by sectarianism — from Sikh militancy to Hindu chauvinism — and by secessionist movements in some of its 25 states, especially Punjab and Assam. Sikh extremists assassinated Prime Minister Indira Gandhi (the daughter of the country's first prime minister, Jawaharlal Nehru) in 1984. Mrs Gandhi's era was marred by questionable economic radicalism and political factionalism, which led to a state of emergency in 1975. She was then defeated in the 1977 elections by the Janata party, but returned to power in 1979. Mrs Gandhi's successor as prime minister and leader of the Congress Party was her son Rajiv. He was ousted in the elections of 1989, but remained the most powerful single politician until he, too, was assassinated in May 1991.

INDONESIA

Population 185 million/per capita GNP $550/ republic

The roots of Indonesia grow from the Indian-influenced Hindu and Buddhist kingdoms that formed in Sumatra and Java from the 7th century, and then from the impact — from the 14th century onwards — of Islam (Indonesia is now the world's largest Muslim country). Later came the Portuguese colonialism of the 16th century and finally the colonialism of the Dutch, who in the 19th century conquered most of what is now Indonesia. During the Japanese occupation, from 1942 to 1945, Indonesian nationalists, led by Sukarno, organised themselves for independence. This was declared in 1945, but did not become a reality until the Dutch left in 1949. Sukarno pursued a policy of non-alignment. As the economy deteriorated, foreign adventurism became a useful distraction, hence a period of 'confrontation' with Malaysia in the early 1960s and the annexing of Dutch-held West New Guinea to become Irian Jaya in 1963. In 1965 a coup, supposedly inspired by the communists, was savagely defeated; in its aftermath Sukarno, suspected of being pro-communist, became a figurehead until he was formally succeeded as president by General Suharto in 1968. Suharto's 'New Order' regime gives a leading role to the military and, through the concept of *Pancasila* (belief in God, national unity, democracy, justice, and humanitarianism), insists on consensus at the expense of adversarial debate. Indonesia has immense natural resources, from rubber to petroleum; its weakness is its ethnic diversity, spread through an archipelago of more than 13,000 islands. Among the islands is the former Portuguese territory of East Timor, whose disputed annexation took place in 1976.

JAPAN

Population 124 million/per capita GNP $23,500/ constitutional monarchy

The world's most successful industrial nation was for 200 years or more a remote mountainous land, keeping itself in deliberate isolation. This changed in the middle of the 19th century when America's Commodore Perry began the pressure that forced Japan to re-open its markets to international trade. By the turn of the century Japan had become a modern power able to defeat tsarist Russia, conquer China, and annex Taiwan and Korea. This power was spurned by the Western powers at the Versailles peace treaty following World War I, a snub that helped fascist militarists become dominant in Japan. They saw expansion abroad as the cure for domestic economic depression, hence the invasion of China and South-east Asia and, in 1941, the attack on Pearl Harbor, Hawaii. Japan's modern miracle is to have built a rich economy despite the atom bombs dropped on Hiroshima and Nagasaki in 1945. Part of the reason was the measures introduced by the American victors: land distribution, the breaking up of monopolies, and the installation of a multi-party democracy (the emperor remained, but without power). Another part was Japan's social cohesion and discipline. These have helped the Liberal Democratic Party rule since 1948, despite periodic scandals. The economy has naturally benefited from the political stability. The paradox is that despite its economic power overseas, Japan remains politically timid in foreign affairs. This, however, will change.

LAOS

Population 4.2 million/per capita GNP $180/communist republic

Landlocked Laos, once known as the Kingdom of a Thousand Elephants, emerged as a separate country in 1353. But it soon became a vassal state of its Vietnamese and Thai neighbours until, in the 1890s, it became a French protectorate. After the French granted independence in 1953, Laos endured two decades of civil war between the American-backed Royal Lao Government and the communist Pathet Lao. Eventually, just as in adjacent Vietnam and Cambodia, the communists were victorious, establishing the People's Democratic Republic of Laos in 1975 with the 'Red Prince' Souphanouvong as president and with Vietnamese soldiers and advisers installed in all key areas. Although communism brought stability, it did not bring prosperity. Some 85% of the population live from subsistence farming. As in neighbouring Burma, parts of the country are devoted to opium-growing, outside the control of the authorities in Vientiane.

MALAYSIA

Population 18 million/per capita GNP $2,300/ constitutional monarchy

Blessed with natural resources ranging from rubber to oil, Malaysia is a federation of 11 states on the Malayan Peninsula and Sabah and Sarawak on the island of Borneo. The peninsular states came under British influence in the late 18th century, and under British rule a century later. From 1840 until the Japanese occupation in 1942, Sarawak was ruled by the 'white rajas' of the Brooke family; from 1882 until the arrival of the Japanese, Sabah was ruled by the rubber producer, the British North Borneo Company. In 1957, Malaya (the peninsular states) became independent within the British Commonwealth; the Federation of Malaysia, including Singapore, Sabah, and Sarawak, was formed in 1963. Two years later, Singapore, most of whose people are Chinese, was forced to leave lest it challenge the principle of Malay dominance (the king is elected for a five-year period from the hereditary sultans of nine peninsular states). The Malays now make up half of the Malaysian population; Chinese, imported by the British, make up about a third; most of the rest are Indians, also imported by the

British. The result is an uneasy racial co-existence which, in 1969, broke into serious riots. Nonetheless, since defeating a communist insurgency in the 1950s, Malaysia has prospered economically, especially during the 1980s, which were dominated by Prime Minister Dr Mahathir Mohamad.

MALDIVES

Population 200,000/per capita GNP $470/republic

A chain of atolls lying south of India, the Maldives depends for its livelihood on fishing, shipping, and — increasingly — tourism. The Sunni Muslim country was a protectorate of Britain from 1887 until independence in 1965. Rule by traditional Muslim sultans has given way to an executive presidency, elected by a citizens' council. Each atoll, however, has considerable autonomy and there are no political parties. In 1988 India sent troops to defeat a coup against President Maumoon Abdul Gayoom mounted by a group of Maldivians and Sri Lankans.

NEPAL

Population 19 million/per capita GNP $170/ constitutional monarchy

The Hindu kingdom in the Himalayas — it ranges from Mount Everest down to a fertile plain on its southern border — is one of the world's poorest countries, depending for its livelihood on foreign aid, foreign tourism, and economic access to India. Until 1951, when King Tribhuvan was returned to power, the country was effectively ruled for a century by a family of hereditary prime ministers, in close co-operation with the British in India. In 1960, Tribhuvan's son, King Mahendra, abolished parliamentary government and instigated his personal rule backed by the non-party Panchayat assembly. In the 1970s and '80s his son, the Western-educated King Birendra, came under increasing pressure to allow more democracy. After violent demonstrations in 1990 in which 500 died, the king agreed to a constitutional monarchy and multi-party parliament.

NORTH KOREA

Population 21 million/per capita GNP $1,100 approx/ communist republic

Since the end of Japanese occupation in 1945 and the declaration of the Democratic People's Republic of Korea in September 1948, the country has been domi-
nated by Kim Il Sung. Formerly a resistance fighter against the Japanese, President Kim inherited the industrialised North and the economy should, therefore, have outpaced the agrarian South once World War II ended. In practice, Kim wasted the North's initial advantage by imposing a regime of unreconstructed Stalinism combined with an awesome personality cult embracing both him and his son, Kim Jong Il. Further waste came through spending on the military, which is thought to absorb about a quarter of GNP. Exports were virtually impossible to the non-communist world because North Korea had defaulted on its foreign debt. Until the late 1980s, Kim was able to play his two allies — China and the Soviet Union — against each other. Following the Sino-Soviet reconciliation of 1989, this was no longer possible — and both China and the Soviet Union then made plain their intention to build relationships with the South. At the start of the 1990s North Korea and Japan made tentative contact. In May 1991, the North announced that it would apply for United Nations membership separately from the South.

PAKISTAN

Population 115 million/per capita GNP $365/federal republic

Created by the 1947 partition of British India into Muslim and Hindu areas. Muslim Pakistan originally had two, widely separated, parts. Govern-
ments changed by military coup until December 1970, when Zulfikar Ali Bhutto's Pakistan People's Party won the first free elections in West Pakistan while Mujibur Rahman's Awami League won in the east. In 1971 East Pakistan seceded, after a civil war in which it was backed by India, and emerged as independent Bangladesh. The Bhutto era, marred by corruption and regional tension, ended in 1977 with a coup by General Zia-ul Haq. Bhutto was controversially convicted of murder and hanged. Zia, who enforced many Islamic strictures, died in 1988 in a

mysterious air crash. In subsequent elections the country returned to civilian rule under Bhutto's daughter, Benazir. She failed to win military support and was ousted by presidential decree in August 1900; elections in October brought to power a coalition led by Nawaz Sharif.

PAPUA NEW GUINEA

Population 3.7 million/per capita GNP $980/ parliamentary monarchy

Much of the eastern half of the giant island of New Guinea (the western half is Indonesia's province of Irian Jaya) is still in the Stone Age, divided by myriad tribes and languages and unaffected by the influence of German, British, and Japanese colonial masters in the century up to World War II. From 1949 until the granting of self-government in December 1973, the country was administered by Australia. In 1975, Papua New Guinea became an independent nation within the British Commonwealth, with Queen Elizabeth as head of state and represented by a governor-general. Until 1980 Michael Somare, of the Pangu Party, was prime minister; since then an election roller-coaster has brought in various prime ministers, including Somare. The country possesses valuable reserves of copper and other minerals, but is challenged by separatist movements (especially on the racially different island of Bougainville), tribal fighting, corruption, and by the difficulty of distributing mineral revenues to a population in which only 20% or so of the work-force has formal employment.

THE PHILIPPINES

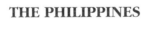

Population 62 million/per capita GNP $730/republic

Discovered by Ferdinand Magellan in 1521, the archipelago of the Philippines became part of Spain's empire in 1565. One lasting consequence is that the Philippines is Asia's only Roman Catholic nation; its culture and its people are a mix of Malay, Chinese, and Spanish that has little in common with neighbouring Asian countries. The Philippines became independent from Spain in 1898 but two years later was taken over by the Americans, to whom the country had been ceded by

Spain at the end of the Spanish-American war. After the Japanese occupation from 1941 to 1945, the Philippines was granted independence by the USA in 1946. America, for which most Filipinos have a strong affection, helped crush the communist Hukbalahap rebellion of the 1940s and '50s, but during the 1970s and '80s the Philippines experienced another, unresolved, communist insurrection and a Muslim struggle for autonomy in the southern islands. Under Ferdinand Marcos, president from 1965 to 1986, the resource-rich country moved from prosperity to poverty, not least because of the corrupt practices of the president and his cronies. The assassination in 1983 of Marcos's chief opponent, Benigno Aquino, as he returned from exile, began the downfall of Marcos. In early 1986, parts of the army combined with a massive demonstration of 'people power' in the streets of Manila to drive him to flight. This led to the restoration of democracy under President Corazon Aquino, Benigno's widow — but not to a sustained economic revival. Disaffected units of the armed forces several times attempted to overthrow her.

SINGAPORE

Population 2.7 million/per capita GNP $11,500/republic

Britain's Sir Stamford Raffles in 1819 arrived in a small Malay fishing village midway on the sea-route from India to China, and so began the creation of modern Singapore. In 1832, the island of Singapore became the centre of government for the Straits Settlements, trading posts that stretched along the Malay peninsula. The British brought in Chinese (who now make up three-quarters of the population) and Indian workers to develop the island's prime advantage, its sheltered, deep-water port. In 1959, Singapore became internally self-governing and in 1963 it joined the new federation of Malaysia. Two years later, it was forced out of the federation and so became fully independent just as Britain was about to withdraw its economically vital naval base. Singapore reacted by investing in labour-intensive, export-oriented industrialisation, adding value to its role as the entrepôt for South-east Asia. Over the years, the labour-intensive industries have been replaced by knowledge-intensive ones, enabling Singaporeans to be among Asia's most materially advanced people. The credit is mainly due to Lee Kuan Yew, whose People's Action Party has governed strictly, but without corruption, ever since 1959. Lee stepped down as prime minister in November 1990 but remained as the 'Senior Minister' in the cabinet of Goh Chok Tong.

SOUTH KOREA

Population 43 million/per capita GNP $5,570/republic

After centuries as an independent kingdom, the Korean peninsula was annexed by Japan in 1910. After Japan's defeat in 1945 in World War II, Korea was divided into a Soviet zone in the North and an American one in the South. These became separate republics in 1948, with the South led by President Syngman Rhee. In June 1950 troops from the North invaded. A three-year war, with Chinese troops fighting for the North and United Nations troops, mainly American, fighting for the South, cost 500,000 lives and ended in stalemate. Subsequently the South prospered, helped by land reform and export-oriented industries — but at the cost of political repression. Rhee was toppled by student riots in 1960 and the country moved into a period of military dictatorship. In 1979, after seven years as president, Park Chung Hee was assassinated. There followed a year of relative liberalism under Choi Kyu Hah, before the emergence as dictator of General Chun Doo Hwan. Chun was persuaded to leave office in 1987, amid a wave of student riots, by his military classmate, Roh Tae Woo. In December 1987, in free elections, Roh became president. He then proceeded to make overtures to the South's traditional foes, the USSR, China, and the North. In 1990 he was rewarded by full diplomatic relations with the Soviet Union.

SRI LANKA

Population 17 million/per capita GNP $430/republic

Occupied since the 16th century by first the Portuguese, then the Dutch, and finally the British, the island of Ceylon — as Sri Lanka was known until 1972 — became independent in 1948. Violence has frequently scarred its politics. In 1959, prime Minister Solomon Bandaranaike of the Sri Lanka Freedom Party was assassinated by a Buddhist monk. He was succeeded by his wife, Sirimavo Badaranaike, who imposed harsh socialism after an uprising by young Sri Lankans in 1971. The consequent economic hardship led to a sweeping victory in the 1977 general election for the United National Party of Junius Jayewardene. He established an executive presidency and remained in power until his retirement in 1988. New elections for the presidency were narrowly won by

Ranasinghe Premadasa. Sri Lanka's democracy, however, has failed to prevent a sustained and bloody conflict between the Sinhalese, mainly Buddhist, majority and the mainly Hindu Tamils (who make up about 18% of the population). Various Tamil groups in the north of the island, often supported by the Tamils in southern India, have been fighting a civil war for a separate Tamil state since 1983. In the south of the island, Marxist Sinhalese have waged a terrorist campaign to prevent government concessions to the Tamils.

TAIWAN

Population 20.5 million/per capita GNP $8,000/republic

The island of Taiwan, which was ruled by Japan from 1894 to 1945, is the last redoubt of the Kuomintang (KMT) government forced to flee from the Chinese mainland in 1949 by Mao Zedong's communists. Officially, therefore, Taiwan is a province of the Republic of China, since the KMT claims to be the legal government for all of China. The technical state of war with the mainland remained until it was signed away by President Lee Teng-hui on 1 May 1991, thereby extending the political liberalisation begun by his predecessor, Chiang Ching-kuo, in 1987. Chiang, who died in 1988, had succeeded C.K. Yen as president in 1978. Yen had become president on the death of Chiang Ching-kuo's father, Generalissimo Chiang Kai-shek, in 1975. Lee is the first Taiwan-born and -bred president. This has helped calm the animosity some Taiwanese feel towards the mainlander-dominated KMT (when Chiang Kai-shek's 1.5 million soldiers arrived, some were appallingly brutal towards the 8 million Taiwanese). Another palliative is the enormous economic success Taiwan has enjoyed under the KMT. Although advocating Taiwan's independence from a united China is an act of sedition, full democracy at the end of the 1980s gave a voice to the opposition Democratic Progressive Party, many of whose members want independence. The issue, however, is hardly pressing, since political liberalisation has coincided with freedom for Taiwan's inhabitants to visit the mainland and with a huge growth in trade between Taiwan and China.

THAILAND

Population 57 million/per capita GNP $1,400/constitutional monarchy

Alone in South-east Asia, Thailand has never experienced colonial rule. After 1932, when the absolute power of the monarchy was abolished, Thailand was ruled (apart from a chaotic civilian period between 1945 and '48) by a succession of military strongmen, each seizing power by a coup d'état and each able to make acceptable accomodations with outside powers, be they British, French, Japanese, or American. Civilian democracy was instituted in 1973, but the military intervened again in 1977. The 1980s were a decade of relative political stability: the unelected prime minister, General Prem Tinsulanond, survived two coup attempts and oversaw a period of rapid economic growth in which an array of political parties gained ground. In July 1988, he resigned and was replaced by Chatichai Choonhavan, the first elected prime minister for 12 years. Chatichai, whose administration had become flagrantly corrupt, was ousted by a military coup in February 1991. The business world, however, seemed unconcerned by the armed forces' intervention.

VIETNAM

Population 67 million/per capita GNP $200/communist republic

More than any other country in Asia, Vietnam is marked by war. In the late 19th century, the country was forced to become a protectorate of colonial France. This lasted until the Japanese invasion in World War II. The nationalist leader Ho Chi Minh took advantage of Japan's defeat to declare independence in 1945 — but the French returned. When Ho's communist Vietcong guerrillas finally defeated the French at Dien Bien Phu in 1954, the Geneva Agreement divided the country into North and South, pending elections. The American-backed South refused to hold elections, and Ho's guerrillas stepped up their attacks from the Soviet-supplied North. American troops landed in 1965 and stayed to prop up the South until 1973. Two years later, with the fall of the Southern capital of Saigon to the communists — it was renamed Ho Chi Minh City — Vietnam was united. Peace, however, did not bring prosperity. The country's occupation of neighbouring Cambodia was expensive; an American trade and aid embargo was an effective commercial stranglehold. At its December 1986 congress, the Communist Party forsook orthodox Marxism and began a programme of economic reform — particularly necessary as Soviet financial support came to an end.

One

People Power

'**People are the most valuable resource'** — **Chinese Communist Party slogan in the 1950s.**

J apan's modern artists dominate Christie's first auction in the series 'Art
of the 21st Century' . . . The Thai finance minister says second cars are
luxuries, and will be taxed as such . . .

(one version of Asia 2000)

C rime, violence, drug abuse — in Asia's over-populated cities the social
order is under siege. An armed gang from among Shanghai's three million
vagrants seizes the Exhibition Centre and threatens to kill hostages, including the mayor . . . Voters in Jakarta demand a return to the early 1980s,
when vigilantes killed thousands of suspected criminals without trial . . .

(another version)

Asians rarely consider themselves
Asian. There is no single thread of Asian genius linking the lustrous Taj
Mahal to China's Great Wall; no cultural bond to tie Buddhism in the same
knot with Hinduism, Confucianism, Maoism; no shared bloodline tracing
Indian and Chinese to a common ancestor.

What unites Asians is an accidental presence on the same land mass. In
the past, they were invaded, intimidated, colonised. Now, they are too
numerous, or too rich, to be controlled by outsiders. Hong Kong and Macao
are the only colonies left in Asia — and the foreigners will be gone before
the year 2000. For better or worse, Asia's people, different and divided, are
in charge of its destiny.

Whatever the politics and economics of Asia in the year 2000 and
beyond, one prediction is a certainty: more than six out of every ten people
on this planet will be Asian. Their economic and political force will be
dominant — and irresistible. They will make an ethnic mosaic, from Tamils
and Bataks to Igorots and Samoans — but some colours in the mosaic will
dominate more than others: of the 3.75 billion Asians, one in every three will
be Chinese, one in every four Indian.

By contrast with these billions in the land masses of China and the Indian
subcontinent, there will be fewer than 130 million Japanese; around 80
million Koreans, including those from what in 1990 was still the Democratic
People's Republic of North Korea; and fewer than 25 million Chinese on the
island of Taiwan. Asia's poor will vastly outnumber Asia's rich.

The imbalance is already dangerous, especially for the poor and for
those who seek to govern them. Poverty is the common denominator in all
of Asia's present armed conflicts: the simmering Afghan civil war; the

intractable ethnic violence of Sri Lanka; the struggle for Cambodia; the communist and Muslim insurgencies in the Philippines. Poverty is a factor even in the separatist movements of Irian Jaya and East Timor, since they are in part reactions to the immigration of poor Indonesians from over-populated Java. Peace and poverty are incompatible. In short, any nation with an annual per capita income in 1990 values of $600 or less is at risk.

That lesson will come home to every Asian government that fails in the 1990s to increase real living standards for its people — and, even in the world's most dynamic region, there are bound to be failures.

They will happen not because natural resources are in short supply (in fact, the worst failures will happen in the countries most blessed by nature), but because governments will lack the managerial skills and financial support to extract greater productivity from growing populations. Instead, their efforts — well intentioned and financed by huge donations from Japan, Taiwan, and multilateral aid institutions — will be thwarted by demographic imperatives: the need to provide new schools, houses, and jobs.

Take just one example. In 1960 the Philippine population was almost 30 million; by 1990 it was 60 million; by 2010 it will be nearly 90 million. This exponential increase in humanity has already humbled two presidents of totally different character: the brilliantly flawed Ferdinand Marcos and the sincere but naive Corazon Aquino. It will threaten Mrs Aquino's successor likewise. How could it be otherwise? Some 1.3 million people a year are joining a Philippine work-force in which one in ten is usually without a job and one in three has only part-time work. Meanwhile, in a staunchly Roman Catholic society, the typical Filipina will have four, even five children during her childbearing years.

What is true in the Catholic Philippines is true for other societies, too, be they Muslim, Buddhist, Hindu, or whatever. 'Total fertility' consists of the number of babies a woman is likely to have during her childbearing years. In India, Vietnam, and the Philippines the rate at the end of the 1980s was about four or five births per woman; in Pakistan, Bangladesh, Laos, and Nepal, the rate was around six.

The reasons are a mix: traditional agricultural societies value more children for their help on the land; religious strictures sometimes forbid contraception; better health care — including something as simple as a water pump for a village — increases life expectancy; it takes at least a generation of material ease before, as in Taiwan and Hong Kong, families limit their own growth.

But at least the process is familiar and certain. There is a direct connection between contraception, fertility, and wealth. The chain is simple: more contraception equals lower childbirth rates and greater per capita incomes.

At the end of the 1980s Singapore had a very high use of contraception, the world's lowest fertility rate, and Asia's highest per capita income outside Japan and Hong Kong. At the other end of the scale, only one Pakistani couple in ten used contraceptives; a Pakistani woman would expect to bear at least six children; and Pakistan's per capita income was a miserable $350 or so a year.

Figure 1   *Contraceptive Prevalence For Selected Countries and Years*

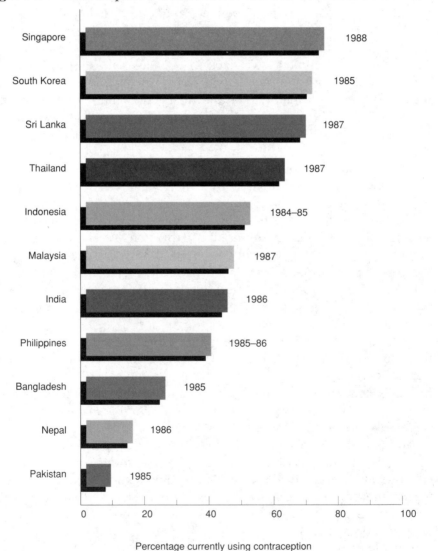

Percentage currently using contraception

Source: Analysis of Population Trends and Projections in Asia, 1980–2020, Part One, Executive Summary. A report prepared by the East-West Population Institute, East-West Center for the Agency for International Development/Washington, May 1990.

Figure 2   *Total Fertility Rates For Selected Countries, 1989*

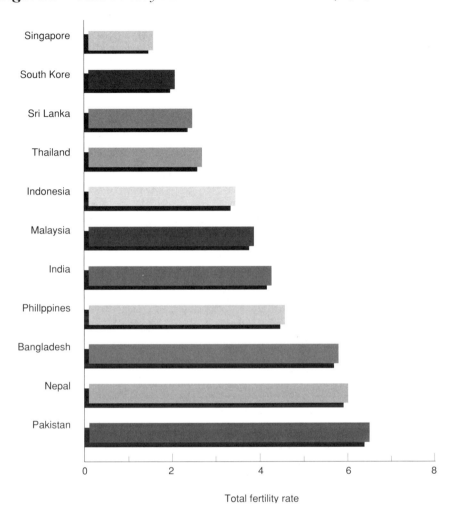

Total fertility rate

Source: Analysis of Population Trends and Projections in Asia, 1980–2010, Part One, Executive Summary. A report prepared by the East-West Population Institute, East-West Center for the Agency of International Development/Washington, May 1990.

The question is how the links in the chain fit together: does more wealth encourage people to have fewer children, or do smaller families create more wealth? China decided in 1979 that it could not reach economic take-off if couples had more than one child. The 'one child' programme remains unpopular, incomplete, and unproven. By contrast, senior churchmen in the Philippines will argue in the 1990s, as Cardinal Jaime Sin did so vigorously during the Aquino administration, that people are a resource to be cultivated — not limited.

The churchmen will have a point: rich European countries (eg, Britain and Holland) commonly have population densities far higher than in Asia They will also have allies outside Asia: in the United States the so-called 'Pro-Life' movement will try to forbid American economic aid to countries that encourage contraception.

The question, in fact, has no ready answer. Population growth is only one element in the complex recipe of development. More important ingredients are unfettered market forces — which explains why, regardless of population policies, Asia's communist countries over the past two decades have fallen so far behind Asia's market economies (compare North and South Korea in 1990, or Taiwan and China, or Vietnam and Thailand).

That, however, does not mean that market economies are any more protected from population pressures than command economies. When too many people gather too quickly in the same place, capitalism's solutions are no more effective than communism's.

At peak periods the Tokyo subway system is so busy that white-gloved employees physically push passengers, like so many sardines, into the trains. In Taipei, motorbikes and mopeds — hundreds of thousands of them — weave a precarious way through mammoth traffic jams. In Bangkok, it may take an hour to drive two miles from the Chao Phraya river to the Sogo department store.

Such is the price of progress. In rich Asia, only Singapore has escaped the tyranny of the traffic gridlock: in 1975, the government of Lee Kuan Yew instituted a system of licences to drive at rush hour into the central business district; in 1990, new regulations were brought in auctioning the right to own a car.

But what works in Singapore is culturally unacceptable outside Singapore. Rich and poor Asia alike will have to use different methods — new subways, tunnels, roads, and railways — to cope with the fastest rate of urban growth the world has ever seen. The process will be difficult enough to manage even for the rich urbanites of Japan, Korea, and Taiwan. For the relatively poor, in Bangladesh, or Indonesia or the Philippines, the process will rarely reach beyond simple survival.

The reason is that the sheer weight of numbers will defeat the efforts of town planners, engineers, and financiers. The urban population of Asia was 271 million in 1955; three decades later, it was 747 million; by the end of the century Asia's city-dwellers will number almost 1.2 billion. The cities, offering more work and pleasure than the countryside, act as magnets of such force that the urban populations of Thailand, Indonesia, the Philippines, and India will double in less than 20 years.

Any city with more than 4 million inhabitants is a 'mega-city', in the jargon of the academics. Until the 20th century there were no such urban monsters. Indeed, the concept seemed incredible (remember that in 1900 the population of the Philippines, for example, was a mere 7 million). In 1950 there were only five mega-cities in Asia: Tokyo, Calcutta, and the Chinese cities of Shanghai, Beijing, and Tianjin. Their combined population was 33.5 million — equivalent almost to the population of modern Spain.

Yet today at least 18 of the world's 30 giant cities are in Asia. In 1985, these 18 mega-cities, ranging northwards from Jakarta in Indonesia to Osaka in Japan, had a population of just over 123 million — equivalent to France, Belgium, and Britain combined. By the end of this century, there will be 28 mega-cities in Asia: they will attempt to house, feed, educate, and give work to a population of 260 million — more than the population of the United States.

The task cannot be done well, everywhere. Where it will be managed best is in North-east Asia. In Japan, and despite a total fertility rate of only 1.7 births per childbearing woman, the Tokyo-Yokohama area will have over 20 million people by the year 2000, and the Osaka-Kobe area another 10 million. Fortunately, Japan has industrial skills, money, an efficient bureaucracy, formidable social cohesion — in short, the strengths to cope. Its key decisions will be the provision of new, affordable, housing complexes and the enhancement of public transportation. This will allow easy commuting on high-speed 'mag-lev' trains between Osaka and Tokyo, a distance of 200 miles. By the end of the century, Tokyo's commercial districts will start expanding out to sea, using conventional land reclamation and also, as building foundations, floating caissons — a technique first used in the oil industry.

Korea will, as so often, follow the path of Japan. As the population of Seoul expands by a third, to almost 14 million, so Korea will expand its mass-transit system and build huge new housing estates. One advantage is that much of the infrastructure for growth already exists, laid down before the 1988 Seoul Olympics by far-sighted planners. Another advantage, assuming the re-unification of the Korean peninsula, is that the addition of North Korean workers to the economy will keep Korea's work-force cheap and its exports competitive.

Where the task will be done worst is fairly obvious: in the Third World metropolises which have already failed to cope with the population influxes of the 1970s and '80s — and which will now have to cope with even greater influxes.

The list of probable failures is depressingly long: in the Indian subcontinent; Bombay, Calcutta, Madras, Dhaka, Karachi, and Lahore. In

South-east Asia, Manila. In China; Shanghai and Tianjin. The list could get longer, to include, for example, Bangkok, Jakarta, and Taipei. But the betting is that Thailand's sustained economic boom will be enough to improve Bangkok's woefully inadequate infrastructure so that by the year 2000 the city's 10 million people will enjoy a reasonable quality of life. The same will be true of Taipei, where in the late 1980s the authorities embarked on a programme of massive infrastructure investment, from a Mass Rapid Transit system to a new sewage network. By contrast with the domestically derived strengths of Bangkok and Taipei, the successful adjustment of Jakarta to the population pressure will depend on outside factors: Indonesia will need higher petroleum revenues if it is to invest adequately in its capital. Those revenues, in turn, will obviously depend on the world balance of energy supply and demand. In particular, Indonesia's revenues will be tied to Japan's rising consumption of liquefied natural gas.

The big question, of course, is whether the increase in city populations can be limited — or even reversed. It looks unlikely. Even though total fertility rates are falling as countries in Asia get richer, absolute numbers are still increasing. Japan's population, for example, will increase from 123 million in 1988 to 129 million in the year 2000, even though the total fertility rate of Japanese women is now a mere 1.7 births.

What is true for Asia's richest country is much more so for its poorer ones. In Bangladesh the total fertility rate has fallen from 6.8 births in 1965 to 5.5 in 1988 — and is expected to fall to 4.3 in the year 2000. But its population will rise from 109 million in 1988 to 145 million in the year 2000; it will not be until 2025 that Bangladesh's population simply replaces itself — by which time the population, if the demographers are correct, will have reached 219 million. But that is not the 'stationary' size of the population: by the time Bangladesh has a birth rate constant and equal to its death rate, a stable age structure, and a zero rate of growth, its population theoretically would be 346 million.

So much for the figures — and bear in mind that if Malthus had been right we would barely have standing space on our planet. The underlying truth is that the more people there are, the less chance they have of finding jobs in the countryside — and so they come to the cities, whose populations are increasing anyway and which are the natural centres for industrial investment, and so for jobs. It is a symbiosis: rural migration to the cities provides the manpower for factories in need of labour. Moreover, investment breeds investment: where one factory starts up, another will follow — and so take advantage of the pool of labour and an infrastructure of roads, banking, advertising, and so on. As more people leave the countryside, so the services available in the countryside — health and education — decline, making the cities still more attractive. Meanwhile, the cities expand outwards, encroaching on what before was farmland.

The result is the mega-city and the fastest rate of urbanisation the world has ever known. In the period between 1965 and 1988 the proportion of the population in Indonesia living in cities rose from 16 to 27 per cent; in the Philippines from 32 to 41 per cent; in Japan from 67 to 77 per cent; in Thailand from 13 to 21 per cent; in Malaysia from 26 to 41 per cent. As this century unfolds, the proportions will get higher. Usually, just one city in the country will account for at least 25 per cent of the total urban population — and the more this is so, the fewer the city's links to the country around it. As one Asian Development Bank analyst noted in 1990 (but in private, such are the Bank's diplomatic sensitivities), 'Cities like Manila and Bangkok may have more in common with Tokyo and Washington than with their own rural hinterlands.'

What, though, of China, which will have more mega-cities than any other country in the world? By the year 2000 China's population, 1.1 billion in 1990, will have reached 1.275 billion. Already, half of them live in an urban setting — from small market towns in Yunnan province to enormous industrial cities such as Shanghai — compared with 18 per cent in 1965. The United Nations projects a population for China of 1.566 billion in the year 2025. Statistically (and alarmingly) a stationary population for China will number 1.835 billion — a tad less than the similarly alarming 1.862 billion for India. No wonder China is so determined to discourage, if necessary by force, what comes naturally to all human beings.

As this century ends, China's schools, factories, and universities will be dominated by spoilt, selfish, undisciplined teenagers. Cynics say this is already true throughout the world — but in China, the teenagers will be male, and they will be the sole offspring of their parents. At the moment they are toddlers and infants; they get presents galore (a traditional favourite is the peaked cap of the People's Liberation Army) from doting grandparents; their proud parents make them fat with the extra titbits produced by the economic liberalisation of the 1980s.

These brats are the product of the world's biggest experiment in social engineering since Herod and Hitler, both of whom admittedly had more evil and pernicious aims in mind than China's well-intentioned family planners. One day the brats will grow up to rule the world's most populous nation.

China's one-child policy is a relatively recent development. In 1979, with the excesses of the misnamed 'Cultural Revolution' long over, the supposedly liberal regime of Deng Xiaoping decreed that Chinese couples should have only one child each. There were exceptions: ethnic minorities in remote areas; Han Chinese — the vast majority of all Chinese — living in hilly or mountainous areas (ie, among the despised minorities); couples whose first child had died; and farming couples whose first child is a girl.

The policy is the result of fear. Already, a fifth of the world's population is living on just 7 per cent of the world's cultivable land (7 per cent, that is, using today's methods). China's planners draw a simple conclusion: unless China's breeding habits are dramatically reined in, the population will grow beyond the nation's ability to feed itself — and famine and strife will once again afflict the Chinese people. The obvious alternative is to export manufactured goods in order to import food. But the alternative cannot be a complete solution: China's exports are low in quality. In any case, relying on 'foreign devils' is part neither of Chinese tradition nor of Maoist self-reliance.

The fear of too many mouths for the nation to feed was born long before the one-child decree. Back in the 1960s, birth control was advocated 'in the interests of planned economy'; in 1970, the government introduced the policy of 'late marriage, child spacing, and fewer children' — which meant that registrars could refuse to issue marriage licences to couples under the approved age (usually, late twenties) and that factories and rural communities would receive a quota of permitted births for their work units.

The problem is that the policy goes against the cultural grain. The Chinese proverb says: 'If you do not have children during the lean years, who will help you reap the harvest?' Since Mao's revolution was based on mobilising the peasantry, it is hardly surprising that China's early communists wanted to increase, rather than reduce, the population. In 1949 Mao wrote, 'It is a very good thing that China has a big population. Of all the things in the world, people are the most precious.' No wonder, then, that in the 1950s Professor Ma Yinchu, the president of Beijing University, was dismissed for his advocacy of birth control; his 'rehabilitation' was delayed until 1979, by which time his view had become China's conventional wisdom.

Arguably, the cultural resistance will weaken as China continues to industrialise. Since the communist 'liberation' in 1949, China's agricultural sector has shrunk from almost half of the economy to barely a third; for industry, the share has grown by the same proportions. Couples who live in small apartments in urban settings now balance the expense and political disapproval of having a second child against the cost of buying new consumer items. In 1990, one housewife in a Sichuan village showed her television set and tape recorder to a foreign reporter and asked: 'If I had lots of kids, how could I afford these things?'

But the resistance will not crumble into nothingness. After all, a nation without a culture cannot exist. Despite the ephemeral intrusion of Marxism, the true loyalty of the Chinese (and many others in Asia) is to their ancestors. It is a loyalty, codified by Confucius, that goes back through millennia. A man's life is a link in a family's unending chain. To quote the late David Bonavia, 'Parenthood in the Confucian world view is a compact, both with those who came before and those who will come after.'

Quite so. But because daughters go off to their husbands' families when they marry, the compact is made with the sons. Parents who have no son have no one to worship them after death. It is fear of the family's oblivion that drives the desperation of so many Chinese couples to have a son. The result is not just the spoiled boy toddlers; all too often the consequence, despite government propaganda urging sexual equality, is also the abandonment or murder of girl babies.

All of this suggests that China's birth-control programmes will continue to have problems, regardless of how strictly they are enforced. At the moment, compulsion comes in various guises, from the gentle to the outrageous. Every Chinese employee belongs to a *danwei*, or work unit, which controls housing, medical care, and retirement benefits for its members. Once the *danwei* has negotiated with the authorities a quota of births for its members, it will select those women allowed to become pregnant. Woe betide those who disregard the quota: their penalties may include social ostracism, the cutting off of their water and electricity supplies, huge fines, and more-or-less forced abortion.

Fortunately, however, the penalties will become fewer and less harsh as the 1990s draw to a close. One reason is that urbanisation and rising materialism have reduced the desire for children; another is that China will become increasingly dependent on the outside world to help its economic development. That help will come with strings to tie China to a better observance of human rights. China's leaders will remember at least one lesson from their bloody repression of the student democrats in Beijing's Tiananmen Square in June 1989: namely, that it caused a suspension of much needed foreign loans. One specific warning on the enforcement of the one-child policy came in 1988: the United States gave asylum to a Chinese couple studying in America, Dr Li Quanbang and Ms Ping Hong, after Ms Ping's Chinese employer threatened punishment on her return if she gave birth to her second child. Again, in May 1990, the United States gave refugee status to Li Jinlin, 37, and his wife, Wang Saizhen, 34. They had entered America illegally after fleeing China when Ms Wang became pregnant with their second child.

The real question is how well China's policies have worked. In 1950, when the Communist party's victory theme for the people was 'the more the better', China was home for about 552 million, and the average woman would have six children in her lifetime. By 1988, Chinese officials claimed the total fertility rate had fallen to 2.31 births (the World Bank reckoned 2.4).

That drop is dramatic — and also misleading. In 1985, for example, the typical woman would be expected to have only two children in her lifetime, so the statistics have in fact become less dramatic. The reason is twofold: the harsh enforcement methods of the early 1980s — women's sanitary pads, for example, were checked and abortions were virtually compulsory — were abandoned; and rural couples, beneficiaries of the agricultural reforms of Deng Xiaoping, were specifically allowed in 1988 to have a second child.

Remember, too, that birth-control policy is just one of several government decisions that affect a country's population figures. Largely because of better medical care, especially from the 'barefoot doctors' who, with rudimentary training, treated the peasants, China's death rate has fallen spectacularly under communism, from twenty deaths for each thousand people in 1949 to eleven per thousand in 1958 and to seven per thousand in the late 1980s — which is the same as Canada's rate and less than Britain's.

But there was a disastrous upward blip in this otherwise smooth decline of the death rate: the inappropriately named 'Great Leap Forward' of 1958. Some 127 million peasants were organised into 26,578 'people's communes' with the task of maximising agricultural output. 'Communism is paradise,' the Party said, 'and the people's commune is the ladder to it.' The ladder slipped. Natural disasters, the lack of personal incentives, and the overuse of the soil combined in a terrible famine from 1959 to 1961, in which about 30 million Chinese died. And the people's reaction? The total fertility rate shot up from a rate in 1960 of four births per woman to a rate in 1965 of six births.

The consequence is that however Draconian the government's measures in the past, China's population is bound to increase for the next twenty years. Between the end of the famine in 1961 and 1975 some 180 million female babies were born. If each of these has just one child by the age of 24, the population will obviously increase by 180 million — but the one-child policy did not begin until 1979 and, in any case, can only be closely monitored in the cities. Meanwhile, more than one in every four Chinese is under the age of 15.

The inescapable fact is that there will be a 'baby boom' in the 1990s and China will miss its target of zero growth in a population of 1.2 billion by the year 2000. Instead, China's population will continue to grow by about 14 million people a year — the equivalent of a new Chile or Ghana or Holland. A more likely outcome for the year 2000 is 1.275 billion. Indeed, a generation after that, the population could well be 1.5 billion or more.

The lesson from all this is not that government population policies do not work, but that they do not work as governments intend them to. That, of course, is a lesson that Singapore for one will stubbornly seek to change in the 1990s.

'We are not going to sit passively watching ourselves become extinct. The New Population Policy is in place. The measures will take some time to work. They will be effective only when people understand the problem and change their private choices. Attitudes must change — towards marriage, having children, making careers.' So declared Brigadier-General (Reserve) Lee Hsien Loong, as Singapore's minister for trade and industry, in 1987.

It is hard to think of any other government, except perhaps China's, being quite as outspoken in defining goals for its people's most private behaviour.

But Singapore will always be a test-tube for social engineers, both now and well into the next century. Experimentation is part of the political culture of the People's Action Party, founded by 'B-G' Lee's father, Lee Kuan Yew, four decades ago. What encourages the experimenters is that the country is a laboratory offering near-instant feedback. After all, the island republic is only 25 miles or so by 17, and in 1990 had only an estimated 2.7 million people.

The question is whether the experiments are the right ones — and whether they actually work. Singapore's fear in the early years after independence was that the population would grow too fast. At the end of the second world war, Singapore's population was less than a million; by the mid-1960s the number had doubled. Between 1960, when there were 1.6 million Singaporeans, and 1965 the population grew by 2.8 per cent a year. In 1966 an alarmed Lee Kuan Yew government promulgated a 'Stop at Two' policy, lest the island be swamped by its own people.

The policy worked. Relentless propaganda in favour of small families made third or subsequent children feel unwanted by society; and parents who had a third child suffered financially, for example losing the right to paid maternity leave and state health insurance for the birth. In 1969 abortion and sterilisation were legalised.

But the policy worked too well, slowing the nation's birth rate much too quickly for the government's comfort. In the early 1960s in Singapore there were 34 births a year for every thousand people; in the early 1970s just 21.2; and in the early 1980s only 17. In the year before the New Population Policy, Singapore's total fertility rate dropped to 1.44 births per fertile woman — the lowest in Asia. The long-term threat was that Singapore's population would grow to reach about 3 million in the year 2010 — and then shrink sharply because the 1960s baby boom found no echo in the 1980s and '90s.

Such hypothetical calculations will obsess Singapore's planners through the 1990s. After all, what permanence can an already tiny state claim in the next century if its population is growing both older and smaller?

But the government has an added worry: that the population will change not just in size and age, but also in racial substance. In the past decade between 76 and 77 per cent of Singaporeans have been ethnically Chinese; between 14 and 15 per cent have been Malay; between 6 and 7 per cent have been Indian. The remainder are mainly Eurasian. This is the mix of racial ingredients that Mr Lee and his colleagues are comfortable with — a mix, they argue, that has brought social stability and material prosperity.

In other words, change the mix and Singapore is in peril — which is why the government monitors even fractional changes in the percentages with a zeal that borders on an obsession.

If the population is to replace itself so that Singapore's ethnic proportions are stable, then each woman should have 2.1 children (the decimal point accounts statistically for premature deaths, spinsters, and so on) during her childbearing years. Unhappily for the social engineers, only the Indians at the end of the 1980s were reproducing at the required rate. The Malays, who are the poorest, least educated segment of Singaporean society, were breeding at a total fertility rate of 2.31 per cent. By contrast, the Chinese were, quite simply, not doing their duty. Their total fertility rate was 1.88 per cent in 1989 — and had been as low as 1.26 per cent, probably the lowest rate in the world, in 1986.

Will Singapore's Chinese do their duty ready for the next century? Probably not, even though encouragement has come and will come in many forms, including the uncatchy exhortation 'Have three, or more if you can afford it' and the establishment, in 1983, of the Social Development Unit. This is an organisation that tries to encourage eligible graduates — and now some appropriate non-graduates — to meet and marry (and so, perhaps, to breed). To many Singaporeans the unit, which arranges group parties and even holidays, is comically like a 'Love Boat' farce. Others regard it as a pragmatic remedy to a real problem: the reluctance of Singaporean women graduates to marry their educational inferiors and the willingness, even preference, of male graduates to do the reverse. Graduates, male and female, are overwhelmingly Chinese, indeed disproportionately so. Lee Kuan Yew worries, in public, that Singapore's human stock will decline in quality as well as quantity.

Unhappily for Mr Lee, exhortations are likely to fall on deaf ears; more effective will be financial incentives and superstition. In 1988, for example, there were 52,957 births in Singapore — the highest for 21 years. Why? Because eight is a lucky number, and so 88 is doubly lucky; and because 1988 was an auspicious Dragon Year in the Chinese zodiac. But even the highest birth rate for 21 years brought the total fertility rate only up to 1.98, still below the replacement rate — and the following year showed a drop down to 47,735 births.

What, then, of financial incentives? They undoubtedly have a big impact, witness the success of the 'Stop at Two' campaign. They have, too, had their impact in the 'Three or More' campaign. By 1989, tax incentives first introduced in 1986 had increased the number of births each year by a quarter — and had more than doubled the number of babies born to better-educated women. It was results like these that prompted the finance minister, Richard Hu, to introduce a new set of tax rebates in his 1990 budget specifically designed to persuade more women to have more children earlier. If a mother had a second child before the age of 28, she and her husband would have a tax rebate of S$28,000 — and the rebate would be reduced by S$5,000 for every year she delayed her second baby.

But these and other bribes will still not bring the changes the government wants. The Singaporean role model in the 1990s will continue to be the independent-minded careerist — male or female — who in his or her twenties prefers to put material acquisitions, from a new car to a second holiday, before the duty to procreate. The only option then left to the government to preserve the racial balance will be to encourage immigration, especially from Hong Kong, where 98 per cent of the population is Chinese — many of them hoping to escape the transfer of sovereignty, due in 1997, from Britain to China.

That remedy will, naturally, bring social problems. Will the aggressive Cantonese of Hong Kong integrate into Singapore's docile society? Will Singaporeans resent the provision of benefits to the newcomers — who will not even have done the national service that all Singaporean men must complete? In practice, it will be too late to worry. The truth is that any population policy, including immigration, breeds both challenge and difficulty — be it in China, Singapore, Japan, or anywhere else in Asia.

As dawn breaks in Hong Kong, old people — men and women — gather in Statue Square to go through their daily ritual of *tai chi*. Their arms trace graceful arcs through the air; their weight moves, slowly and smoothly, from leg to leg. It is the Chinese version of the West's obsession with jogging: each dawn, the parks of China, Taiwan, and Singapore are sprinkled with elderly Chinese staying fit in the traditional manner.

But it is not just the Chinese who are staying fit and so living longer. All over Asia life expectancy is rising — and will continue to do so. In 1960, a Japanese could expect to live to perhaps 68, the lowest expectation in an industrial market economy. Today, Japanese life expectancy is 78, the world's highest. The Chinese, wherever they may be, will live to the age of

70 or older (which in poor mainland China is an amazing achievement). The Koreans and the Malaysians will also live beyond 70. Soon, too, the Thais.

When this century ends, the only people in Asia condemned to die before the age of 70 will be the masses of the Indian subcontinent and Indonesia, and the poor in the Indochina crescent curving from Burma, through Laos and Cambodia, to Vietnam. Even they will live ten or more years longer than their parents did.

There is no mystery to this growth. It is the straightforward result of better water supplies, sanitation, food, and health care. A vaccination programme carried out in the 1950s or 1960s will still be keeping people free from disease in the 1990s. Deadly epidemics in Asia are becoming rare (and the coming one, AIDS, will never be as prevalent in Asia as it is in America, let alone Africa).

But do not think of Asia's rising life-expectancy as an 'age bomb' on an ever-shorter fuse. In reality the bomb exploded long ago. Since 1650, the population of China has grown ten times over; before then, the population for centuries varied between 50 million and 100 million. In India, the population has increased by two-and-a-half times — at least — since 1920.

A better metaphor for the aging of Asia is the python: a 'baby boom' generation shows as a bulge first at the mouth of the population snake — and then the bulge, as it ages, goes further through the snake's body, until with death it narrows to nothingness at the snake's tip. When the bulge is healthy, vigorous and of working age, it feeds the whole snake. The question is how to feed the snake when the bulge gets too old to work.

Figure 3   *Japan's Population Pyramid (1920-2025)*

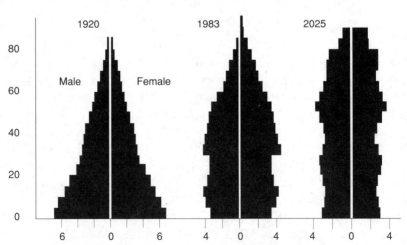

Source: Institute of Population Problems, Ministry of Health and Welfare, Japan.

The problem is not unique to Asia. Indeed, the only Asian country to be acutely affected during the 1990s will be Japan. But almost every Asian country will suffer eventually (save, perhaps, Malaysia, which has toyed with a grandiose — and probably foolish — ambition actually to raise its population, from 17 million in the late 1980s to a target of 70 million in the 21st century). The simple equation is that as wealth increases, fertility rates decline — which means that the unproductive elderly form an ever-larger proportion of the population.

What may make Asia unique is the speed of the process. It took most European countries anywhere from 45 to 135 years before the percentage of their citizens aged 65 and over rose from 7 per cent to 14 per cent. Japan is expecting the same doubling to happen within 26 years — a single generation. At the beginning of the 1990s, the proportion of elderly was 12 per cent, so the doubling is imminent. By the year 2025, one in every four Japanese will be 65 or older, and half of these senior citizens will be 75 or older.

The age division is not arbitrary. Populations conveniently fall into three categories for demographers: children aged up to 14; youths and adults aged from 15 to 64; and the old, starting at the age of 65. The convenience is, of course, economic. The first and last categories cannot fend for themselves, and so must live off the efforts of the middle category. The smaller the middle category, the more pressure on its efforts.

That explanation can be fuzzy around the edges. In India, for example, child workers, working in sweatshop factories, are an important part of the economy. The same is true in many other of Asia's poor countries: the small factories and workshops of Jakarta and Manila depend on the illegal employment of children. Meanwhile, Asia's unmechanised agriculture will continue to depend on children helping their parents in the fields — the reason that peasants are so slow to use contraception.

There is even a little fuzziness, too, for the category of the old. The elderly are not a one-way drain on an economy's resources: they provide economically useful services such as child-minding, which frees more women to enter the work-force. In Singapore, there has been a bureaucratic attempt also to lighten the burden of the old on society: the Central Provident Fund, a compulsory savings scheme, is self-funding — the money a worker pays in to the CPF is available to him on retirement, unlike in most countries where the pensions of the retired are paid from the contributions of those still working. In theory, a retired Singaporean is a burden on nobody, because his needs are met by his own past CPF contributions.

But the essence of the explanation is true enough. Asia's economic dynamism is at least partly the energy of youth. The proportion of productive

Japanese — those aged 15 to 64 — in Japan's population has been growing for the past four decades. Disciplined and hard-working, they created the steel, shipbuilding, and automobile industries that formed Japan's post-war economic miracle. By 1990, their share was over 70 per cent, the highest in any large industrial country. But that will be the peak: the challenge for Japan is that early next century their share of productive workers will be the lowest in the industrialised world.

Where Japan leads, the rest of Asia will follow — albeit at varying paces. Singapore, Hong Kong, Taiwan, and South Korea all have the human characteristic that brought success to Japan: a population young enough and disciplined enough to work hard. In each of these 'Newly Industrialised Economies' at the end of the 1980s, some 70 per cent of the people were aged over 14 but below 65.

Moreover, this productive proportion will last because it will be fed by 'baby booms' that occurred way back in the 1950s and 1960s. A child born in Seoul or Singapore in 1953 will not end his working life until, say, the year 2013. Asia's declining fertility is a relatively recent phenomenon: even in rich Taiwan, Singapore, and South Korea, (and poor, contraception-keen China) the proportion of people aged 65 and over will not exceed 10 per cent for another twenty years or so.

U nhappily, many of the 'productive' will, in reality, be idle and unproductive. Whereas young and growing work-forces provided the foundations for the economic growth of Japan, Korea, Taiwan, Singapore, and Hong Kong, elsewhere they threaten to be the dead weight that prevents economic 'take-off'.

The reasons are complex, even confusing. In a country such as Thailand, a population of almost 60 million is seen as a viable domestic market, helping to create a self-sustaining economic development (indeed, this is one reason why neighbouring and 'under-populated' Malaysia is so keen to increase its numbers). Yet in the Philippines, a population only slightly bigger than Thailand's is considered an economic hindrance. Whereas the Thais have taken advantage of a growing labour force, the Filipinos have not. Some 1.3 million Filipinos each year join a work-force in which the unemployment rate hovers around 10 per cent and the underemployment rate around 30 per cent.

Part of the difference, clearly, lies in counting heads by age as well as by number. The Thai birth rate is declining much faster than the Philippine one, which means that the population pressure in Thailand is easing while in the Philippines it is still increasing. Between 1965 and 1980 the Thai population rose by 2.9 per cent a year — the same as in the Philippines. But in the 1980s the Thai growth rate plummeted to 1.9 per cent a year, while the rate in the Philippines dropped only to 2.5 per cent. In the 1990s, the gap between the two countries will grow still wider: the Thai population will be growing by just 1.3 per cent a year while Filipinos will increase in number by 1.9 per cent a year.

Transpose those growth rates to the size of the labour force, and the impact is dramatic: in each decade since the end of the 1960s, the Philippines' work-force has grown faster than in the previous decade — and the acceleration will continue until at least the second decade of the 21st century. In Pakistan and Bangladesh the speed of the increase is astonishing, with their work-forces expected to be growing more than three times faster by the end of the 1990s compared with the 1970s. But in most of rich Asia, the process is the reverse. The Thai work-force, for example, will be increasing at the start of the next century at only half the speed of the 1960s. One hopeful sign for Indonesia is that the growth in its work-force — now over 71 million — will start slowing early next century.

The hope, of course, is relative. Each year in Pakistan, India, Bangladesh, the Philippines, and Indonesia the work-force increases by over a million people. How can their governments possibly find what amounts to 3,000 new jobs for each day of the year?

The answer is that they cannot — and possibly should not. The command economies of Indochina have been even worse at creating employment (and everyone in a Marxist state is supposed to have a guaranteed right to work) than the least effective of Asia's market economies. For proof, compare Vietnam with the Philippines, or Burma with Indonesia.

The economies in the 1990s and beyond that will deal best with the pressure of the work-force will be those that give the freest play to market forces. The biggest reason for Thailand's progress in the past two decades compared with the Philippines has little to do with political instability, the present curse of the Philippines. Indeed, Thai politics since the second world war has been far less stable than Filipino politics, which became unbalanced only at the end of the Marcos era in the mid-1980s.

Instead, the reason for Thailand's advance over the Philippines is that Thai entrepreneurs (most of them, at least in part, ethnically Chinese) have been forced to make unsubsidised decisions. Their Filipino counterparts (also often ethnically Chinese) have been allowed to get rich from a status quo that protects them from outside competition — and so preserves the inefficiencies of Philippine industry and agriculture. It is no accident that almost all Japanese investment in Asia in the 1980s was to Thailand, Singapore, and Malaysia, with a liberalising Indonesia becoming latterly attractive. By contrast, the non-communist laggards in Asian development, especially India, have squandered their potential by protecting their markets too well and for too long. In practice, that means protecting the feudal interests of a few families, who see no reason to invite in foreigners to share the cake — even if foreign help would bake a bigger cake.

This explanation for who wins and who loses in Asia may sound a touch simplistic — and it is certainly less than complete. For example, one factor common to the economic rise of Japan, South Korea, and Taiwan was land reform after the second world war. The consequence of giving or selling land to the people who tilled it was to increase agricultural productivity while giving the previous landowners the incentive to invest in industry. The parallel failure of land reform in the Philippines has meanwhile bred popular insurrection, lowered agricultural productivity per head, and stifled investment.

Another factor is the ability of a given country to train and use its people's brains. The triumph of Japan and Asia's 'Tigers' (or 'Dragons', as Singapore, Hong Kong, South Korea, and Taiwan are also known) is partly one of education. In Japan and Korea virtually everyone can read and write; the remaining 'Tigers' are almost as advanced, since only one in every ten or eleven of their adult inhabitants is illiterate. But in poor Asia, illiterates abound. In China, for example, three in every ten adults are unable to read and write; in India, the figure is five or six in every ten; in Pakistan a depressing seven out of every ten. Those figures are collective totals: if women were judged separately, their illiteracy rates would easily outstrip men's, such is the low value put on women in developing countries. The basic equation is that low education equals low achievement.

There can, of course, be exceptions. Filipinos, for example, are highly literate — only 14 per cent or so of adults cannot read and write — and yet they have managed to achieve a worse standard of living than the less literate Malaysians.

But the exceptions are just that, exceptions. The norm is that to manage the transition from an agrarian economy to an industrial one, the work-force must be literate and educated. This does not mean creating an élite of highly educated; it means breeding a competence among the barely educated. The more workers who can read an instruction booklet, or even a simple safety sign, the more productive the factory. India's enormous output of PhDs and computer scientists is insignificant, and ineffectual, when set against India's background of child labour, abject poverty, and non-existent schooling.

The problem is to find the money to build the schools and provide the teachers. School enrolment in countries with high birth rates, such as Bangladesh, India, Pakistan, and the Philippines, will be two, three — even four — times higher in the year 2000 than it was in 1980 (the actual rate will depend on the willingness of parents to send their children to school, and the willingness of governments to enforce schooling). This means that those governments, which have a duty to provide, if not jobs, certainly education, will have to increase the number of teachers, schools, and books. Most governments will fail in this duty.

By contrast, the governments that will succeed are those that are rich already: in South Korea, for example, school rolls will fall in the first decade of the 21st century because of the decline in the Korean birth rate in the 1980s and '90s. Given that education must compete for its share of government budgets, the rule of thumb will be that the smaller the school population, the more spending per pupil — and so the better the education. A child in Taiwan in the 1990s will get a much higher standard of education than his counterpart in the southern Philippines or the mountains of Sumatra.

But it would be wrong to exaggerate this phenomenon by which the favoured get more favours while the unfavoured must keep on struggling. One aspect common to all Asian countries is the popular regard paid to learning. Education in Asian countries, rich and poor, will improve dramatically because its customers — the schoolchildren — want it to. In the poor Muslim villages in southern Thailand, children have a passion to learn and a respect for the teacher that do not exist in countries such as the United States and Britain. In Singapore during examination times, schoolchildren spend hours in the airport terminal and in fast-food restaurants so that they can revise in air-conditioning and away from family distractions. In Japan, the authority of the teacher has remained absolute despite the post-war explosion of wealth — and Japanese children work so hard that their educational ratings (including intelligence quotients) consistently exceed American and European averages. A Japanese boy of eleven will have the mathematical skills of an American boy of fifteen. What is true of Japanese schoolboys will be true in the 1990s of other nationalities, too, starting with the Singaporeans, Hong Kongers, and Taiwanese.

With luck, the 1990s will be the decade in which this enthusiasm for education will combine with declining birth rates to ease Asia's poor countries out of the trap of their own poverty and population pressures.

In practice, only some countries will be lucky. They will be the ones which create opportunities attractive enough to entice investment from rich Asian countries such as Japan and, increasingly, South Korea, Taiwan, and Hong Kong. The investment will consist not just of capital, but also of technical and managerial skills. Some countries, notably Malaysia, Thailand, and Singapore, made their own luck during the 1980s: Sony, for example, transferred its Aiwa subsidiary to Singapore because the island republic offered competitive labour costs, an attractive tax regime, and a reliable legal framework.

The unlucky countries will be those that see import substitution almost as an end in itself, protecting the domestic market so completely that no domestic producer will ever be efficient enough to win export orders. This has been the hallmark of India — despite Rajiv Gandhi's free market rhetoric in the mid-1980s — and, of course, the Philippines. A cautionary tale for Asian development is that four decades ago the Philippines was Asia's richest country after Japan; now, it seems determined to join the poorest.

How will the lucky and the unlucky recognise themselves? Easy: lucky, ie rich, countries in Asia will be those, like Japan, Taiwan, Singapore, and Hong Kong, that import workers from abroad; the unlucky, or poor, countries will be those, like the Philippines, India, and Pakistan, that need to export their workers. There is a third category that straddles the divide: Thailand and Malaysia are labour exporters that are, nonetheless, clearly enjoying a sustained economic boom.

There is, also, another way in which the fortunate and less fortunate can judge themselves. Rich countries will soon face the problem of bored and affluent young people unwilling to subscribe to the work ethic of their parents. In Japan, the signs are already there with the pleasure-seeking, consumption-minded *shinjinrui*; in Singapore, the signs are the trendily dressed groups of teenagers patrolling Orchard Road with the simple aim of being seen and admired.

Poor countries, meanwhile, will face the problem of equally bored young people, often unemployed, who see no chance of affluence. They already crowd the streets of Shanghai, Manila, New Delhi, Jakarta, and Ho Chi Minh City, or Saigon as most people will soon start calling it again.

For the politicians of Asia, solving the problems of the young rich will be a lot easier than alleviating the misery of the young poor. The question is whether they realise the severity of the problems in the first place.

Two

The Politics of Change

'You cannot mock a great leader in an Asian Confucian society. If he allows himself to be mocked, he is finished.'

Singapore's Lee Kuan Yew, after the 1989 student protests in Beijing's Tiananmen Square

*R*ight-wing factions in the Japanese parliament demand the expulsion of
foreign workers . . . India's new prime minister promises no mercy to the
fomenters of sectarian violence . . . A Philippine senate inquiry concludes
that democracy has failed to diminish feudalism . . . In Malaysia, the
fundamentalist Parti Islam blames its electoral rout on fraud and
government propaganda . . .

(some political possibilities for Asia 2000)

Asians talk politics in different ways.
Indians argue every detail with obsessive passion; Filipinos embark on long
flights of ornate eloquence; Indonesians are addicted to allusion; and the
Chinese, experts at the non-committal phrase, talk freely only to those they
know and trust.

So much for clichés — any traveller through Asia could soon provide
many more, and many an Asian might dispute them. But clichés invariably
contain at least a kernel of truth. If Asia is not culturally and racially
homogeneous, how could it possibly be uniform politically? There are
obvious differences even in similar institutions. India's Parliament, in its
handsome Lutyens building in New Delhi, is virtually the same — with its
British colonial origin, its legislative ritual, even its language — as the
Singapore Parliament, which nestles in the white-washed colonial buildings
opposite the Cricket Club. And yet no one would mistake one for the other.
In India, the members of Parliament storm through points of order, quote
Shakespeare and Macaulay, and hurl carefully crafted insults at each other.
In Singapore, the members read their speeches with a robotic lack of fire;
their ministerial colleagues report to Parliament rather as company directors
report to shareholders — and with even less likelihood of being challenged
from the floor.

What is different between India and Singapore becomes still more so
elsewhere. China's National People's Congress, hundreds of well-behaved
delegates gathered each year in the awesome Great Hall of the People, is
the equivalent of the Philippine Congress — whose House of Representatives
squabbles in endless intrigue and whose two dozen (usually ineffectual)
Senators make speeches worthy of Demosthenes. Meanwhile, opposition
members of Taiwan's Legislative Yuan throw punches and chairs — as well
as simple invective — at the representatives of the ruling Kuomintang. It is
hard to remember that until 1987 Taiwan had been under martial law for 38
years.

In other words, political comparisons in Asia are of contrasts, not
likenesses. The adversarial politics of the Indian subcontinent is the legacy

of Westminster, and therefore of ancient Athens; East Asia, from China to Indonesia, has the obedient cast of Confucianism, which considers challenge to authority to be akin to barbarism — and to be contemplated only when authority abuses its power to flagrant excess.

But that crude contrast hides more subtle ones: in Pakistan, the co-existence of secular democrats and theocratic Muslim fundamentalists; in China, the proletarianism of Marxism and the hierarchies of Confucianism; in the Philippines, the rhetoric of nationalism and the nostalgia for imperial America. Across Asia, from Afghanistan to the Pacific, there is a spectrum of political systems. Parliamentary democracy in India, military dictatorship in Burma, communism in China, colonialism in Hong Kong — these are the strong colours; the weaker colours include the quasi-one party system of Japan, the race-based parties of Malaysia, the family fiefdom of the Sultanate of Brunei. Travel across Europe, and the political tapestry has the underlying colour of democracy first mixed in Athens; systems of proportional representation and the like are shades of a uniform colour. Travel across Asia and the tapestry is a rich pattern of different colours.

None of Asia's contrasts, crude or subtle, is likely to blur before the end of this century. Indeed, several will sharpen as Asia attempts to adapt to the fastest process of change the world has ever seen. The most obvious pressure will be demographic: the more people there are, the greater the need for jobs, schools, hospitals, and so on. But other pressures will be insidiously urgent, too: the deterioration of the environment; the erosion by wealth of the values of the past; the impact of information, carried to the smallest villages, in India or in Papua New Guinea, by the miracle of the transistor — consider, for example, the popularity of 'Dallas' and other American soap operas in rural Asia, or the avid following in Singapore and Malaysia for British soccer matches transmitted live in the pre-dawn hours of the South-east Asian day. The pressures will vary from country to country, but together they will add up to a political challenge that is both enormous and complex.

That challenge coincides with perhaps the only phenomenon common to otherwise heterogeneous Asia: the inevitability of political change. The strong leaders of the post-colonial era are dying — and the systems they created will grow weak without them. By the end of this century, the gerontocrats of the Long March will all be dead — and the People's Republic of China will no longer pretend to the revolutionary zeal of 'the Long March spirit'. In Burma, Ne Win, dictator since 1962, will no longer be fit, or even alive, to pull the strings of power. The same will be true of Indonesia, where General Suharto assumed power in 1965, and in North Korea, ruled by the 'Great Leader' Kim Il Sung since 1948. Even in Japan, Asia's most developed nation, there will be an almost tangible change of generations, as the factional leaders of the post-war era pass away and leave the Liberal Democratic Party to younger men (one of whom, Toshiki Kaifu, became prime minister in 1989).

But who, or what, will replace Asia's post-colonial generation? Whatever the possible answers, none has yet commanded general support. East of India, no country in Asia has yet managed to change its government by the peaceful use of the ballot box. Either the ruling party has kept on ruling — as with Japan's LDP, Singapore's People's Action Party, Taiwan's Kuomintang, Malaysia's United Malays National Organisation — or it has been turfed out by force. Even the restoration of democracy in the Philippines, in 1986, was achieved outside the electoral system; Ferdinand Marcos was toppled not by Filipino votes (he had, in any case, rigged the ballot) but by the 'People Power' of hundreds of thousands of demonstrators in the streets of Manila, and by the defection of a handful of senior military officers.

And yet an answer to the challenge of transition cannot be postponed indefinitely. In practical terms, economic progress cannot happen within a framework of political instability. Asia's strongest economies — Japan, South Korea, Taiwan, Hong Kong, and Singapore — have all had a secure political base, albeit derived from different sources (including military dictatorship for most of South Korea's post-war history and colonial dictatorship for all of Hong Kong's). The next strongest economy in the 1980s was probably Thailand's — and Thai economic progress accelerated as soon as Thai generals stopped mounting coups d'état. The fact that the generals overthrew the elected government of Chatichai Choonhavan in February 1991 does not in itself mean the pace of progress will slow. Indeed, many businessmen saw the coup as the only way to end the rampant corruption of the Chatichai government. What matters for the economy is if one coup leads to another, destroying business confidence in the process. With luck, Thailand's political stability will reassert itself because all political players have a vested interest in a stable economy.

In human terms, too, delay will be costly. Sri Lanka, bloodied and scarred by civil war and ethnic hatred since the early 1980s, is perhaps the world's most obvious victim of political failure since Lebanon. And yet Asia could provide many more examples as it entered the 1990s: sectarian violence in India; guerrilla warfare in Cambodia; ethnic insurgencies in Burma; separatist movements in Indonesia and Papua New Guinea; communist and Muslim rebellions in the Philippines. All these are issues which defy military solutions — and which, therefore, will demand political remedies.

The conventional cure advocated by Western liberals is representative, multi-party democracy. The argument is that economic prosperity is achieved by economic freedom — and that economic freedom cannot exist without political freedom. That may well be true. Certainly, where political freedoms are scarce or non-existent, as in Burma, Vietnam, or China, economic progress lags or even halts. But to Asian minds, the argument begs many questions: what is freedom — or natural justice, or human rights, or any of the other abstract concepts that underpin the Hellenistic democracy of Westminster and Capitol Hill? As one senior Kuomintang official once remarked to this writer: 'In the West, you are born with individual rights; in the East, we are born with social obligations.'

In essence, he must be right (and bear in mind that the Taiwanese, dynamic and full of *joie de vivre*, are arguably the most individualistic Chinese). Western-style democracy is an adversarial process: decision through combat. The Confucian cultures of east Asia prefer agreement: decision after the painstaking search for consensus. Only in the Indian subcontinent, largely untouched by Confucius, and in the Philippines, a colony first of the Spanish and then of the Americans, is the adversarial style popular — elsewhere, it merely provokes embarrassment. In Indonesia, for example, it is unthinkable for politicians to attack each other in the direct, personal terms that their counterparts in Britain, Australia, or the United States take for granted. Instead, criticism must be through allusion and inference; no one should ever be made to 'lose face'. The logical (at least to Indonesian minds) conclusion of this is the system — both political and philosophical — of *pancasila*, the five principles on which Sukarno founded independent Indonesia.

It is hard to quarrel with any of the five: Belief in One Supreme God; Just and Civilised Humanity; the Unity of Indonesia; Democracy led by the Wisdom of Deliberations among Representatives; Social Justice for the Whole of the People of Indonesia. They are as wholesome as motherhood and apple pie — and in practical politics they provide a basis for suppressing the sectarian and inter-communal strife that might otherwise tear apart a nation spread across 13,600 or so islands and 3,000 and more miles. Other governments in South-east Asia acknowledge the benefits brought by *pancasila*, especially in the era of President Suharto. But the suspicion lurks that *pancasila*'s roots are shallow. Because they attempt to bind different cultures, languages, sects, and religions, they are embedded in no single culture — and therefore exist courtesy only of a strong, authoritarian leader. What happens when that leader, General Suharto, leaves the political stage? However much Indonesia's fellow Asians may admire *pancasila*, the truth is that they must look elsewhere for a political model. What will help is that some models are now known to be failures.

The biggest failure in Asian politics is communism. It has failed on two counts: economically, it has been unable to match the achievements of capitalism; politically, it has failed to provide a smooth transition of leaders, witness the power struggles within the Chinese Communist Party.

In short, communism, however adapted to Asian ways, has been a disaster. With the exception of Bangladesh, even the poorest non-socialist countries, such as Indonesia and the Philippines, now enjoy higher living standards and personal incomes than those of Asia's Marxist nations. The most obvious contrast is between China and Taiwan: in 1949, when Chiang Kai-shek and his Kuomintang government moved to Taiwan in flight from Mao Zedong's victorious People's Liberation Army, Taiwan and the Chinese mainland had much the same miserable, war-wrecked economies. Today, the Taiwanese have an income per head at least sixteen times bigger than their relatives on the mainland—which means most of Taiwan's households have washing machines, refrigerators, and televisions, and most of China's households do not. There are two other glaring contrasts between countries that started off as equals: North and South Korea; and Burma and Thailand. As Asia approaches the end of the 20th century, only North Korea pretends such contrasts do not exist.

It was not always so. For almost three decades after the defeat of Japan in World War II, it could be — and was — legitimately argued that communism was an irresistible tide sweeping through Asia. First, Mao emerged victorious in China, the world's most populous country; then, the Korean south was saved from the communist north only by the intervention of United Nations troops, mainly American; finally, Ho Chi Minh, who had defeated the French in 1954 at Dien Bien Phu, seized all of Vietnam for communism in 1975 by capturing Saigon from American-backed South Vietnam. Meanwhile, as Laos and Cambodia fell to communist regimes, underground communist movements were active throughout South-east Asia. Not surprisingly, Thailand, Malaysia, and Singapore feared they might, in the metaphor of the times, be the next dominoes to fall.

But the dominoes did not fall, and any that do in the next decade will be communist ones. The most obvious reason is the economic one, that Asia's communist regimes have failed to deliver the goods. The communist insurgencies of Thailand and Malaysia abandoned the fight in the 1980s because in a period of sustained economic growth they could offer no credible alternative to the legal governments. Now, the only communist rebellion of note in Asia is that of the Philippines' New People's Army. But more than two decades of communist struggle in the Philippines (five, if the Hukbalahap guerrillas' fight against the Japanese during the second world war is included) have failed to bring decisive gains — despite the Philippines' wretched slide into debt and poverty during twenty years of President Ferdinand Marcos.

Why will Philippine communism continue to fail in such ideal conditions for revolution? Probably because NPA fighters, red bandanas around their heads and lucky amulets around their necks, are every bit as inefficient as the government's Armed Forces of the Philippines. As with much else in the Philippines, a flamboyant show is often more important than the dull quest for genuine achievement — which is why many guerrilla raids are comical as well as bloody. When guerrillas accidentally drop their ammunition magazines, or attack empty buildings, it is hard to take them seriously. Also, the Philippines remains a deeply Roman Catholic country, emotionally at odds with Marx's atheism. But the biggest reason is that even at its most feudal and most corrupt, Philippine capitalism still appears to most Filipinos, especially in Manila, to offer a way out of poverty — and no communist neighbour, certainly not Vietnam, has been able to show a convincing alternative.

Yet the economic reason cannot be the only excuse for communism's failure in Asia. In China, for example, the populace — albeit much poorer than the people of Taiwan — is still vastly better off than it was in the corrupt and chaotic days before Mao's victory. Moreover, this populace did not revolt against communism during the economic nightmare of the Great Leap Forward, at the end of the 1950s, nor during the social nightmare of the 1966–76 Cultural Revolution. Whatever the unrest that simmers in the cities, among both students and factory workers, China's rural inhabitants — all 750 million of them — have no particular reason to reject the Party. 'Socialism with Chinese characteristics', as paramount leader Deng Xiaoping named his 'open door' policy of economic liberalism, has made today's peasant generation rich beyond the dreams of their parents. In other words, the economic failure of communism is relative rather than absolute.

What has reinforced the economic evidence of communism's failure is a combination of external force and internal doubt. The outside force was the determination of the United States, even after her humiliating defeat in Vietnam, to block communism's tide. The evidence was concrete in the vast American military facilities at Clark Air Base and Subic Bay Naval Base in the Philippines; human in the shape of military advisers to the army of Thailand; financial in the form of economic aid to capitalist South-east Asia and a ruthless embargo on trade with Vietnam. As one Singaporean minister, Brigadier-General George Yeo, explained in late 1989: 'Americans may have mixed feelings about the Vietnam War but that containment of communism gave ASEAN (the Association of South-East Asian Nations) the years of peace and stability it needed to take off economically.'

But what of the internal doubt? In essence, it is East Asia's pride in its own cultures, and attendant suspicion of foreign, 'barbarian' concepts. Whatever the universality Karl Marx claimed for his ideas, to Asia both he and his ideas were foreign. The result is that Asia only borrowed Marxism — it did not, and will not, absorb it into the cultural bloodstream.

Arguably, China is a huge exception, since — unlike Eastern Europe — it became communist not by an invasion but through an indigenous revolution. And yet China's communism was never the same as Russia's: from Mao to Deng, China's communist leaders have behaved just like the Chinese emperors of old. In practice, Asia's communism has been a method of control and repression for which the Leninist system is ideally suited — but the same system, even over four decades, has never managed to eradicate the innate entrepreneurism of the Chinese and Vietnamese. It may be a mistake to consign Marxism to an Asian oblivion. After all, powerful ideas — witness Christianity — have the habit of survival, even of re-invigoration through re-interpretation. But for at least the next decade Asia's communism will surely be moribund.

The same will not necessarily be true of Asia's other political failure, the rule of the military. As Asia approaches the end of this century, be-medalled generals command the political future of half the continent. Sometimes, their rule is overt, as in the military junta in Rangoon that in 1990 simply ignored the result of Burma's general election. At other times, their presence is in the background: for example, ABRI, the armed forces of Indonesia, whose support has underpinned the rule of President (and former General) Suharto; or the Thai generals who regularly provide ministers (and prime ministers) for a parliamentary system ever aware that civilian rule has its limitations — as demonstrated by the military's bloodless ousting in February 1991 of the civilian government of Prime Minister Chatichai.

In Pakistan, too, it is the generals who, ultimately, call the political shots: in 1990, the military establishment, in league with President Ghulam Ishaq Khan, helped provoke the election that dismissed the civilian prime minister, Ms Benazir Bhutto, from office. In China, where Chairman Mao was careful to subordinate the military to the control of the Communist Party, it is nonetheless the People's Liberation Army that gives each new 'emperor' the means to wield his power. No Chinese leader can rule without the PLA's backing, which is why a presence in the Central Military Commission is worth more than a seat on the Politburo; no Chinese government can make the system of political docility, often repression, work without the support of the seven military regions. As Chairman Mao used to say: 'Power grows out of the barrel of a gun'. Even in Singapore, which prides itself on representative democracy, there is a strain of militarism in the political mix: several leading members of the People's Action Party have an army background — not least ministers Brigadier-General (Reserve) Lee Hsien Loong and Brigadier-General George Yeo — and all able-bodied men are required to perform regular bouts of military service.

Does this military influence really matter? Arguably, not as much as Western democrats, trained to treat military men with suspicion, usually believe. It is, after all, undeniable that in most developing countries — from South America through Africa and on to Asia — most of the available and readily deployable talent is concentrated in the armed forces. The sequence is simple enough: independence from colonialism breeds patriotism and the concept of national defence, which, in turn, attract the best and brightest into the military — which is also the sector of society most likely to offer the resources of discipline and education to make best use of the best and the brightest. That includes the ability to send young officers for training abroad, to Britain's Sandhurst or America's West Point. The natural consequence is that the officer corps of a Third World army becomes a tightly knit, intensely proud intelligentsia for whom ideas and their application are much more easily linked than in the mature democracies of Europe and America, where the military has long been out of fashion.

The problem is that this concentration of talent can distort both the political and economic process. Young officers of the Armed Forces of the Philippines at first supported the fall of Marcos in 1986 and the restoration of democracy under Corazon Aquino. But they then became impatient with the obvious imperfections of that democracy, and their reaction, conditioned by the politicisation of the armed forces under Marcos's martial law, was to plot against Mrs Aquino. The Reform the Armed Forces Movement — cheerfully known, with an allusion to actor Sylvester Stallone's Rambo character, as the RAM-boys — saw itself as the saviour of the state; so did its less right-wing offshoot, the Young Officers Union. Arguably, their arrogant idealism is a delusion that has inspired fascist movements throughout history — for example, in Franco's Spain or Pinochet's Chile. Unarguably, their activities did much to worsen the Philippines' plight by distracting its government and destroying the good wishes of foreign investors for the post-Marcos nation.

But the pernicious antics of disaffected military idealists in the Philippines do not automatically mean that the military should have no role elsewhere in Asia. The need to separate the military from a nation's political life is a Western prejudice that not all emerging nations agree with. In Indonesia, for example, the *dwifungsi* — dual function — of ABRI, the Indonesian Armed Forces, is guaranteed by law. And why not? It was Indonesia's armed forces that, by guerrilla warfare, finally wrested the nation's independence from the Dutch after the second world war.

Victory did not automatically give Indonesia's military a politically decisive role. Indeed, President Sukarno — 'Bung (brother) Karno' to the mesmerised masses — mistrusted some of his generals and promoted political parties as a counterweight, especially the well-organised communist PKI.

But weight and counterweight did not produce a stable balance. From 1950 to 1957 six cabinets fell in rapid succession, making Sukarno as well as ABRI exasperated with the behaviour of the parties. The result was martial law. But since martial law meant an enhanced role for ABRI, Sukarno sought to limit ABRI's influence by favouring the PKI — a process which provoked ABRI into setting up rival grassroots organisations managed by serving army officers. These eventually coalesced into the 'Functional Group', or Golkar, an amalgam of interest groups — from farmers to soldiers, to civil servants, to women's organisations and so on — that is easily Indonesia's biggest political party, not least because the PKI was bloodily outlawed in the unsuccessful, supposedly communist, coup attempt of 1965. Given that background, Golkar's connection with the military is like a child's to its parent.

But is it healthy for the connection to be too close? After all the child grows up and demands the freedom to make its own mistakes. Too much parental control stunts the child's development. In 1980 ABRI filled over half of the posts in government at the national provincial and district levels — and a third of the posts in the foreign service. To their credit, some military thinkers, and not only from the younger generation, believe that Golkar must become more independent of ABRI (indeed, in the 1987 elections, the military adopted a determinedly neutral stand). They reason that while a strong political force may 'guarantee the creation of national stability to sustain development', in the words of the academic Ibrahim Ambong, 'that situation tends to create monolithic life, which in fact is incompatible with the dynamics of development.' Better, therefore, for ABRI to assume a more professional role, and not to flaunt its responsibilities as the guardian of the nation-state.

Easier said than done. The best model east of Turkey was probably Thailand's military — until the coup of February 1991, the 17th (successful or otherwise) since the abolition of the absolute monarchy in 1932. But even despite attempted coups in 1982 and 1985, and the successful one in 1991, the military has in general tempered its fierce loyalty to the monarchy with a growing readiness to encourage pluralistic party politics. An inferior model is Pakistan's armed forces, ever impatient with the corrupt frailties of civilian democracy. But all have their flaws: the tendency of the military to intervene too readily, or to demand bigger budgets, or to ignore basic civil and human rights. And then there is corruption. In contrast to their Western counterparts, Asia's generals regularly have assets and life-styles grossly in excess of their official earning power.

In robust economies such corruption may not be too damaging — and some would say it acts as a necessary lubricant for the economy. Moreover, the failure of military rule in Asia is total only in Burma, where Ne Win and his generals reduced a nation of wealth and promise to a state of poverty and despair in just a generation. But partial failure does not qualify as success. It is no accident that in Asia's richest nations, the military are barely noticed; and no accident that in the poorest, the military are always prominent. The best answer, therefore, to the challenge of transition must surely be a civilian one.

'The People's Liberation Army loves the people. The people love the PLA.' So went the official slogan in late May, 1989. It was true. The perfect family in modern China is a hard-working couple in their early thirties with one young child — a boy. On family outings the boy is invariably dressed in the uniform of the PLA. Springtime crowds, bicycling through Beijing, are dotted with PLA caps, perched by doting parents on the heads of their offspring. At the Great Wall, the souvenir for Chinese and foreign tourists alike is a military cap with the Red Star of the revolution. Love for the army is simple and genuine: the PLA freed China from Japanese occupation and Nationalist chaos; it organised the countryside; it brought education to the masses; it rescued the nation from the lunacies of Chairman Mao's Cultural Revolution. All this is within the lifetime of hundreds of millions of Chinese, so no wonder there is a reservoir of popular affection for the PLA.

But the reservoir is fast leaking. When armoured columns of PLA troops drove along Beijing's Changan Avenue in the pre-dawn hours of June 4th, 1989, the PLA's 'love of the people' was exposed as a deceitful myth. As student demonstrators fled Tiananmen Square — the vast expanse linking the Gate of Heavenly Peace with the Great Hall of the People and the Forbidden City — hundreds, some say thousands, of ordinary Chinese were torn down by volleys of machine-gun fire or crushed under tank tracks. Literally overnight, Beijing's mood of popular euphoria was transformed by the sullen acceptance of repression. In the ensuing hunt for the 'black hands' who had attempted a 'counter-revolution' against the State, scores were executed and thousands more summarily imprisoned. Once again, as in the days of the Cultural Revolution, foreigners were shunned, lest innocent conversations be misinterpreted by the ubiquitous secret police. Blithely setting aside the liberalism that had accompanied a decade of economic reform, the official media set about reviving all the old slogans of Marxist, indeed Maoist, orthodoxy — including the injunction to 'love the PLA'

The endeavour will not succeed. The 'Beijing massacre', as the outside world called the tragedy of June 4th, 1989 (China talks only of the 'June 4th incident'), is one reason. Yet the reservoir of affection for the PLA and, by extension, respect for the political system as a whole, had been leaking and evaporating long before the student protests that had occupied Tiananmen Square since the previous April.

Ironically, it was the 'open door' economic policy brought in by Deng Xiaoping at the end of 1978 that began the process. First the peasantry and later the urban masses (economic reform reached the cities in 1984) saw an alternative to the way of life enjoyed or endured ever since the 1949 Revolution. That way of life decreed that the Communist Party decided where citizens should live and work, whom and when they should marry, how many children they should have, when they should retire. It also decreed that a career in the PLA was both worthy and coveted: a peasant boy from an impoverished province such as Gansu or Shaanxi would not only be fed and educated if he entered the PLA, but he would also join a brotherhood with a network of self-help that spreads all over China.

The alternative proposed by the Dengist reforms was essentially simple: to make money. As Deng observed, in contradiction to the late Chairman Mao: 'To get rich is glorious.' Millions took him at his word. The Dengist reforms introduced the idea of profit: once a farmer or a worker had fulfilled his contract to provide the State with a set quota of production at a set price, the rest of his labour was for him to profit from. Some prices and quotas were still set by the State — but other prices were increasingly freed, often allowing fixed and free markets to co-exist in the same goods. The results were immediate and astounding: for a decade China's economy grew on average by more than 10 per cent a year, the world's fastest pace apart from the petroleum-rich Sultanate of Oman; farmers, tilling the land as they, not the Party, thought fit, grew rich — and filled new 'free markets' in the cities with fresh fruit, vegetables, and meat; factory workers, flush with bonuses from their extra output, bought refrigerators, television sets, and even (as smugglers from Hong Kong were quick to spot) video-cassette recorders.

The success came with a price tag: cynicism, corruption, and inflation. If a taxi driver in Beijing, alert to the black market opportunities provided by dealing with foreign businessmen, could make ten times the money of a surgeon, why should anyone become a surgeon? If a middle-ranking Party official could buy machine parts — or pork and grain, for that matter — at a low price fixed by the State, he would be a fool not to hoard them so that he could illegally sell them later on a rising free market. It was what Western economists call 'arbitrage' — and what normal people call 'corruption'.

Meanwhile, more people had more money and expected a better quality of life, and so prices steepled in an inflationary rise not seen since the corrupt and chaotic days of the Nationalists.

Traditional communism had banished inflation: when both output and prices are fixed, unsatisfied demand (which is what causes inflation) exists in the form of queues outside State shops with empty shelves. Now Deng's 'Socialism with Chinese Characteristics' was letting the genie out of the bottle. In 1988, inflation reached a perilous rate of 30 per cent a year. The way to beat inflation and 'the system' was to use *guanxi* — or connections — and the people with the best *guanxi* were invariably members of the Party. In retrospect, the student occupation of Tiananmen Square in April 1989 was the inevitable reaction to China's economic crisis and social decay, which added to the cynicism many, if not most, Chinese had felt for the Party ever since the Cultural Revolution, with its thousands of arrests, executions, and imprisonments. No wonder the leadership, old, isolated, and fearful that worker sympathy for the students would become overwhelming, decided martial law, followed by military assault, was the only solution to preserve the Party's monopoly on power.

But can the monopoly survive even the 1990s? The weakness of the Party will become ever more obvious, not least to its own leaders as they regard the wreckage of communism in the Soviet Union and Eastern Europe. The Party's thinkers realise that a return to Maoist isolation — the brand of security North Korea has practised under Kim Il Sung — is impossible. The 'open door' policy has made China dependent on foreign trade for a third of the nation's income; around 50,000 students, half of them on government scholarships, are in the United States; foreign debts can be repaid only if the Special Economic Zones, neo-capitalist enclaves dotted along the coast, make deals with foreign investors. In short, the Party will have to grope for an accomodation with the liberalism imported from a non-communist outside world.

It will find the going tough, not least because, paradoxically, the Party's opponents have no clear idea of what to put in the Party's place. When Deng Xiaoping proclaimed the need for economic reform, he talked of the 'Four Modernisations' — a programme to improve agriculture, industry, defence, and science and technology. A young intellectual, Wei Jingsheng, then added a fifth — 'Democracy' — and was given fifteen years in prison for his impudence. A decade later, the students in Tiananmen Square made the same plea; their impudence was to erect a plaster-of-Paris 'Goddess of Democracy' statue, facing the portrait of Chairman Mao and uncannily resembling the American Statue of Liberty.

But what do the Chinese mean by democracy? The students have no clear definition, because they have no experience of any system except

Marxism. 'Democracy' they see as the ability to express an independent thought; it does not necessarily involve a battle of ideas between political parties. Meanwhile, the Communist Party regards such battles, the essence of Western politics, as anathema. More than a year after the Tiananmen tragedy, the official *People's Daily* declared: 'Socialist democracy is one million times better than bourgeois democracy.' The Party considers itself democratic because it says it represents the masses; bourgeois democracy, by contrast, is a Western system to favour capitalists by exploiting the masses. At all costs, China must, the Party argues, guard against economic progress tempting the nation into a 'peaceful evolution' to bourgeois democracy.

This hypocrisy insults any mainland Chinese who has travelled beyond North Korea, or who has met Chinese visitors from Taiwan, Singapore, and Hong Kong. What keeps the hypocrisy intact is that China is still ruled by a clique of old men 'allergic', as one Western diplomat observed, to any hint of political change and hence of instability.

But by the end of the century, the old men will all be dead or at least incapable. In 1990, for example, Deng Xiaoping was 86, President Yang Shangkun was 83, and economic theorist Chen Yun was 85. The succeeding generation of Party leaders, less dogmatic and also less powerful, will be unable to resist the economic and social pressure for greater political freedom. If they try, by maintaining a regime of repression, they risk ultimately a popular uprising that will destroy the Party and fragment China into provinces at economic (or even military) war with each other. More likely, they will try to adapt by copying Asia's apparent political successes.

T he nation which other Asians envy — sometimes openly, often reluctantly — is Japan. Its economic power, they assume, is matched by political strength and continuity. The evidence is the Liberal Democratic Party, supreme in government ever since its formation — from a merger of the Japan Democratic Party and the Liberal Party — in 1955. In comparison, the opposition parties are pygmies, too small to threaten the LDP individually and too fractious to form a menacing coalition. Talk to opposition members of the Diet, or parliament, and you soon realise they have no expectation of power — and some would be terrified to receive it.

None of this will change in the 1990s. Barring some catastrophic error, the LDP will continue to rule Japan virtually without challenge. Indeed, most Japanese believe the rule will continue just as smoothly beyond the '90s. No wonder, then, that the ruling parties of East Asia look to their

Japanese counterpart. The LDP, it seems, has found the elixir of life and the key to national prosperity. Copy the LDP and the future will bring success.

At the end of the 1980s, Taiwan's Kuomintang, facing a small but vigorous Democratic Progressive Party, was examining the LDP's way with the opposition; Singapore had introduced multi-member constituencies in some ways similar to Japan's; and, on 9 May 1990, South Korea's Democratic Justice Party merged with two of the three opposition parties to become the Democratic Liberal Party — deliberately designed to rule, like the LDP, for ever.

The imitation is a sincere form of flattery. On the surface, Japanese politics has solved the quandary that faces all Confucian societies: how to cope with the conflict of ideas in a culture that abhors confrontation. The answer is that the LDP is made up of competing factions. Because no single faction is powerful enough to dictate its terms to the others, ultimately the survival of all depends on reaching a consensus. The same approach then influences dealings with the opposition. In a society that lives by consensus, the LDP will only rarely dictate its terms, knowing that if it does, it risks an embarrassing boycott of parliament by the opposition parties. Western politicians might say, 'So what?' To the Japanese, however, it would mean a break in the consensus, and so a loss of face for everyone. In 1990, Prime Minister Kaifu wanted to send troops to help America in the crisis caused by Iraq's invasion of Kuwait; in the end he abandoned the controversial plan, even though he had the arithmetical support needed for parliamentary approval. Mr Kaifu's compromise was to help the Americans with Japanese cash instead of Japanese manpower.

But however sincere the flattery, the imitation may be mistaken. The 1990s will present the LDP with challenges which will reveal its flaws more than its strengths. The paradox is that the greatest weakness of all is the factions, normally seen as the LDP's essential strength. The reason is that the factions revolve around personalities, not ideas and policies. Their very names reveal as much: the Tanaka, Suzuki, Fukuda, Nakasone, and other factions bear the names of politicians, not ideologies. They operate not by the persuasion of ideas but through the ties of marriage, personal loyalty, and, especially, cash. Their function is simple: to collect money from LDP supporters and distribute it to LDP candidates.

The function exists because politics in Japan is an expensive business. In multi-member constituencies, with elections at least once every four years to the lower House of Representatives, it can cost up to $4 million to get elected. Collecting that cash needs organisation — and inevitably spawns corruption and nepotism. In the 1970s LDP politicians, in a scandal that reached Prime Minister Kakuei Tanaka, took huge bribes from the American Lockheed corporation; in 1989 the equivalent scandal centred on payments by an employment and property company called Recruit, and the victims included another prime minister, Mr Noboru Takeshita. That scandal led to the loss of the LDP's majority, for the first time in its history, in the upper House of Councillors — but the loss was soon balanced by an impressive victory in the lower house.

The problem for the 1990s is that the corrupting demands of money-politics will coincide with problems the LDP is ill equipped to meet. Hitherto, the LDP has been able to conceal its flaws: the Japanese constitution, imposed by America after the second world war, renounces war — and so implicitly encourages industrial advance by peaceful methods. That is precisely what Japan under the LDP has spectacularly achieved, thereby allowing the Japanese in general (including politicians) more-or-less to ignore the political world beyond Japan.

But the outside world will increasingly intrude into Japanese politics. Already, the West in general and the United States in particular is demanding an end to Japan's trade surplus — the greatest single source of friction in Japan's dealings with its allies. In the 1990s the surplus will shrink, but that will not lessen the demands on Japan to use its financial and economic strength less selfishly — which means not just opening up Japan's domestic market to foreigners (a process well under way) but also reforming a tax structure which favours protected farmers (who vote for the LDP). Even then, there will be the potentially more difficult task of adjusting foreign policy to needs that go beyond economics. How will Japan react when America, pleading poverty, withdraws still more of the troops and weapons that have kept the Pacific more-or-less pacific since the end of World War II? As Japan's military power inevitably increases, how will her politicians reassure not just other Asians but their own citizens? After all, Japanese militarism in the past has brought only misery, both at home and abroad.

These are the kinds of questions that are bread-and-butter to Western political parties, ever eager to argue competing solutions. But to the LDP such questions are uncomfortable: factions are about power and money, not ideas. Until Yasuhiro Nakasone became prime minister in 1986, no Japanese leader had been particularly concerned with foreign policy issues — and the collective apathy to such issues will not fade overnight. The truth is that the LDP has not solved the Confucian quandary, how to accommodate the battle of ideas in a consensual system; Japan has simply been rich enough and protected enough to ignore the quandary.

If communism and militarism cannot meet Asia's challenge, and if the success of the LDP is a mirage, where else will Asia look? The answer, right or wrong, will be to Asia's own roots. Most Asian countries will search, regardless of the overall political system, for strong, authoritarian leaders of the kind who dominated the immediate post-colonial period. Indonesians will want a commanding figure in the mould of Sukarno and Suharto; the Chinese will want a new emperor, whether he calls himself communist or not; the Koreans, re-united or not, will want not megalomaniacs like Kim Il Sung but smoothly decisive men like Roh Tae Woo. Certainly Asia will become more 'democratic', with richer, better-educated populations demanding a say in the way they are governed — but Asia's version of democracy will shelter beneath an umbrella of authoritarianism.

There are two reasons for this prediction. The first is the influence of Confucius. Two and a half thousand years ago the Chinese sage taught 'Order and Stability' by dividing human relations into five categories: those between the ruler and his deputies; those among friends; those between husband and wife; those between parents and children; and those between elder and younger brothers. Only in the relationship between friends is there equality; the other categories all involve obligation (for example, 'A wife must obey her husband'). Through social obligation comes social harmony. The result is a culture of authority and obedience. True, Confucius's follower, Mencius, justified the killing of a bad emperor — but in practice, the bad had to be very bad to inspire revolt. How else can one explain the longevity of inefficient rule in modern China, North Korea, and Vietnam? Confucian stability is all too often at the expense of economic stagnation.

But Confucianism is a phenomenon of East Asia; it has had little impact, for example, in the Indian subcontinent. Whereas the pedestrians of Seoul, Taipei, and Singapore wait patiently for the lights to change even on empty roads, the self-willed citizens of Delhi and Bombay jaywalk with the insouciance of Londoners. What, then, is the second reason for predicting that the Indians, like the Chinese, will share an Asian desire for authoritarianism — or 'strong rule'? Why do Indians, Pakistanis, Bangladeshis, and Sri Lankans feel a nostalgia for autocratic leaders such as Mrs Gandhi, Zulfikar Ali Bhutto, or Mrs Bandaranaike and Junius Jayewardene?

The answer is essentially simple. Because Asia's political institutions are still fragile, and will remain so for some years to come, only strong individuals can hold them together. The mature systems of America and Europe react with barely a tremor to even the greatest of shocks — witness the Watergate scandal in America. By contrast, Asia feels vulnerable to even the smallest threat — witness the use of the Draconian Internal Security Act (a colonial invention) in both Malaysia and Singapore to arrest seemingly innocuous critics of the regimes. Witness, too, the Singaporean practice in the late 1980s of restricting the sale of foreign newspapers which allegedly 'interfered' in Singapore's domestic politics.

Lee Kuan Yew, Singapore's prime minister from 1959 to 1990 (and still, in 1991, secretary-general of the People's Action Party), was bluntly to the point in his justification. As Lee told Hong Kong's Foreign Correspondents' Club in October 1990: 'When the marketplace contest of ideas has been practised in newly independent nations, it has ended in less than happy results. This has happened in Sri Lanka and India. Both are heterogeneous, multiracial societies. In both, there are intense racial and regional disagreements on important, emotional issues, such as race, religion and culture. In both, a plethora of media propound divergent and incompatible policies, mobilising sectional constituencies and arousing emotions. In both, the result has been confusion and dissension, rather than enlightment and consensus.'

The Singapore solution of Mr Lee is to take the Western institutions with which Singapore began its independence — a multi-party parliament, an independent judiciary, and a free press — and over the years to cocoon them within the authoritarian embrace of Confucianism. Part of the process is age: as Lee grew older, he became ever more conscious of his Chinese-ness (and to an extent that may well have been offensive to many Malay and Indian Singaporeans). Another part is example: the 1969 race riots in neighbouring Malaysia — in which 196, by the official count, were killed — is part of the political folklore on how the contest of political parties can let racial sensitivities explode into violence.

But the final part of the process is more recent. As Lee says: 'The growing strength of the economies of East Asia and their social advances have altered Asian views of the value of the British and American systems as models . . . The mood in Asia is changing. There is self-confidence in their capacity to modernise and compete. There are new models to emulate. An obvious one is Japan. Japan's successful economy is based on her political and social stability, her orderliness, low crime rates, negligible drug-taking, and strong communitarian values. Asians are in little doubt that a society with communitarian values where the interests of society take precedence over that of the individual suits them better than the individualism of America.'

Maybe so. The consequence in Singapore is a deliberate attempt to smooth friction at its source. Lee's People's Action Party, even as its share of the popular vote declines, dominates Parliament because of the 'first past the post' system (in the 1988 election only one opposition candidate was elected). But of the 55 constituencies, 13 are 'group representation constituencies' — they elect three members each, of whom at least one must be from an ethnic minority. This certainly favours the organisational strength of the PAP, but it does also give a voice to Malays and Indians. Similarly, a new category allows up to six 'Nominated Members of Parliament' — a way of ensuring a place, albeit with slightly reduced powers, for the opposition. Put all this together with a docile, managed media and with a judicial system that no longer allows an appeal to the Privy Council in London: the result is a political and social vehicle especially designed to take Singapore from the strongman rule of the Lee era into the 21st century without sacrificing the benefits of authoritarianism. Indeed, one feature of Singapore's immediate future is the attempt to have firm, Confucian government without it taking the dynastic shape common to such governments. Lee's son, Brigadier-General (Reserve) Lee Hsien Loong is undoubtedly a future prime minister — but only after Goh Chok Tong has had a turn. Similarly, the elder Lee will undoubtedly become the nation's elected president (hitherto they have been chosen by Parliament) — but not the first one.

The question is how well all this will work. The answer will be exasperatingly vague. The Lee formula will succeed for Singapore because Singapore is a small, malleable community — only a third or less the size of New York. Given competent administrators, almost any system could therefore be made to work. But the Lee formula will also fail his people: in the late 1980s, Singaporeans were emigrating — especially to Australia — at the same rate as Hong Kong Chinese. But the Hong Kongers were driven by their fear of China's takeover in 1997; the Singaporeans were driven by boredom and by a feeling among many that the Chinese and the best educated (often the same people) had an unfair advantage that went beyond the aggressive meritocratic norms of Singapore.

Moreover, despite the comprehensive range of Lee's political vision, it is difficult to see his formula taking root beyond Singapore. Sometimes this will be because the Lee vision cuts across vested interests. In Malaysia, for example, the number one issue for the 1990s will be — as in previous decades — how to give more economic power to the politically supreme, but materially disadvantaged Malay half of the population. Somehow, this will have to be done without alienating the third of the population who are Chinese — and who have done most to advance Malaysia's economic progress. For better or worse, the issue will be decided by a political system which, unlike Singapore's, is avowedly racist. The leading member of the ruling coalition is UMNO Baru, or the 'new' United Malays National Organisation; its leading partners are the Malaysian Chinese Association and the Malaysian Indian Congress. The opposition is similarly based on racial lines (although in practice rather than ideal theory). Since the prime purpose of each party is to protect the interests of its own race, the potential for ethnic tensions is obvious. Even though racial violence has been extremely rare (the 1969 riots are the famous example), it is hardly a system one would invent from scratch. But it exists because it has evolved, and, clearly, none of the parties will legislate itself out of existence.

The same is true elsewhere. Many, probably most, South-east Asians revere Lee and his Singaporean solution. In the Philippines, many have already called for a Lee Kuan Yew figure to take over from the ineffectual Mrs Aquino; in Hong Kong, some toy with the idea of Lee as an adviser, even as a transitional governor, in the run up to 1997; in Taiwan, Lee's services as an intermediary with mainland China are valued and exploited. Indeed, even in China itself, Lee is lauded. It was his colleague Goh Keng Swee who advised China on how to set up the Special Economic Zones; and it is Lee that many Chinese intellectuals use when they advocate 'neo-authoritarianism' as the next stage in freeing China from the strait-jacket of traditional Marxism.

But the reverence will not automatically lead to imitation. Philippine culture, with its essential flavours of corruption and forgiveness, simply cannot breed the accountability, verging on the vindictive, that characterises a Lee Kuan Yew. The best the Philippines can hope for in the 1990s is a leader as brilliant and inspiring as Ferdinand Marcos — but without the selfish and excessive venality. Taiwan and China provide much better breeding grounds for leaders to emulate Lee, but they will still have to work within the existing systems of the Kuomintang and the Chinese Communist Party. After all, the alternatives are considered too dreadful by people and leaders alike. The alternative to the KMT would be parties demanding Taiwan's independence and the *de jure*, as well as *de facto*, abandonment of the dream of a reunited China. This, in turn, would probably mean war with the mainland's communists, who, like the KMT, oppose Taiwan's secession from the motherland. Meanwhile, the alternative to the Chinese Communist Party is what? The most likely answer is bureaucratic chaos, economic dislocation, provincial warlordism — and, therefore, civil war. Such a process, or one near to it, is alarmingly evident to China's leaders in the collapse of communism in eastern Europe and in the fragmentation of the Soviet empire, and, indeed, the Soviet Union.

Yet to be forewarned does not necessarily mean there will be enough protective arms in readiness. The great political challenges that will face Asia in the next decade already outstrip the abilities of Asia's political institutions. Reunification between Taiwan and China, and between North and South Korea; a settlement in Cambodia; a rapprochement between India and Pakistan; peace in Afghanistan — all these developments are probable, certainly possible, by the end of this century. They will be the result of popular will, particularly in the case of the Koreas, and economic necessity. But they will all be achieved by individual leaders, determined and far-sighted, rather than by political parties and institutions. It was Deng Xiaoping, not the Chinese Communist Party, who eventually decided, in 1989, to accept the olive branch offered by Mikhail Gorbachev and so end thirty years of Sino-Soviet hostility. It was the late Chiang Ching-kuo, not the KMT, that decided in 1986 to set Taiwan on the course of political liberalism and better relations with the mainland; and it was Chiang's successor, Lee Teng-hui, who in 1991 formally ended the state of war with the mainland. It was Roh Tae Woo, not the South Korean parliament, who, at the end of the 1980s, began the push for better relations with the communist world — from China to Russia and even North Korea. Arguably, the transfer of Hong Kong to China's sovereignty in 1997 will be an institutional process — but only because Deng Xiaoping devised the notion of 'one country, two systems' in the early 1980s.

All those are challenges that cut across national boundaries. Yet the same reliance on the strong leader will apply also to intrinsically domestic issues: sectarian strife in India; civil war in Sri Lanka; economic and political reform in China; economic recovery and political stabilisation in the Philippines.

In the past, strong leaders gained their legitimacy from revolution and the struggle for independence — witness Mao Zedong and Deng Xiaoping in China; Mahatma Gandhi and Jawaharlal Nehru in India; Sukarno and Suharto in Indonesia; Lee Kuan Yew in Singapore; Ho Chi Minh and Le Duan in Vietnam. Sometimes, the strong leader begets a dynasty, by blood or marriage: Nehru's daughter was Indira Gandhi, whose son Rajiv succeeded her; in Pakistan, Zulfikar Ali Bhutto, a civilian strongman executed by Zia ul-Haq, a military strongman, was eventually followed to the premiership by his daughter Benazir; in Taiwan, the reforming President Chiang Ching-kuo was the son of Generalissimo Chiang Kai-shek. In North Korea, Kim Il Sung hopes (probably in vain) that his son Kim Jong Il will prove a durable successor.

But the legitimacy tends to fade with the memory. The challenges of tomorrow will demand a new crop of leaders to face a complex mix of demographic, economic, and social pressures. Those pressures will test all of them and, as has already happened with President Aquino in the Philippines, bewilder some. Leaders, however, are created as well as born: the underlying question, therefore, is how well Asia can make them.

Three

Poisoned Success

'It is hardly the sun's fault if your branches have no leaves' — Chinese proverb

*B*angkok hospitals overflow with casualties from the latest disaster to hit
the Thai chemical industry . . . Cyanide and dynamite bring Philippine fish
stocks close to exhaustion . . . Beijing's luxury hotels issue tourists with
smog masks . . . Cancer becomes Asia's biggest killer . . .

(plausible aspects of Asia's environment in the year 2000)

Asia's cultures emphasise the
harmony of man with his environment. The Chinese talk of *fung shui*, wind
and water; South Korea's flag is the symbol of *yin* and *yang*, the balance of
complementary forces; Buddhists, Taoists, and Hindus believe in a self-
renewing life source that pervades all existence.

But none of these cultures is an adequate defence for Asia's natural
environment before the destructive growth of Asia's people and their cities.
While North America and Europe will spend the 1990s cleaning their
industrialised economies, most of Asia — especially China and India — will
become dirtier with every added unit of gross domestic product. With few
exceptions, the pursuit of affluence will be literally poisonous.

There are two reasons for this gloomy, but certain, prediction. The first
is that Asia's population is growing at a speed which will outstrip
governments' ability — financial and managerial — to provide adequate
housing, sanitation, and industrial controls. The second is that — apart from
Japan, Singapore, South Korea, and Hong Kong — Asia is still near the
beginning of the upward curve of industrial development. Since that curve
creates pollution, the further a country has to travel along it, the more
pollution it will create on its journey. What compounds the problem is that
until a country is industrially advanced, as Japan now is, it rarely has the
money, or the pressure from an environmentally aware population, to
clean up its act. Instead, the pressure is the opposite, and polluting, force
of consumerism.

The evidence is already clogging Asia's roads and clouding its skies. Asia
is taking to the motorbike, car, and truck with an enthusiasm unmatched in
the century of the internal combustion engine. Stand by the roadside in
Tokyo or Seoul and you see the traffic crawling through a shimmer of
exhaust haze; in Manila, you are choked by diesel clouds belching out of
garishly decorated 'jeepney' taxis — a long wheel-base version of the old
American jeep. In Bangkok, thousands of *tuk-tuks*, motorised tricycles,
assault the senses with the noise and smoke of over-stressed two-stroke
engines. But as the *tuk-tuks* disappear with Thailand's increasing prosperity,
they will be replaced by the motorcar — and so one source of pollution will
be followed by another.

It is hard to exaggerate Asia's enthusiasm for motorised transport, harder still to appreciate how that enthusiasm has been expressed — and how its polluting effect has, until recently, been simply ignored. Little more than a generation ago few Asians, even in Asia's richest countries, could afford to buy and operate a car, or even a motorbike. Today's Japanese teenager expects, almost as a right of citizenship, to own first a motorcycle and later a car. His grandfather, however, had to save for years to become motorised. The change came when the economic miracle of modern Japan filled workers' pockets with yen to spend. Suddenly, the father of today's teenager was able to transport himself and his family wherever there were roads to take them. The number of Japanese who owned a vehicle of some kind rose from 32 million in 1977 to over 50 million just a decade later. The skies of Osaka and Tokyo can no longer be cleaned, regardless of today's insistence on catalytic converters for car engines and controls on exhaust emissions. The sad truth of Japan's economic miracle is that it involves diesel and gasoline particles rising constantly into the air that people breathe.

Where Japan leads, the rest of Asia tends to follow. Consider the situation in Taiwan at the start of the 1990s: a population of 20 million crammed into a small island and buying new cars at the rate of 10,000 a month — which add themselves to 2 million cars already on the roads, all of which do battle with 7 million motorcycles. The Taiwanese, of course, take this for granted; it is the foreign visitor who gasps (literally, thanks to the air quality) at the gridlocked insanity of Taipei traffic.

The same foreigner will struggle to breathe in Bangkok and Manila, sprawling capitals whose vehicle populations have doubled in a decade and whose environmental safeguards are either fictional or absent. Not even the 'clean' cities of South-east Asia, Kuala Lumpur and Singapore, are immune from the pernicious encroachment of the car. Each year, the number of people buying cars in Malaysia goes up by 10 per cent. In Singapore, despite huge taxes on car and truck ownership, and despite rules that more-or-less compel the buyer of a new car to reduce an old one to scrap metal first, the number of vehicles on the roads almost doubled during the second half of the 1980s. The government's reaction? Determined that the 'garden city' of Asia should not become a fume-filled car park, it decreed in 1990 that vehicle ownership would henceforth be decided by quotas, for which intending purchasers must bid; in addition, owners of cars more than ten years old would have to pay surcharges to keep them on the road.

What happens next? Simple: no other country will attempt, like Singapore, to slow the advance of the car. Popular reaction would be too adverse, and vested interests in car sales are too powerful. Instead, through Asia's 1990s, the growth of automobile ownership will accelerate. The poorest people will get rich enough to buy mopeds; less poor people will move from mopeds to cars; the rich will move from small cars to larger ones (in the decade to 1988, Japan's small-car fleet fell from 2.4 million to 1.7 million).

All this will involve a frightening acceleration in vehicle ownership, and so in the growth of pollution. At the start of the 1980s, almost 800 million Indians had barely a million vehicles between them. At the start of the 1990s, no more than a few million of the one billion Chinese had been inside a motor car (indeed, there were only 35 cars for every 10,000 Chinese). When you start from such a small base, consumer growth becomes phenomenal. Once China, for example, takes away the bureaucratic bars to the private ownership of the motor car, every peasant in Guangdong will take his savings from under the mattress, or get money sent from relatives abroad, to buy a car — the modern world's symbol of affluence and proof of mobility. And, as it brings new freedoms to its driver, each car will foul the atmosphere for everyone. So too, of course, will coal-fired power stations, inefficient steel mills, out-dated chemical plants, and all the other necessary trappings of the industrial age.

Inevitably, the air of Asia will get nastier to breathe wherever industry takes root or expands. But the dirtiest atmosphere will undoubtedly be China's. At the start of the 1990s the per capita value of China's goods and services — its gross domestic product — was around $330 (although some analysts, reworking China's Byzantine statistics, reckon it was almost $500). That is the result of a sustained economic growth which among the world's other nations is matched only by Oman, an Arabian sultanate with a population of only 1.5 million (or less than two thousandths that of China), and by the rival Chinese island of Taiwan. In the four decades since the Communist revolution, mainland China's economy grew by an average of 6 per cent a year — and almost all of the growth came from the spread of heavy industry, fuelled by low-quality, dirty Chinese coal.

The consequence is a pollution problem more than equal to the horrors of Eastern Europe. In July 1988, China's air was so clouded with coal smoke that the city of Benxi, in the north-east, disappeared from satellite photographs. In nine out of every ten Chinese cities, the quality of air (measured by the quantity of suspended particles) regularly falls below the nation's minimum standard — which is itself the lowest level approved by the World Health Organisation.

But air quality, or lack of it, is not the only reason that China is Asia's greatest environmental nightmare. A fifth of China's rivers and waterways are dangerously polluted with industrial and human waste. As the 1990s began, some 90 per cent of China's 434 registered cities had no sewage system, and the rest could only handle about 5 per cent of each day's waste. Each year in Shanghai, some 450,000 tonnes of excrement pours into the slow muddy swirl of the Huangpu river. Not surprisingly, in early 1988 Shanghai suffered an epidemic of hepatitis-A that struck more than 290,000 of the city's residents and left patients piled up in hospital corridors. Since neither sanitation nor personal hygiene in China will improve overnight, there will certainly be similar outbreaks in the future.

Sometimes, China's pollution amounts to wilful poisoning: a metal processing plant in Nanchang was forced to close in 1989 after discharging 10 tonnes of chromium-laced waste into the city's drinking water. Doubtless there were — and are and will be — many other cases either undetected or unpunished. Because of the economic reforms of the 1980s, China's factory managers are under pressure to make profits by cutting costs, so why spend money on keeping the industrial process clean? Moreover, an individual factory manager can hardly change the system around him. If the municipality does not provide disposal facilities, the factory is bound to dump its waste wherever and whenever it can. Some municipal irresponsibility is frightening: as landfill sites are filled to overflowing, sanitation workers from some cities simply dump garbage by the roadside. In Heilongjiang province, in China's far north, garbage is dumped on the frozen surface of the Songhua river — and so the river is clogged with rubbish as soon as the ice thaws.

Bad air, poisoned water — and, increasingly, poor land. Soil erosion, by the passage of wind and water, has afflicted China for thousands of years. The Yellow River, for example, carries almost half of the silt load of all the world's rivers and has been controlled for centuries by dykes and canal systems. But what worked once will not necessarily work always. Estimates of China's deserts vary widely: some experts say the deserts cover 13 per cent of the nation's land area; some say 33 per cent — and some say the deserts have expanded by around 30 per cent over 30 years. Whatever the exact figure, the fact is that the world's most populous nation is losing huge amounts of topsoil each year, and that some form of soil erosion affects roughly one sixth of the country.

The reasons are plain: the land is falling victim to population growth and the encroachment of industry. Grassland is overgrazed; trees are cut for firewood; some 440 million tonnes of plant stalks are burned each year instead of being ploughed back into the soil to sustain its fertility; and chemical fertilisers, instead of night soil brought from the city, are used to produce more frequent crops — regardless of the law of diminishing returns. Meanwhile, the economic reforms of the 1980s have spread a rash of light industry across what was previously agricultural land. If present trends continue, by the year 2000 China will have doubled its non-arable land within the space of 50 years.

Can the trend be reversed before then? Probably not, but at least China's authorities appreciate that the problem exists. Since 1982, some 200 million people have planted an average of five trees a year, normally on 'National Afforestation Day'. The idea is to halt the soil-stripping winds that sweep in from the west by building a 'Great Green Wall' of trees and shrubs across China's north and north-west. Practice is another matter: the central and provincial authorities who pay for the wall are perennially pressed for funds — and farmers are understandably reluctant to provide tree seedlings without prompt payment. The result is a patchy wind-break, vulnerable to fire and the depredations of insects. Dust in China is as intrusive and pervasive as in the arid Middle East.

All this, inevitably, adds up to little hope for environmental salvation, at least not in the 1990s. Towards the end of the 1980s, the declared ambition of Deng Xiaoping, the paramount leader who ten years earlier had set China on the path of economic reform, was to quadruple China's per capita gross domestic product (GDP) to $1,000 by the end of this century. That means that China will have to grow through the 1990s by around 7 per cent a year to reach the level of national prosperity now enjoyed by Thailand, Botswana, and Cameroon.

It will not be done by observing the niceties of pollution control. Present environmental regulations are either insufficient or ignored. Fines, for example, for releasing contaminated water are so small that they amount to barely half the cost of purifying the water — so why would any rational factory manager bother? Moreover, since the State owns almost all of China's industry, individuals rarely bear personal accountability and so have little incentive to change their behaviour. By 1992, the State is supposed to raise spending on environmental protection from the current 0.7 per cent of GDP to 1 per cent — an amount that the director of the Environmental Protection Agency admits will be 'largely insufficient'.

Instead, China will reach for its goal by doing more of the same: more heavy industry, such as steel mills and petrochemical plants; more light industrial sprawl from township enterprises that make cheap toys, textiles, and plastic goods. All this will demand an increase in electricity that will be met by burning poor quality fossil fuels — mainly coal — in inefficient power stations.

It could hardly be otherwise. China, with 15 per cent of the world's coal reserves, is the world's largest producer and user of hard coal, burning some 900 million tonnes each year. By the year 2000 it will burn probably 1.5 billion tonnes a year — and will have made little effort to switch to other forms of supply. Inherently cleaner energy from hydro-electric stations is underused because there are neither enough dams nor enough money to build them. Natural gas reserves are mainly in the west and south-west, with no transportation system to bring them to the consumers in the east. True, the alternative of nuclear power is being pursued (the Daya Bay nuclear power station, just 33 kilometres east of a nervous Hong Kong, will come onstream during the early 1990s), but slowly, and amid justifiable fears of managerial and technical incompetence. In other words, economic growth will depend on using coal that has an average ash content of 27 per cent and sulphur content of 5 per cent. Since this coal is priced well below free, world market levels, there is no incentive to wash it at the pit-head to reduce its ash and sulphur. China, therefore, is doomed to get dirtier as it grows richer.

T he rest of Asia can hardly be immune from China's pollution. The noxious air is carried by winds that obey no frontier. The poisoned rivers flow into international waters, or, in the case of the Pearl River, swirl into Hong Kong's already polluted sea.

In which case, the rest of Asia has all the more reason to be as clean as it can be. The chances are not good.

Ironically, where they are worst is in Asia's least industrialised countries. The logic behind this paradox is that in rich Japan and Taiwan, people know — and loathe — the reality of pollution. They march in the streets or disrupt the annual shareholder meetings of polluting companies. Eventually, governments will have to appease them with stricter environmental safeguards. By contrast, Asia's poor know, and care, little about the damage they do to their surroundings. As one director of the environmentalist group, Greenpeace, said at the 1990 summit of Commonwealth leaders in Malaysia, 'Environmental protection is a luxury people can only afford when they have a full stomach.'

True enough. It is difficult to explain to the dirt-poor tribes of the hills of Laos, or Burma, or northern Thailand the harm for the world of the 'slash-and-burn' technique by which they clear the forest. They know nothing of the forest's role as the lungs of the planet, releasing oxygen into the atmosphere and extracting carbon dioxide; the 'greenhouse effect', when carbon dioxide accumulates in the air, is a buzz phrase they have never heard, let alone understood. Poor peasants from India across to Indonesia and the Philippines just see a need to clear trees in order to plant crops. And why not? It is exactly what America's pioneers did as they moved west — and exactly what Europe's hordes did a thousand and more years earlier. Dr Mahathir Mohamad, prime minister of Malaysia, was not alone in 1990

Figure 4 *Dirty Air*

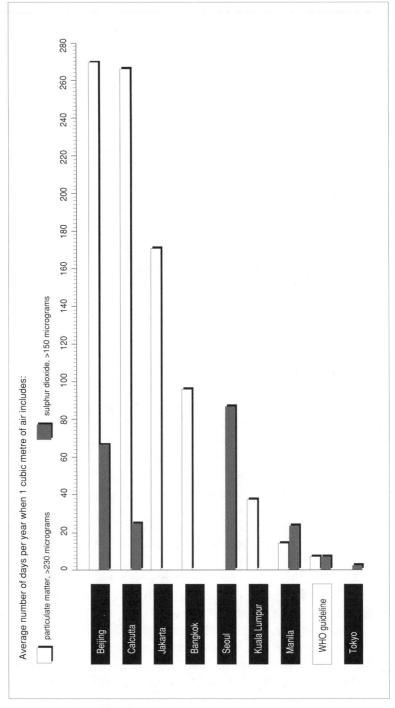

Average number of days per year when 1 cubic metre of air includes:

☐ particulate matter, >230 micrograms   ▨ sulphur dioxide, >150 micrograms

Beijing
Calcutta
Jakarta
Bangkok
Seoul
Kuala Lumpur
Manila
WHO guideline
Tokyo

Source: World Resources Institute
Printed by permission of *The Economist.*

Figure 5   *Dirty Water*

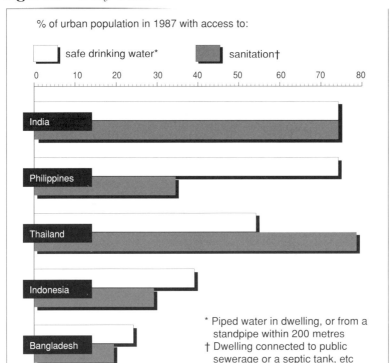

% of urban population in 1987 with access to:

safe drinking water*   sanitation†

India
Philippines
Thailand
Indonesia
Bangladesh

* Piped water in dwelling, or from a
standpipe within 200 metres
† Dwelling connected to public
sewerage or a septic tank, etc

Source: World Health Organization estimates
Printed by permission of *The Economist.*

in suggesting that environmental pressures from the West were a new, and hypocritical, form of imperialism.

It is equally difficult to persuade the villagers of South-east Asia that their traditional agricultural industries bring pollution as well as prosperity. An ordinary sugar mill, for instance, produces huge volumes of organic wastes — which normally pour into the local water system. The same is true of the factories that process coconuts, or palm oil, or rubber, or timber — the products that underlie all the 'resource economies' of South-east Asia: Thailand, Malaysia, the Philippines, Indonesia, Burma, Laos, Cambodia, and Vietnam. And it is true of the South-east Asian shrimp farms that supply the insatiable appetite of the Japanese. Even China's piggeries are a hazard: their waste all too easily runs off into the adjacent water supply (which is why in the mid-1980s Singapore banned all livestock farming).

Unhappily, the tendency to pollute does not apply only to traditional rural industries. Low-technology light industry in developing countries involves a witch's brew of poisons such as cyanide, arsenic, cadmium, and mercury. The proof is in the effluent that spills from the electroplating factories of Indonesia and Hong Kong or the dyeing factories of Taiwan. All too probably the shiny chrome on the car fenders of Philippine jeepneys, or the batik shirts bought by tourists in Bali, or the fake designer handbags sold on Bangkok sidewalks will have poisoned the environment at some point in their manufacture.

It would be naive to believe that the tendency can be suppressed sooner rather than later. Light industry is spreading throughout the poorer parts of Asia: through the islands of Indonesia, the villages of India, and along the coasts of Thailand. Increasingly, factories, mills, and workshops will dot the landscape of Vietnam and the rest of Indochina. Assume peace in Cambodia, and the whole fertile swathe of Indochina, from the Gulf of Tonkin to the Bay of Bengal, will suck in foreign investment — from Asia's 'Tigers', South Korea, Hong Kong, Singapore, and Taiwan; from prospering Thailand and Malaysia; from rich Japan; and from Americans and Europeans who spy the world's next opportunity to reap huge rewards from small outlays. Yet much of this investment will be 'new' in form rather than substance: industrialists from rich countries will transplant to the poorer countries the outmoded and polluting plant and equipment that they can no longer use at home. They will be following a well-trodden route: from the mid-1980s onwards, Taiwan's small and medium-sized manufacturers have been installing old, but working, equipment in mainland China in order to escape Taiwan's rising wage rates and stricter pollution controls. The same type of industrial migration will cross the next frontier of direct foreign investment — Vietnam, a country ravaged and despoiled by half a century of constant war, and the rest of gnawingly poor Indochina.

If the polluting tendency cannot, in the short term, be stopped, can it at least be slowed? With luck, yes. The first reason for a qualified optimism is that Asia knows much more about industrial intoxication than it used to. In Japan, for example, there are more than 2,000 officially recognised survivors of Minamata disease — and there are probably thousands more who could also qualify for compensation for a disease that began in 1956, when the chemical wastes of the Nippon Chisso Hiryo company began to poison first the fish and then the people of Minamata, in the south of the country. India, too, has been made painfully aware of industrial pollution — ever since 1985, when a cloud of poison erupted from the Union Carbide chemical plant in Bhopal.

A second reason is that checking pollution is technologically feasible, even for poor countries. Zinc plating, for example, can be done without using cyanide as an agent; waste coconut water can be fermented to produce vinegar; sulfur can be recovered from chimney stacks and be used to make gypsum; sewage sludge can be anaerobically digested to make methane gas.

The problem, however, is that it is usually only the rich, or at least prospering, countries that have the management skills and bureaucratic determination to introduce clean technology. In Japan almost all incinerators have energy recovery devices that generate steam for heating and electricity. Moreover, Japanese recycling techniques have become so efficient that well over 90 per cent of all scrap metal and wood chips is recovered for later use. Singapore is equally efficient, treating sewage effluent to provide industrial water and methane gas. Malaysia has dramatically cut the pollution from its palm oil mills by introducing the 'polluter-pays principle' — ie anyone who wants to damage the environment must pay a fee to do so. The higher this penalty, the more willing industrialists are to invest in cleaner, more modern facilities. In early 1990 Singapore took the polluter-pays principle a clever step further: having signed the Montreal Protocol to reduce the use of ozone-damaging chlorofluorocarbons (CFCs), the island republic — often derided as 'squeaky clean' — made users of CFCs bid for a share of a fixed allocation. The idea worked: the electronics industry, which uses CFCs as a solvent and cleaning agent, started investing in water-based cleaning systems before the CFC auction became too expensive.

But what of the poor countries? However sincere their motives, their attempts to secure a cleaner environment will be thwarted, time after time, by lack of money, skills, and personnel.

Take the Philippines as an obvious contrast to Singapore. In theory, the Philippine regulatory code is every bit as comprehensive as Singapore's. Any new industrial venture in the Philippines — be it mining, or forestry or smelting — must be preceded by an environmental impact study and so be dependent on the approval of the grandly named Department of Environment and Natural Resources. But in practice, whereas Singaporean officials from the Pollution Control Department vet industrial plans and patrol factory areas, their Filipino counterparts are rarely seen — and when seen are then ignored. The reality of the Philippines is that at the start of the 1990s a field engineer for the Department of the Environment was paid between 4,000 and 8,000 pesos a month ($165–330), scarcely enough to resist a timely bribe from a sugar planter who would otherwise have to invest $650,000 in a waste-treatment plant. Meanwhile, the incorruptible machines erected in the Manila streets to monitor air pollution are permanently out of order. It is blowing in the particle-laden wind to imagine that the Philippines has the ability to clean up its act within the next decade.

Unhappily, what is true of the Philippines is true also of China, Indonesia, the Indian subcontinent, and, often, Thailand. For years to come, they will do depressingly little to correct their collective faults.

Unless, that is, public opinion in Asia shifts so far that it begins to resemble Western attitudes to environmental issues. Arguably, this could happen — especially as television in the 1990s reaches into almost every Asian home. Generally speaking, it is true that Asia's masses, uneducated and uninformed, have little sense of the way development wobbles the ecological scales. But in most Asian countries there is now an emergent middle class that has some understanding of the problems of development, and is willing to express its discontent.

The obvious example is Taiwan, where, because the richest stratum of society is only about five times wealthier than the poorest, six out of every ten people consider themselves part of the middle class. As soon as the late President Chiang Ching-kuo abolished martial law in 1987 and allowed political freedom, this middle class allied itself to the working class and began mounting environmental protests at the rate of one demonstration a day.

The protests produced results. In October 1988 the government ended the siege by demonstrators of a polluting petrochemical complex in southern Taiwan by paying 21 local villages compensation of NT$1.27 billion (US$49 million). That set a precedent: the following February, 200 fish farmers in Kaohsiung, the hideously polluted port in Taiwan's far south, marched against the state oil company to demand NT$7 billion in compensation for polluted water. Attempts by the petrochemical industry, which is a pillar of Taiwan's economy, to build new — and cleaner — naphtha crackers have been dogged at every turn by environmentalists.

Arguably, the protests in Taiwan exaggerate the Taiwanese concern for their environment. For some, environmental issues are a way of supporting the political opposition against the Kuomintang government that fled from mainland China to Taiwan in 1949 and has ruled the island-born Taiwanese ever since. Other demonstrators may be as interested in extortion as in the environment — a trick the Japanese learned a generation earlier. Yet, however false the motives of a minority, there is no denying that most Taiwanese are now genuinely worried at the toxic mess they have made of their island in its concentrated, almost obsessive transformation from poverty to wealth.

To a lesser extent the same is true elsewhere. The Friends of the Earth, Western in origin, have friends throughout Asia. In Malaysia, for example, they are known by the literal translation, Sahabat Alam Malaysia. The Korean Green Party and the Environmental Preservation Party both entered the political fray in 1990. In the Philippines, where the national culture encourages eloquence and argument (often for its own sake), the small middle class has spawned scores of environmental groups, the most notable Haribon. Many of their leading lights have, in turn, been co-opted into the Department of Environment and Natural Resources — and the result is a splendid set of environmental rules and guidelines (read, for one example, the Philippine Strategy for Sustainable Development).

But will Philippine middle-class eloquence evoke a response from ordinary Filipinos? Not now, and probably not during the 1990s. The reason is simple: most Filipinos are preoccupied with the struggle for simple survival. That applies equally to the sugar-cane cutters of Negros, who spend much of the year without work, and to the office workers who spend four hours a day going by cramped and noisy jeepney to and from Manila's Makati business district. The office workers appreciate the need for change — but how can they take part in the change when Manila's buses are few and dilapidated? One of the many Philippine absurdities at the end of the 1980s was the decision by the mayor of Quezon City, a densely populated area of metropolitan Manila, to declare his district a 'smoke-free zone' in which cigarette smoking was banned in public areas. Meanwhile, every passing jeepney was belching out the equivalent of a lifetime's cigarette smoke with every single change of gear. Until the means for environmental improvement are available, why should any rational person make an individual effort? That question, of course, applies not just to the Philippines, but to every part of impoverished Asia, be it scruffy Katmandhu or overcrowded Shanghai.

But it begs another question: will individuals make the effort once increasing national prosperity does make the means available? One of the challenges for Asia in the 1990s and beyond will be to ensure both the popular support and the legal framework to enforce environmentally sensible policies.

Fortunately for Asia's future, the base from which it starts is surprisingly good. Virtually every country now has a government department responsible for environmental protection. In Singapore, the Ministry of Environment actually runs ahead of public opinion and pressures from environmentalists; in other countries, the environmental lobby lives in hope of finding like-minded civil servants — as in Taiwan and the Philippines — and then indulges in the fainter hope that these officials will wield clout over the rest of the government.

Less fortunately, there is a tendency in almost all countries for red tape-wielding administrations to bind even the best intentions into a state of inertia. In Hong Kong, for example, the legal system — with its right of appeal and insistence on due process — has the perverse effect of allowing known polluters to stay polluting. So, for a time, did the law itself. Until late in 1990 Hong Kong's *Water Pollution Control Ordinance* gave exemptions from the legal discharge limits to factories that were discharging waste before August 1989 — and then allowed the polluters to increase their discharges by up to 30 per cent. The bizarre logic behind this was that the limits had been set several years earlier during an economic downturn, and so lost their relevance when the economy picked up. A better explanation is that a pro-business administration was excessively timid in its judgement of what industry would accept. As the British colony's governor, Sir David Wilson, said in October 1990 in his annual address to the Legislative Council, the ordinance was 'a licence to pollute'. In India, the bundles of red tape that tangle anti-pollution efforts are frighteningly large — and they are only slightly smaller in Indonesia.

But regardless of the failings in practice, at least Asia has most of its theory right. The polluter-pays principle is jargon that is becoming familiar from India across to the Philippines. Environmental legislation either exists or soon will. Thailand, for example, will specifically address environmental degradation in its seventh five-year plan, beginning in 1992. India, inspired by the Bhopal disaster, has had fierce rules since 1986 on the unlimited liability of a polluter to pay for damage, even damage committed in good faith; in the case of foreign multinationals, the unlimited liability applies to the parent company as well as the local subsidiary.

Perhaps, then, theory will in part be proved by practice: industrialists will learn, willingly or otherwise, that to exploit a country's poverty with cost-cutting pollution must carry a price. The Asian Development Bank, for example, now insists that all its loans and assisted projects are first assessed for their environmental impact. The same scrutiny will be demanded by other donors, and by corporate investors. In 1989 America's Scott Paper withdrew from a proposed wood pulp joint venture in Indonesia for reasons that allegedly were influenced by environmental protests.

But despite the growing public awareness, and the framework of environmental legislation, Asia — especially poorer Asia — will continue to harm itself. The reason is the power of money to pervert policy and to shape the actions of politicians. That power is real throughout the world, witness the squabbles for regional development funds in Europe or for new automobile factories in America; in Asia the power is seen whenever an industrialist wants to build a petrochemical plant, or quarry a mountainside, or construct a tourist resort. It is most evident of all in the felling of Asia's trees.

Most non-Asians view Asia's economy through the prism of their own possessions: the Toyota car and Nikon camera; the contoured tennis shoe (made with the cheap labour of, first, Japan, then Korea, now Thailand and Indonesia, and soon, no doubt, Vietnam); the Hong Kong wristwatch and solar-powered calculator; the Taiwan clone of an IBM personal computer. If they look beyond the personal trappings of their life, they might think of wide-diameter steel pipe made in Japan, or oil tankers made in Korea. But almost certainly their vision would exclude Asia's forests, spreading in a thick green carpet from the eastern border of India across to the Philippine archipelago.

And yet that carpet supplies plywood, chipboard, newsprint, toilet paper, even toothpicks, to much of the world — in particular Japan. At the end of the 1980s Indonesia was providing 70 per cent of the world's need for tropical plywood; a tenth of Malaysia's export earnings came from selling timber in one form or another; almost a tenth of Thailand's GDP was produced by the forestry industry; and Burma was relying on exports of teak and other hardwoods to pay almost half of the interest on its foreign debt. In short, Asia — or more particularly the tropical rain-belt of the continent's south-east — has been taking advantage of nature's bounty. In the words of the Malaysian prime minister, Dr Mahathir Mohamad: 'The West has extracted wealth from its forests by chopping them. It is our turn to obtain some wealth from our forests.'

But for how long? The theory of forestry management is that the industry should be sustainable: only large, mature trees will be felled; young trees will be left to allow the forest to regenerate itself. The result is then a virtuous circle of husbandry and profit — and the virtue extends to all mankind since it is the world's rain forests, from South America to South-east Asia, that supply the air with its oxygen and rain-making clouds. By contrast, kill young trees as well as old, and the world will grow hot and short of oxygen; the polar ice caps will melt and flood low-lying countries such as Bangladesh; some, such as the Maldives, will simply disappear beneath a layer of saline water.

That last sentence smacks of alarmism, and alarmists — from Malthus to the authors of the Global 2000 Report commissioned by President Jimmy Carter — invariably underestimate man's versatility and ability to adapt.

Even so, the alarm is not without cause, as any sequence of satellite photos of the earth's rain forests will show. Since the end of the second world war, half of the earth's rain forests have disappeared before the advance, in Brazil, or the Congo or Papua New Guinea, of pioneer farmers, slash-and-burn nomads or voracious logging companies. By one calculation, 40 hectares of rain forest are lost every minute; in Asia, the loss amounts each year to an area half the size of Taiwan. Clearly, it cannot go on indefinitely.

But who will stop it? Thailand's forest cover fell from 29 per cent of the total land mass in 1985 to only 19 per cent in 1988 — but it was only when devastating floods in 1988 swept through deforested swathes of the country's south that all 301 of the nation's logging concessions were cancelled by emergency royal decrees. The decrees were long overdue:

Thailand had cut so extensively into its forests that by the start of the 1990s it was having to import wood to meet a sixth of its needs. True, in the late 1980s Indonesia banned the export of logs — but only to add value to its forests by exporting plywood and other processed timber, which meant just as much, if not more, pressure on its forests.

The problem is simple. Just as with narcotics, when there is a demand, there will also be a supply. The demand-side 'villain' of Asian deforestation is Japan: its housing and construction industries have a seemingly insatiable desire for wood; its fastidious people throw away some 20 billion pairs of disposable wooden chopsticks a year. As a result, Japan is the world's biggest importer of tropical timber, consuming 15 million cubic metres a year and destroying 750,000 acres of tropical forest a year in the Malaysian state of Sarawak alone. The relative strength of the yen means imported hardwood is cheaper than Japan's own softwood (and, in any case, 40 per cent of Japan's forests are protected); it also means the wood is cheap enough to be thrown away, rather than recycled. Chopsticks are the obvious example (and arguably not an important one, since chopsticks are made from fast-growing, easily replenished softwoods), but the same applies to the plywood boards used for shaping concrete blocks — and often to wooden furniture so cheap that people leave it behind when they move house.

The supply-side has a more colourful list of actors: corrupt politicians in the Philippines; venal Thai generals; 'well-connected' Indonesians; both government ministers and rebel chieftains in Burma. In the Philippines, for example, army officers supervise the export of logs illegally felled on tracts owned by prominent families. At the end of the 1980s, when the aborigine tribes of Sarawak, Malaysia, were blockading the logging roads, the state's environment minister was also the owner of a timber company, while the family of the chief minister held large logging concessions. Much the same thread ties politics to logging in the neighbouring state of Sabah. In Indonesia, the biggest timber tycoon is probably the Chinese-Indonesian Bob Hasan (an Indonesianised name; his Chinese name is The Kian Siang), who is in partnership with Sigit Harjojudanto, a son of President Suharto. In short, it is impossible to separate the logging industry — legal or illegal — from South-east Asia's power élite.

Probably the clearest example is in Burma. As soon as Thailand's logging industry was halted by royal decree, Thailand's generals turned to their counterparts in Burma. The result was, in double quick time, a score and more of contracts that allowed Thai companies to operate directly inside Burma as well as to buy from Burmese companies. In one sense, this was nothing new: Thailand had long bought Burmese timber — but from the insurgent Karen, Kachin, and other tribes who have fought the Rangoon government for the past four decades. What was different this time was that in their desire to get more teak and other hardwood than the rebels could supply, the Thais were dealing with the Burmese authorities and offering them military co-operation against the insurgents.

In terms of business, it was a perfect match: the Thais have an urgent need for timber and the Burmese government has an urgent need of foreign exchange. In ecological terms it will probably prove disastrous. Traditionally, Burma's official loggers have used the 'Burma Selection System', which works to a 30-year cycle of selective logging in any one area and recognises that a teak tree may take a full century to reach maturity. But the greed of both parties to the deal now means that the system is likely to be observed only in the breach. That, of course, is already true in much of the Philippines, Malaysia, and Indonesia. Why should it be different in less developed economies such as Burma's? Vietnam may turn out to be an exception to this rule of environmental rape for profit — but only because Agent Orange and other American defoliants stripped the country of four-fifths of its forests during the Vietnam war.

Is the destruction of Asia's environment therefore both inevitable and inexorable? Up to a point, most certainly. There cannot be economic development without some damage, to soil, water, and air. Even environmentally aware societies such as California's suffer environmental harm in their quest for material comfort.

Figure 6   *Deforestation*

	Area covered with woods or forest %	% annual de/reforestation		% of total land under protection
		1972–82	1982–87	
Asia Pacific				
Brunei	44	-3.2	-3.5	
Hong Kong	12	+0.9	0.0	
Indonesia	67	0.0	-0.1	7.5
South Korea	1	-0.1	0.0	5.7
Macao	*			
Malaysia	60	-1.1	-1.2	4.9
Philippines	37	-2.7	-1.8	1.7
Singapore	5	0.0	0.0	4.3
Thailand	28	-2.4	-1.6	7.8
Centrally Planned				
Burma	49	0.0	+0.2	0.0
Cambodia	76	0.0	0.0	0.0
China	13	+0.7	-0.8	0.2

* less than 0.05

	Area covered with woods or forest %	% annual de/reforestation 1972 82	1982 87	% of total land under protection
North Korea	75	0.0	0.0	0.0
Laos	56	-0.7	-0.7	0.0
Vietnam	40	-0.4	-0.4	0.6
South Asia				
Afghanistan	3	0.0	0.0	0.2
Bangladesh	16	-0.4	-0.3	0.7
India	23	-0.6	-0.1	4.3
Nepal	17	-0.1	0.0	7.1
Bhutan	70	+0.3	+0.2	18.6
Pakistan	4	+1.0	+0.6	9.4
Sri Lanka	27	-0.4	0.0	10.6

Source: The Economist's 'Book of Vital World Statistics, a Complete Guide to the World in Figures' published by Hutchinson Business Books/Random Century.

But the damage can be limited. The best hope for Asia's forests, for example, is not that the loggers will suddenly discover virtue, but that their customers — especially Japan — will.

The hope has at least some justification. In the 1990s Japan, which has only just coined a word to translate the Western sense of 'the environment', will feel rich enough and secure enough to take moral stances on the world beyond its shores. Already, Japanese corporations are becoming sensitive to the bad publicity caused by Japanese-aided projects around the world that dam rivers or build roads through rain forests. Indeed, big business's federation, the Keidanren, now sees the profit to be made not from damaging the environment but from selling anti-pollution equipment — and from taking the lead in meeting ever stricter world standards on issues such as chlorofluorocarbons. After all, the first to meet a standard — for air-polluting automobiles or biodegradable plastics — will grab the biggest share of the market, and so the biggest share of the available profit. That is a lesson Japan learned years ago — and where Japan leads, Asia's other rich countries will follow.

Meanwhile, the rest of Asia will learn that tourism is as much a resource as timber, gold, or copper. Preserve the flora and fauna of Asia, from the Indian subcontinent across to the white-beached islands of the Philippines, and you have a paradise that makes money — as the ecologically alert Australians and New Zealanders discovered long ago.

Put that together with cleaner technology and environmental lobbies, and Asia — notwithstanding the certain nightmare of China — has a chance of providing a respectable natural legacy for its future generations. What those generations will do, socially and politically, with their inheritance, is another question.

Four

Learning to Think

'Learning is as necessary to a nation as water to a fish' — Chinese proverb

'The nail that sticks up, will be hammered down' — Japanese proverb

*S*ingapore celebrates its first Nobel prize winner . . . Japan's Ministry of Education, alarmed by the rise in truancy, says parents must be held responsible if their children go absent . . . Muslim fundamentalists at the University of Malaya fail to gain re-election to the board of the students' union . . . The Philippines launches a 'university of the air' in Tagalog . . . The University of Asia, set up by the Association of South-East Asian Nations, confers its first degrees . . .

(educational possibilities for Asia 2000)

At Singapore's Changi airport teenage bookworms sit cross-legged in the corridors, using the air-conditioned cool to prepare for yet another round of school exams. Near Taipei's railway station, youngsters throng special 'cramming schools', desperate for the extra marks required for university in America. In Hong Kong, immaculately uniformed girls return home from school — to tiny sampan boats moored in the foul-smelling typhoon shelter in Causeway Bay. In the mountains of Pakistan, Pathan toddlers gather in a mud-walled schoolroom to learn the Koran by heart . . .

Throughout Asia, from Trivandrum to Tokyo, education is a serious affair. Truancy and idleness are the un-Asian luxury of Australia and the world's other advanced, self-indulgent nations. The classroom violence of New York and Los Angeles is inconceivable, even in Asia's most deprived and crime-ridden cities.

And so it will remain for at least another generation. Education, allied to the work ethic, is Asia's passport to wealth. The obvious proof is in the near-perfect adult literacy rates of rich and urbanised Japan, Hong Kong, and Singapore. The less obvious evidence is that even poor peasants get richer if they can read fertiliser instructions and calculate prices (by an 8 per cent increase in output according to one study in Africa). Only in Asia's poorest countries do parents want their children to labour in fields and factories instead of learning — and, if there is a choice, the sons will learn and the daughters will work.

But what exactly will Asians mean by 'education'? What they mean now is somewhat superficial: the acquisition, usually by rote, of factual knowledge. For most, this remains the basics of reading, writing, and arithmetic. For the élite, it has evolved to include bio-chemistry, engineering, medicine — even aeronautics. But almost everywhere, the humanities are considered the old-fashioned province of the second-rate scholars: the best brains are directed to medicine, the applied sciences, and law. Literature, philosophy, and fine arts, because they do not lead to obviously lucrative careers, are for inferior minds. Worse still, as in some faculties of Islamic Studies, they may even be for closed minds.

For much of Asia, this definition cannot change for years to come. The challenge for the Indian subcontinent, Indochina, and Indonesia will be to provide the rudiments of literacy and numeracy when education budgets are overwhelmed by population growth. Out of India's 500 million adults, more than half the men and two-thirds of the women are functionally illiterate: they are unable to read and write a short, simple statement on their everyday life. While in China, thanks to the effective literacy campaigns of the one-party State, factory workers can carry out simple written instructions, in India the worker needs a boss's voice. The same is true in Afghanistan, Bangladesh, and Pakistan — anywhere that lacks the infrastructure of schools, teachers, and books.

But for Asia's rich the challenge will be different. How can individuals, regimented into Confucian conformity, begin to think creatively? The question applies to all the 'miracle' economies of East Asia, but most particularly to their leader, Japan. In nine decades of the Nobel prizes, there have been only seven Japanese winners. Even allowing for the Western bias of the prizes, the number is a humbling reflection of how little Japan has given the world besides automobiles and consumer electronics. As one official commission on education in Japan reported in the mid-1980s, the 'principle of putting emphasis on individuality' must now guide all aspects of the nation's schooling: failure to reform 'will have a major impact on Japan's fate in the 21st century'.

Why should that be? Conventional wisdom in the West holds that Japan's schoolchildren are harder working, better behaved, and more intelligent than their American and European counterparts. In standard intelligence tests, the average Westerner — by definition — scores 100. When Japanese students take the same tests, the average is 117. When the International Association for the Evaluation of Educational Achievement (an appropriately grand title for such a portentous issue . . .) carried out a world-wide assessment of standards in mathematics, Japan came first in arithmetic, algebra, and geometry. In contrast, American students came tenth, twelfth, and sixteenth. That was in 1981–82, and subsequent evidence suggests the gap may have widened. By one reckoning, a Japanese high school diploma is worth the same as an American bachelor's degree. Dyslexia is unknown, or at least unrecognised, despite a script that involves two alphabets and 2,000 Chinese characters.

But this excellence carries a heavy price, not just in the 'uniformity, rigidity and closedness, all of which are deep-rooted defects of our educational system', as one official publication puts it, but also in a scholastic misery that lasts from kindergarten to adulthood. Japan's schoolchildren are regimented in ways that the children of Brooklyn and Brixton would neither understand nor accept. Schools require uniforms (some even regulate the colour of a pupil's underwear). Jewelry and cosmetics are naturally out. One in three junior high schools specifies that boys should not have hair longer than 0.9 centimetres. Schoolgirls are told how to fold their socks. Out-of-school behaviour is often as regulated as in-school activities: no going out at night, no trips to the video-game parlour. Break the rules, and the punishment may be deliberate humiliation — for example, having to lick the teacher's foot.

Sometimes, the discipline goes tragically to excess. In July 1990, the Fukuoka school board said it was investigating seven teachers who had buried two students up to their necks in sand and left them, at the ocean's edge, for twenty minutes. The students' sin was to have refused to admit to extorting money from classmates. Amazingly, the school's parents' association supported the teachers' action. In the same month, in Kobe, fifteen-year-old Ryoko Ishida arrived seconds late at her high school. As the school clock chimed 8.30 a.m., a teacher sent the school's heavy gate slamming shut on its tracks — and Ryoko was crushed to death. When the school principal later expressed his regret, he told the school's 1,500 students that they should come earlier to school: 'I would like all of you to think again about your basic life-style.'

The required style is unremittingly harsh. There is no mystery to Japan's schoolroom excellence in international comparisons. It results from hard work and hard discipline. Compulsory schooling — six years of elementary school, three of middle school, and three of junior high school — begins at the age of six, but 90 per cent of five-year-olds attend some form of kindergarten or other pre-school education. For four-year-olds, the proportion is just over half, and for three-year-olds, barely able to dress themselves, the proportion is one in every toddling six. The school week lasts until Saturday lunchtime, and there is a minimum of 210 days of classroom instruction. Add in extra days for field trips, sports, and so on, and the average Japanese school year lasts for 243 days. By contrast, the American year, including field trips, sports, and all other non-academic activity, lasts for 180 days, the British for 192, and the French for 185. Moreover, the Western schools like to cultivate an individual's own talents, from throwing the javelin to acting in the school play. Not so in Japan: throughout, the emphasis is on melding individuals into a cohesive, absolutely uniform group. The all-powerful Ministry of Education decides every detail of the curriculum, down to which Chinese characters should be learnt at what age. Pupils do not question and argue — they listen and memorise, even though there are at least 40 students in each dingy classroom. There are no remedial classes nor streams for different abilities.

Neither the bright nor the stupid gets special attention, and all must do homework that works out at two hours a night compared with the American child's thirty minutes. The average Japanese schoolchild feels worn out, but no wonder his standard outstrips that of his *gaijin* counterparts abroad — he (or she: the same is true for girls as well as boys in the Japanese school system) puts in a great deal more effort.

But the rigours of compulsory schooling are not the only ones for the Japanese child. He (or certainly his parents) must think of his adult future. A quarter of the Japanese labour force enjoys 'lifetime employment' with big companies, like Mitsui and Mitsubishi, who recruit from the universities. The best way to get into a good company is first to get into a good university, and the only way to do that is to excel in the university's entrance examination. One result of this ambition is that while half of Britain's schoolchildren disappear as soon as they reach sixteen, the minimum school-leaving age, nine out of every ten Japanese teenagers continue to highschool in preparation for what the Japanese call 'exam hell'.

This hell claims many victims: two out of every three candidates will fail to get into a university or other college of higher education, so another consequence of the system is that half of all fifteen-year-olds attend *juku*, or cram schools, in the evenings and at weekends in a concentrated — and expensive — effort to improve their chances. There are now at least 35,000 cram schools, often charging thousands of dollars a year. The crammers are crammed (two- thirds of them were founded after 1976) because demand is insatiable: the exam hell that awaits an eighteen-year-old trying to get into Tokyo, Keio, Waseda, or other top universities will determine his life for the next forty years. Those who fail often try again and again, pouring still more yen into the *juku*. They are known as *ronin*, or masterless *samurai*, in an ironic, but not disparaging, reference to feudal Japan. Of the half-a-million candidates a year to all universities, almost half will be *ronin*.

Is it all worth the effort? In career terms, undoubtedly. The four years an undergraduate spends in university are the only interlude of hedonism a Japanese can expect before retirement. Former Prime Minister Yasuhiro Nakasone reportedly called it 'leisureland' — no tests, no papers to write, no need to study at all. The reason is that Japan's companies do their own in-house training; they recruit an employee according to which university he attends, not what he learns there — which is why the 'exam hell' is to enter university, not graduate from it.

Educationally, however, the effort is ludicrous. University entrance examinations are a bizarre form of Trivial Pursuit: Which monarch was involved in the second partition of Poland? Which composer dedicated 'The Musical Offering' to monarch A, Haydn, Mozart, Bach, Handel, Vivaldi? Which country, Indonesia, Thailand, Bangladesh, Burma, the

Philippines, or Malaysia, had the following rice crop? Those are typical questions for Waseda and Tokyo universities — and can be answered only by those who have spent countless hours memorising instead of thinking.

And yet this system is what has produced the post-war economic miracle of East Asia. South Korea has the same exam hell as Japan; Taipei has the same cram schools as Tokyo. Hong Kong and Singapore, with their background of colonial Britain, are spared much of the trivia, but their students still face relentless pressures to succeed in school systems that, unlike Japan's, are avowedly élitist. Each year, the front page of Singapore's *Straits Times* gives banner coverage to the boys and girls with the best exam results — while those who fail know they have lost face for ever. Whatever the country, its classroom graduates will be literate, numerate, conformist, disciplined, hardworking, and obedient (all the things, some would say, that their Western counterparts are not). They are the perfect workers for today's volume industries: in car plants and tourist hotels alike, they provide efficient, error-free service. As one international banker, constantly besieged by job applicants in his Singapore office, observed: 'They can always tell you what, when, where, and how.'

The same banker then added: 'But they can never tell you why.' That, however, is precisely the question Asia's industrialised economies will have to answer in the next decade. Japanese workers are already among the most expensive in the world; Hong Kong's and Taiwan's are up to ten times more costly than workers on the Chinese mainland; Singapore's labour force, with high wage rates and compulsory pension contributions, is surrounded by the cheap masses of Malaysia and, especially, Indonesia. Soon, the workers of Indochina will enter the regional economy and undercut everyone. The only way, therefore, that expensive workers can stay employed is to improve their skills. Whole economies will have to go 'up-market' in the next decade. The Taiwanese artisan who now makes handbags will soon have to make high precision medical instruments; the Singaporean warehouseman will have to operate computerised storage systems. In short, the labour-intensive will give way to the technology- and knowledge-intensive — and that will put a premium not just on efficiency and discipline but also on creativity and initiative.

All this has long been recognised. Japan's continued industrial success is partly because it ruthlessly abandons industries when it no longer has a comparative advantage, ceding much of its steel and shipbuilding to South Korea, transplanting basic electronics to South-east Asia. In Singapore, as long ago as 1979, the government adopted a 'high wage' policy as part of its 'Economic Development Plan for the Eighties': the idea was to force employers into high-tech industries and so replicate the standard of living just reached by Japan. The plan failed because others were attempting to go up-market without raising wages, which meant that Singapore was simply pricing itself out of the market — but the idea behind the idea was sound enough. So too with Taiwan: by the late-1980s, the KMT government had established a special 'science park' at Hsinchu, outside Taipei, and was dangling all sorts of tax incentives to persuade the island's companies to upgrade at home instead of simply moving to cheaper places overseas.

The difficulty rich East Asia will face is that identifying a problem is not the same as solving it. It is simply not possible to carve a California-style Silicon Valley out of the mountains of Korea and Taiwan without also having creative people who prefer long hair and blue jeans to a nine-to-five routine in a grey suit. Likewise, the City of London and New York's Wall Street depend for their innovative financial instruments on people whose heretical ideas belie their pin-stripe suits and buttoned-down collars. Such people are hard to find in a Confucian world which values conformity and fears individualism. Moreover, they are hard to breed: parents and teachers are comfortable with the known, not the unknown. Even if they accept at the intellectual level the need for educational change, they will find it hard at the emotional level. Why should a rational Japanese teacher, living in perhaps the world's most successful modern economy, want to copy the free-form chaos, or so it would seem, of the schools of London and Los Angeles? In South Korea, the Education Ministry worries that while Korean twelve-year-olds score second highest in internationally comparable mathematical tests, Korean seventeen-year-olds scored 23rd — but the same ministry also worries that reformist ideas from the teachers are evidence of a 'leftist' conspiracy. It may be government policy to change educational tradition, but the change will clearly not happen overnight. All societies have a conservative core, and so a tendency towards inertia.

But the change, albeit slow and patchy, will happen nonetheless. Conservatism will be eroded by the pressures of economic development and increased familiarity with other systems. In Japan, for example, Western pressure is bringing financial deregulation — and in its train the system of lifetime employment is breaking down as Japanese and foreign firms compete for labour. An employee's marketability then depends on what he has learned, not which university he went to. Moreover, East Asia is becoming ever more international: there are over 25,000 students from Taiwan, and 24,000 from Japan, in the United States; Japanese companies, from Nissan to Nomura, have overseas plants and offices to be staffed from the home base. Each year, more and more East Asians take holidays in the world beyond their Confucian rim.

The question is how to manage the change. In Japan, the Provisional Council on Educational Reform, set up by Mr Nakasone, spent from 1984 to 1987 wrestling with precisely this problem — and now the Ministry of

Education, hide-bound by tradition, and the stubborn Japanese teachers' union are struggling with the council's recommendations. One idea (anathema to bureaucrats used to determining every detail of a syllabus) is to revise all schools' curricula between 1990 and 1996 in order to introduce more diversity. World history, for example, becomes compulsory while Japanese history becomes optional. Another idea is to use an American-style credit system to lessen the importance of exams, and to have 'exam hell' on several days of a year, to allow a student more chances of entry to a university. The most exciting idea of the Japanese is to go truly 'international' — to open Japanese colleges abroad and have Western colleges in Japan. In March 1990, Teikyo University, a private university in Tokyo, bought into Salem University, in the American state of West Virginia; in return, nine American universities had opened campuses in Japan, and a score more were planning to do likewise. Meanwhile, Adelaide, in South Australia, has been chosen as the site of the Multi-Function Polis — an internationally financed city devoted to high technology and home to up to 200,000 brainy souls. In practice, this is a Japanese idea whose reality will depend on Japan's money and Japan's scientists.

But if the curative measures exist, how quickly they will work is debatable. Whereas the universities of Singapore, Hong Kong, and Taiwan have always looked to the outside world (not least because their professors are often graduates from American and British universities), the universities of Japan and South Korea are smugly introverted: progress for the teaching staff, as in the rest of their societies, depends on seniority rather than merit; research money is equally shared among professors, regardless of need. Susumu Tonegawa, the Japanese winner of the 1987 Nobel prize for Physiology or Medicine, is a tribute not to Kyoto University, where he took his first degree, but to the American universities where he did — and does — his research. If the best brains of Japan and the rest of East Asia are to stay at home, the best hope lies in demography and market forces: by the end of this century the number of Japanese eighteen- year-olds will fall from 2 million at the start of the 1990s to just 1.5 million. That will leave the nation's educational system with a huge amount of surplus capacity — and give students, and therefore employers, the chance to choose. The onus will then be on competing universities to provide an education that is relevant, rather than simply traditional.

The educational problems of Confucian Asia are the worries of the rich. Asia's poor, however, face problems that are more fundamental, and so more serious. Typical adults in Afghanistan, Bangladesh, India, and Laos have one disability in common: they cannot read and write. The same is true in Bhutan, Papua New Guinea, Nepal, and Pakistan. Their illiteracy traps them into the poverty of subsistence agriculture and unskilled labour. Unhappily, the disability will remain despite a pledge by the United Nations Educational, Scientific, and Cultural Organisation (Unesco) to end illiteracy in Asia by the year 2000.

One reason is demographic: stubbornly high birth rates will mean too many children for teachers and too few classrooms to put them in. At the end of this century, the average Indian woman will be one who bears three children during her lifetime; her Pakistani equivalent will bear five or six. Another reason is 'human nature': it will remain easy, and common, for education investment to be siphoned off by corruption. In Pakistan, for example, schools are planned and appear in official statistics — but in fact they remain unbuilt, with venal officials pocketing the financial allocations. Similarly, teachers receive pay cheques but do not turn up, preferring to take second jobs and bribe the school inspectors into silence. The third factor is cultural: a belief, especially in Muslim societies, that it is unnecessary — even harmful — to educate women. Throughout the poor countries of Asia, female literacy rates are lower than male ones. In India, for example, just over half the men can read, but only a third of the women can.

Add up these factors and the result is that out of Asia's three billion or so people, some 666 million are functionally illiterate. There will be little improvement in the next decade. According to Unesco's calculations, by the year 2000 India, Pakistan, Bangladesh, Nepal, and Afghanistan will, between them, have 475 million illiterate adults. Take in the rest of Asia and the figure will rise to around 645 million.

Figure 7 *Table of Education and Literacy*

	Percentage of age group enrolled in education										Primary net enrollment (per cent)		Adult illiteracy (per cent)	
	Primary				Secondary				Tertiary Total				Male 1985	Female 1985
	Total 1965	Total 1987	Female 1965	Female 1987	Total 1965	Total 1987	Female 1965	Female 1987	1965	1987	1975	1987		
Low-income economies														
Bangladesh	49	59	31	49	13	18	3	11	1	5	—	53	67	78
Bhutan	7	24	1	17	0	4	—	1	—	—	—	—	—	—
Laos	40	111	30	100	2	23	1	19	0	2	—	—	16	24
Nepal	20	82	4	—	5	26	2	—	1	5	—	—	74	88
China	89	132	—	124	24	43	—	37	1	2	—	98	31	45
India	74	98	57	81	27	39	13	27	5	—	—	—	57	71
Pakistan	40	52	20	35	12	19	5	11	2	5	—	—	70	81
Sri Lanka	93	104	86	102	35	66	35	69	2	—	—	—	13	17
Indonesia	72	118	65	115	12	46	7	—	1	—	72	—	26	35
Afghanistan	16	—	5	—	2	—	1	—	0	—	—	—	—	—
Burma	71	—	65	—	15	—	11	—	1	—	—	—	—	—
Cambodia	77	—	56	—	9	—	4	—	1	—	—	—	—	—
Vietnam	—	102	—	99	—	42	—	40	—	—	—	—	—	—
Middle-income economies														
Lower-middle-income														
Philippines	113	106	111	106	41	68	40	69	19	38	95	—	14	15
Thailand	78	95	74	—	14	28	11	—	2	20	—	—	9	12
Malaysia	90	102	84	102	28	59	22	59	2	7	—	—	27	34
Upper-middle-income														
South Korea	101	101	99	101	35	88	25	86	6	36	99	99	—	—
Low- and middle-income														
East Asia	88w	125w	—	120w	23w	45w	—	40w	1w	5w	—	—	29w	41w
South Asia	68w	89w	52w	73w	24w	35w	12w	24w	4w	—	—	—	59w	72w
High-income economies														
Singapore	105	—	100	—	45	—	41	—	10	—	100	—	14	21
Hong Kong	103	106	99	105	29	74	25	76	5	—	92	—	12	19
Japan	100	102	100	102	82	96	81	97	13	28	99	—	—	—

1. Some totals may exceed 100% where students older or younger than the relevant age groups are enrolled in educational sectors.
2. 'w' means the percentage is weighted by each country's share in the aggregate population.

Source: Adapted from Table 1 — Basic Indicators, and Table 29 — Education in The World Bank's World Development Report, 1990, published by Oxford University Press, New York.

The human and economic cost of this is incalculable, but certainly horrendous. Uneducated women have more children than educated ones, not least because so many of their children die in infancy. Why do they die? Often because their mothers have no idea of basic hygiene and sanitation. Families wash and defecate in the same river water; in India, millions use the river Ganges, which doubles as a depository for corpses; in Bangkok, the poor who live on the banks of Chao Phraya clean their teeth in its filthy water. The equation is straightforward: female illiteracy leads to high birth rates, high infant mortality rates — and low life expectancy. Consider the contrast between China and India, two huge populations with almost equal per capita gross nation product. Some 70 per cent of adult Chinese can read, compared with only 40 per cent or so of adult Indians — and whereas the Chinese can expect to live to the age of 70 or more, the average Indian will die ten years younger.

But the example of China is proof that illiteracy is not an incurable condition for a poor country. When Mao Zedong's communists emerged triumphant in the 1949 revolution, China's illiteracy rate was around 85 per cent; today, all but the very young and the very old can read the *People's Daily* (if they can work up the enthusiasm). What makes the achievement still more remarkable is the nature of the Chinese language: dialects that bear no relation to the written word and a script, pictographic in origin, that consists of complex characters formed by many strokes. To be literate, an individual must know 2,000 separate characters; to be fully educated, at least 5,000 out of the 45,000 in existence. Because there is no alphabet, arranged, like the Roman script, on a phonetic basis, devising a dictionary is extraordinarily difficult: the barely satisfactory solution is to arrange an order of the 214 'classifiers', strokes of which one is certain to be in every character. Not surprisingly, until this century, literacy in China was a privilege of an élite — those who had the time to achieve a huge feat of memorisation.

What has now made the feat commonplace is an enormous effort of national will. In the early years of the Revolution, schoolchildren taught the troops of the Red Army; then the government established schools and organised night classes for adults; finally, the characters themselves were simplified, so that a character which traditionally (and still today in Hong Kong and Taiwan) had perhaps a score of strokes would now have only ten. Add to that the popular impact of Mao's speeches and writings (including *The Little Red Book*) and the increasing use in literature of colloquial, or *baihua*, Chinese, and the consequence was possibly the most dramatic increase in literacy the world has ever seen.

But it will not be repeated in India, nor in any other country beyond China's borders. One reason is that no country has the revolutionary fervour that inspired the Chinese in the 1950s and '60s. A more important reason is that no government bureaucracy has the organisational ability and the power of compulsion that has characterised Asian communism. Given the horrors that Asian communism has wrought — witness China's Cultural Revolution and the Cambodian genocide of Pol Pot — that may be no bad thing. But, in any case, the parallel is irrelevant since communism is no longer an attractive option for any Asian nation.

The key to establishing literacy will be a combination of money and organisation. The greater the budget for education and the more efficient its provision, the more likely a nation is to teach its young to read and write. Rich Japan conventionally allocates almost a fifth of total government spending to education; South Korea in 1990 dedicated a massive 22 per cent of the national budget to education. By contrast, India's education budget is only about 2 per cent of total government spending; Pakistan's is less than 4 per cent. One Unesco calculation is that it would cost $50 billion over ten years to eradicate illiteracy around the world — and the poor of Asia are in no position to stump up their equivalent share.

But that does not mean the attack on illiteracy is hopeless. Indeed, capitalist Thailand, like communist China, is as impressive an example of the opposite. Fifty years ago only three out of every ten adult Thais could read; now only one in ten cannot. Taiwan is still more impressive: its illiteracy rate in the 1950s was as bad as the Chinese mainland's; now the rate is a mere 5 per cent. The method is simple: provide primary schooling for all children, and supplement it with night classes for adults (which become unnecessary after a generation or so). In all of Asia's rich countries — and those that are becoming rich — primary schooling is compulsory and enrolment rates are virtually 100 per cent. The child of a Hong Kong street hawker goes to school as automatically as the child of a Hong Kong banker; so do the children of Malaysian rubber tappers, Korean car workers, and Thai prostitutes. Even in poor Indonesia and the Philippines, primary school education is now universal.

The challenge is to build on that base. Two problems will dog Asia's campaign for literacy and learning: how to ensure the quality of primary schooling and how to ensure that children go on to secondary schools. Superficially, Thailand is already a success: for the past two decades primary school enrolment rates have been around 80 per cent or higher (today the level is about 95 per cent). But the success has its flaws — only two-thirds of children complete the six years of compulsory primary education, and only one-third go on to a secondary school. If a child drops out of education before getting to the fifth grade — ie, by the age of ten or eleven — the chances are he will grow up illiterate. What prospects are there, then, for a country such as Laos? Its primary school enrolment is 100 per cent (indeed, over 100 per cent if you take in the statistical quirk of counting pupils who are older than the normal primary age group) — yet only a quarter go on to secondary school and just 2 per cent have any tertiary education.

Worsening the situation is the position of girls in the educational process. They are already present in fewer numbers than boys in Asia's primary schools, and in the secondary schools the proportion falls still further. In Asia's least developed countries the average secondary enrolment rate for boys ranges from 6 per cent in Bhutan to 35 per cent in Nepal; by contrast, the girls' enrolment rate ranges from 1 per cent in Bhutan to a top of 24 per cent in Burma. With such figures, few homes will be literate in a Western sense: a Bhutanese mother will spend her time toiling in the fields, not teaching her child from a Peter and Jane reading book. One Unesco study gloomily concludes that while the number of Asia's male illiterates fell between 1970 and 1985, the decline was more than outweighed by an increase in the number of female illiterates.

The problem is a combination of economics and culture. In subsistence economies an educated woman is not seen as a valuable commodity, so what is the point of spending money to educate a girl in a classroom who could be doing useful work in the fields? Meanwhile, cultural and religious beliefs will also keep girls away from learning. The Koranic evidence for discriminating against girls is slender (and the *Hadith*, or sayings of the Prophet Muhammad, can be invoked for almost any purpose), but the fact remains that most Muslim societies like to keep all but the youngest male and female students apart.

True, Indonesia, the world's biggest Muslim nation, tries hard to provide equal educational opportunities for all its children and, in deference to the doctrine of *pancasila*, puts little stress on the strictures of traditional Islam. But Pakistan, whose very creation was an act of religious separation from Hindu-dominated India, has in recent years done precisely the opposite. During the autocratic rule, from 1977 to 1988, of General Zia ul-Haq, the government deliberately promoted the traditional Muslim *madrassah*, or mosque school, at the expense of the secular system inherited from the British. Some 7,500 mosque schools were set up, staffed by *mullahs* whose own education rarely went beyond Islamic studies. Their task in the *madrassah* is really nothing more than to teach the Koran and certain *hadith*, by rote. But the *madrassah* should not be mocked for its own sake. For the Muslim minority of southern Thailand, for example, it is a way of affirming an identity that is different from the Buddhist Thais. Tiny Muslim children from dirt-poor villages learn the Arabic script chalked on the blackboard, and cheerfully recite Koranic passages by heart. For them, the *madrassah* is an addition to their normal education, not its sole content. But for millions of small Pakistani children primary education now consists only of the mosque school — and as soon as puberty approaches, girls are no longer allowed to attend. No wonder female literacy in Pakistan has declined over the past twenty years in every province except the Punjab. Writ large across the country, the inevitable result of stressing an 'Islamic way' of education will be to restrict Pakistan's ability to develop.

But literate nations such as Thailand and, especially, the Philippines should not feel smug in comparison. Literacy is a tool with which to become educated, not an education in itself. Through the 1990s Thailand will suffer a severe 'brain shortage' because of the defects in its system: the high drop-out rate after primary school and the tendency, unusual in developing countries, of university students to choose arts courses in order to enter the socially prestigious civil service. Just when Thailand is consolidating its eastern seaboard industrial zone — one of Asia's biggest industrial schemes for the rest of the century — there will be a critical scarcity of engineers. This will not be properly remedied (foreign experts can obviously be imported temporarily) until the educational process in Thailand can produce universal secondary schooling followed by a re-definition of the purpose of tertiary education.

The challenge in the Philippines is to distinguish between quantity and quality. Philippine enrolment rates are among the highest in the world, from primary school up to university. A quarter of college-age Filipinos are enrolled in college or university; if part-time courses and learning by correspondence is included, the proportion rises to around 40 per cent. The proud boast of many Filipina domestic servants in Singapore and Hong Kong is that they are better educated than their employers — and only the Philippines' poverty has driven them to menial work abroad. The equally proud boast of the government, seeking to attract foreign investment, is that the Philippines has the best-educated work-force in South-east Asia, and that this work-force is reasonably fluent in English.

Unfortunately, the boasts now smack more of delusion than realism. A generation ago, the University of the Philippines was probably the best in Asia, and its private-sector rivals, the Ateneo de Manila and the De La Salle university, were arguably as good as 'UP'. Now, this trio, catering almost exclusively to the young of the nation's social and business elite, is under pressure: they cannot afford to pay their faculty enough to keep good professors from defecting either to private industry or to universities abroad. Today, it would be hard to rank UP alongside the best universities of Singapore, Malaysia, Thailand — perhaps even Indonesia. And if UP caters for the élite, what happens to the majority? The answer is that they go to the 'University Belt', a strip of some twenty-five private colleges in the grimy Quiapo district of Manila. But because increases in tuition fees were subject to a ceiling as long ago as 1973, the University Belt colleges, starting off with much lower fees than the Ateneo and De La Salle, are in a worse mess by far than the élite universities. By the end of the 1980s, a University Belt professor, teaching full time and paid by the hour, could make only 2,500 pesos (around $120) a month — a sum below the official poverty line for the average Filipino family.

The reasons for this unhappy state of affairs lie in the corrupt, twenty-one-year regime of President Ferdinand Marcos, who managed to transform one of Asia's most successful economies into a near-bankrupt disaster. Education was one of the more vulnerable items in the national budget, especially after 1983, when the International Monetary Fund demanded Marcos change profligacy into austerity. But the consequences have been tragic: Filipino schoolchildren score lower in science tests than their counterparts in Singapore, South Korea, Thailand, and Hong Kong; youngsters now enter college after ten years of formal education with, according to the government, the international equivalent of only seven years' education; and pass rates to the Philippine bar (the country is as over-lawyered as the United States of America) have fallen by half. Whether the students themselves realise any of this is doubtful: the Philippine desire for learning and a paper qualification is such that many of the girl students in the University Belt pay their way through college by selling their bodies in the bars and discos adjacent to their colleges.

The question is how quickly the Philippine government can first halt and then reverse the slide in the quality of the nation's education. The immediate prospects are not good. Education now accounts for less than 3 per cent of the country's gross national product — higher than the 1.6 per cent low in 1986 when Marcos was overthrown, but much lower than the 5.5 per cent common in the developed world. The country's problem is simple, and the solution difficult. How can the government devote more money to education when servicing its foreign debt — the millstone inherited from Marcos — absorbs a third or more of its export earnings? There can be no easy answer, but what will complicate the answer in the 1990s is the growth of Philippine nationalism. In economic terms, that will mean a political campaign to repudiate part of the foreign debt, or at least to put a cap on the amount of the nation's regular repayments. In educational terms, it will mean a move away from English as the country's language of university instruction towards Tagalog, or its slightly different variant, Filipino — in which case, the boast of an educated, English-speaking work-force will become somewhat hollow.

O
f all the educational issues that will beset Asia in the future, the most sensitive will be language. Asians divide themselves with hundreds, indeed thousands, of languages and dialects. It is part of Asia's fascination: language reflects culture, and any journey through Asia reveals a myriad of cultures. The Tamils of south India are different from the Hindus of the north; in Pakistan the Punjabis are different from the Sindis; in Indonesia, the Balinese are different from the Bataks. And so it goes, across the breadth of Asia. The truly cohesive, homogeneous nation state — like Japan or Korea — is a rarity. More common is the swirling diversity of the Philippines, India, and Indonesia. Even China, with its innate sense of itself as the centre of the universe, is in fact a country divided by language and dialect—for example, Cantonese and Fukkienese in the south, Mandarin in the north.

If they are left to deepen, these divisions will threaten to break Asia's countries apart. The archipelagos of Indonesia and the Philippines will scatter into an array of competing islands. China will break into warring provinces; India into rival states; Malaysia into racial blocs. The prospect, inevitably accompanied by bloodshed and terror, is one no sensible government would relish. The obvious way to avoid it is to require a common language — and so to superimpose a shared culture. But which language?

So far, there have been three answers: the language spoken by the most people, or the language left by a colonial power — or a combination of the two. The Philippines, for example, has both Tagalog and English; India has Hindi and English; Malaysia has *bahasa* (language) Malay and English; Indonesia requires everyone to learn *bahasa* Indonesia. In Thailand, the teaching of Thai to the hill tribes of the north and to the Muslim minority in the far south helps create a link of national identity with the Thai majority. Meanwhile, China has made the Mandarin of the north the official language for all regions — and, indeed, calls it *putonghua*, or 'common language'.

The problem is living with the answers. Choose the colonial language, and there is either a lingering taste of colonial inferiority or a division of the nation into those with real fluency in the colonial language and those who have only an accented smattering. In the Philippines, a pop singer called Freddie Aguilar became wildly successful in the mid-1980s not only because he braved Marcos and sang for Corazon Aquino — but also because he sang in Tagalog, the language of the masses.

But choose the main vernacular and inevitably groups speaking a country's less popular languages will feel left out. In Malaysia, the Chinese and Indians see *bahasa* Malay as a medium deliberately favouring the Malays. In Brunei, which also speaks *bahasa* Malay, one bar against Chinese residents qualifying for full citizenship is the need for fluency in Malay — and there are inevitable charges that the language hurdle is made impossibly high in order to deprive the Chinese.

Not that the problems are insuperable. *Bahasa* Indonesia is acceptable from Sumatra to Kalimantan because everyone knows the alternative would be linguistic chaos. Moreover, a lingua franca fits seamlessly into the umbrella of *pancasila*. Similarly, Tagalog raises no ire in the Philippines: popular films have made Tagalog understood by nine in every ten Filipinos — compared with one in two who understand English.

The question, however, is the economic, not just the cultural, value of choosing a native lingua franca for linguistically fragmented countries. All too often, the values are at odds. The language of international business and of science and technology is English — not Tagalog or *bahasa* Malay or Tamil or Hindi. It must be true that a child will learn better if taught in his mother tongue, but what if there are no books and other learning materials in that mother tongue?

A case in point is Hong Kong: 98 per cent of the 6 million-strong population is Cantonese, and, taking in China's Guangdong province, Cantonese is the mother tongue of at least 50 million people. Yet the tendency, especially from the 1970s when secondary education became universal, for Hong Kong's schoolchildren to be taught in Cantonese — with English, the previous medium of instruction, taught now as a second language — has proved, at best, controversial. Undoubtedly, the British colony's standard of English has slipped dramatically. Employers complain that they cannot get local staff competent in English to work as bank tellers, hotel clerks, travel agents — anywhere where English is needed in a city that lives through its connections to the outside world. Since the employers complain, so do Hong Kong's parents: they want their children to get good jobs, and so they demand that English once again be the medium of instruction in the colony's public schools. Such pressures will enrage many educationalists, who point out that English-medium schooling benefits only an élite and leaves the majority floundering. But without that élite, how will Hong Kong fare as an 'international' city if its law firms, practising British law, cannot recruit graduates able to draft accurately in English; if its bankers cannot communicate fluently with their counterparts abroad; if its businessmen have to search for translators for every transaction? Much of the 1990s in Hong Kong will be spent resolving the dilemma: possibly more teachers will be imported from England (a pilot scheme was begun in 1987), or possibly Hong Kong's free market will spawn English-language 'cram schools' on the lines of Taipei.

One thing is certain: if Hong Kong fails to improve its English, more of its business will go to Singapore — which has always thought deeply and acted cannily on the issue of language. One of Lee Kuan Yew's cleverest moves thirty years ago was to promote English, the language of the departing British. The cleverness was twofold: a command of English gave Singapore ready access to international business, and none of Singapore's ethnic groups — Chinese, Indian, or Malay — could complain that the choice of language favoured another community. The result is that Singapore now has a plethora of tongues: the government's count is four official languages, Malay, Chinese, Tamil, and English; one national language, Malay; and one language of administration, English. In practice, this means that English is the language of all official business, and most private business. But there is also another language, a lingua franca that enables all Singaporeans, regardless of race, class, and education, to converse with one another. This is what Singaporeans laughingly call 'Singlish' — an accented, somewhat distorted English that outsiders can barely understand.

But if a language is more than just a business tool, can imported English or derivative Singlish satisfy Singapore's cultural needs? The danger is that Singaporeans, cut off from their cultural origins, will end up truly fluent in no language at all. A typical Chinese Singaporean might speak the Hokkien dialect at home, English in the office, and Singlish in the streets — and be unable to express abstract concepts in any of them. Is there a language-driven answer to prevent Singaporeans becoming, in the words of Lee Kuan Yew, 'a people who have lost their cultural self-identity . . . [without] emotional and cultural ballast . . . pseudo-Westernised, alienated from our Asian background'? Lee's solution in the 1980s was the decade of the 'Speak Mandarin' campaign (the government loves to speak in upper case imperatives, repeated constantly on television and in the government-controlled newspapers). The idea was that within fifteen years, by the mid-1990s, Mandarin would replace Hokkien, Teochew, Cantonese, and the other dialects of the Singaporean Chinese — and would at the same time reinforce 'real' Chinese culture, by spreading literacy (the Chinese script is the same regardless of dialect) and the traditions of a China that the Singaporean Chinese left fifty or more years ago.

The campaign, backed by a ban on imported Cantonese TV programmes, is working. Chinese shop assistants who five years ago would have chatted among themselves in Singlish or Hokkien now use Mandarin. Two-thirds of Chinese primary school children speak Mandarin at home. Probably, too, the inculcation of Mandarin is meant — as with the imposition of English a generation earlier — to be an economic weapon. Singaporeans who speak Mandarin will flourish in an awakening China far more easily than rival overseas Chinese: the Hong Kongers, for example, will be confined by Cantonese.

But there remains a risk that Mr Lee has been too clever by half. Language is an emotional issue, tied to race and culture. The government is careful to stress that Singapore's Malays and Indians should cultivate their own cultural roots. The stress, too, is on mutual understanding (Lee and his son, B-G Lee Hsien Loong, meet the ideal qualifications — they are fluent in English, Mandarin, and Malay). But the fact is that 76 per cent of Singaporeans are Chinese: the more they speak Mandarin, the more they will think of themselves as distinctively Chinese — and the more the ethnic minorities will suspect they are victims of a subtle form of discrimination.

In practice, discrimination based on language is a fact of life throughout Asia — and will remain so. In India, for example, entry to the senior civil service can only be achieved by fluency in English. This means that an 'old school tie' network enmeshes the whole of the administration: the favoured civil servant has been to a posh public school (in the English, fee-paying, sense of the term) like the Doon School or Mayo College, and then on to St Stephen's College, Delhi University. He will be a high-caste Hindu and use English, the language of both school and university, as the language of the office and home. The same is true in the Philippines: the Filipino élite have all been educated in English, and have often studied in America. Ironically, it is this élite, playing with the idea of national identity, who argue for the replacement of English with Tagalog — which results in the bizarre spectacle on television chat shows of Filipino politicians, absolutely fluent in English, competing with each other to throw into the discussion bits of stumbling Tagalog.

The irony, of course, does not invalidate the argument that Anglophone Asia is suffering from linguistic imperialism. It is true that emphasising a foreign language deprives the majority of their full potential. It is also true that education in the vernacular can be made universal. In 1982, the first Malaysian students taught entirely in *bahasa* Malay entered university, products of a policy switch from English-medium instruction almost a decade earlier. Theoretically, the University of the Philippines is pledged to switch to Tagalog by 1995, and a bilingual education policy has been law in Philippine schools since 1974.

The problem is that adopting either a vernacular education or proper bilingualism will always carry a political and social cost, as well as an unquantifiable economic cost. To argue that Thailand, Indonesia, and South Korea are progressing without the benefit of English schooling does not convince a parent or an employer in the Philippines. Since the stress on Tagalog in the mid-1970s, English skills in the Philippines have dropped dramatically except for students educated in élite, private schools. In Malaysia, the vice-chancellor of the University of Malaya, Professor Syed Hussein Al-atas, says he is appalled at the decline in English. His argument is compelling: 'Those opposed to the study of English will only succeed in making Malaysians backward. They are not true nationalists. They can harp on the need to develop *bahasa* Malay, but without emphasising the need for English, they would only prevent Malaysians from improving.' The government seems at least partly persuaded, hence its present determination to improve English standards.

But will English be Asia's only 'imperial language' in the 1990s? It will certainly be the main one, but the likelihood is that as Japan's industrialists and bankers direct more and more of the Asian economy, so too will Japan's language become increasingly common. Two decades ago, the number of foreigners learning Japanese was less than 100,000; today, the number is well over 700,000 — and that does not include the immigrant workers, from Filipina 'entertainers' to American stockbrokers, who pick up Japanese as they go along. Nor does it include Asia's shopkeepers and hotel staff, increasingly aware that a smattering of Japanese will lead to bigger purchases and better tips.

Those numbers, however, are paltry compared with the number of Japanese learning English — first as a compulsory language at school and then as a tool of business in the internationalisation of Japan. The reality, therefore, is that English will increasingly be Asia's lingua franca even as the natural homes of English, Britain, America, and Australasia, decline in their relative economic — and political — importance. The question then is how Asia will add value to this lingua franca. With luck, the Confucianists of East Asia — especially Japan — will use English as a way to prise wide the narrow minds of domestic tradition and to engage in original research. With luck, all of Asia will use English as a means to boost foreign trade, and so grow rich or richer. But what next? The challenge facing a prospering, better-educated Asia is to learn to enjoy itself.

Five

Playtime

'A day of leisure is a day of immortality' — Chinese proverb

*Tokyo travel agencies offer adventure holidays in Sarawak for Japanese
professionals bored with Singapore and Hong Kong . . . Philippine feminists
say the Ministry of Tourism is encouraging prostitution . . . A Japanese
yacht, equipped with a radical new keel, wins the America's Cup . . . Thai
businessmen plan a new chain of beach resorts in Vietnam . . . The
international squash tour welcomes its first player from Taiwan . . . The
Perth Casino advertises for Japanese and Chinese croupiers . . .*

(future thoughts for Asia's leisure industry)

The world's best hotels, biggest fleets
of jumbo jets, largest market for designer labels (both real and faked): all are
in Asia. So, too, are the most expensive golf clubs — and the busiest
McDonald's outlets. In Hong Kong, there are more Rolls-Royces per head
than anywhere else in the world (although West Palm Beach and London's
Mayfair run it close). In Tokyo, you can drink the world's richest coffee —
it comes laced with gold. In Macao, you can bet with the world's most
determined gamblers.

What the superlatives have in common is the spending of money. Asia
is famous for its propensity to save; in the 1990s it will become more famous
for its ability to spend. The simple reason is that money has no value unless
it is used. As Asia's economies grow, so its people must buy — whether by
investing in Australian and American real estate, eating more hamburgers,
or taking more holidays abroad. The consequent certainty is that rich Asians
will spend in the pursuit of leisure, and non-Asians and poor Asians will
benefit from the chase. Moreover, because Asia's wealth is based on a broad
platform of manufacturing and services, the pursuit will retain its momentum
almost regardless of the world's economic cycles: the parallel is with the
wealth of America and Europe, not the evanescent fortunes of the Middle
Eastern oil producers.

But who are the rich of Asia? Each year *Forbes* magazine compiles a list
of the world's greatest fortunes, from supermarket owners to royalty. The
1990 list makes intriguing reading. The United States is still the greatest
breeding ground of the super-rich, with ninety-nine dollar billionaires, but
next comes Japan with forty — which means that in less than fifty years
Japan has risen from radioactive defeat to produce as many billionaires per
head as its conqueror. Tiny Hong Kong, with seven, has the same number
of billionaires as Britain or France; Taiwan, with six, is equal to Italy; Korea,
with four billionaires, is only two behind not just Italy but also Switzerland
and Saudi Arabia; Singapore and Indonesia, with two each, are on a par
with Spain; Malaysia can boast one billionaire, as can India. And, of course,

most people would add (*Forbes* does not) the Sultan of Brunei, arguably the world's richest man given the fuzzy line between his own wealth and that of his country.

The Sultan excepted, what is remarkable about the list is its relative anonymity. The whole world knows the name of Donald Trump, a has-been billionaire; much of the world can remember the song lyric 'as rich as Rockefeller'; most of Europe is aware of Giovanni Agnelli, the boss of Fiat, or Sir James Goldsmith; no educated American will quickly forget Wall Street's fallen wizards, Michael Milken and Ivan Boesky. Yet surely no ordinary person outside Asia, and precious few within it, have heard of Yoshiaki Tsutsumi and Taikichiro Mori — let alone Liem Sioe Liong and Robert Kuok.

No matter: if the man-in-the-street does not know them, the international banker certainly does. Mori and Tsutsumi have the biggest real estate empires in Japan (which now means the world). Liem, a Chinese-Indonesian with close ties to President Suharto, dominates his country's cement, steel, cloves (needed for Indonesia's *kretek* cigarettes), and flour trade; he also has three banks in America and an international investment company, First Pacific, based in Hong Kong. Robert Kuok is a Chinese-Malaysian once known as the 'sugar king' of South-east Asia, and now the man behind the Shangri-La hotel chain. Meanwhile, Li Ka-shing, the richest man in Hong Kong, with interests ranging from container ports and property to supermarkets and satellites, walks to his office unrecognised even by bankers. Indeed, the only Asian business billionaire whose name is known world-wide is probably Sony's founder, Akio Morita — the rest are known only by their products.

One other attribute distinguishes the *Forbes* billionaires: almost invariably the non-Japanese have made their wealth by their own efforts. Liem left impoverished China at the age of twenty and started in Java as a peanut-oil trader; Li began his business career peddling plastic toys at the age of thirteen. The Japanese are different because Japan was an industrialised nation a generation before its war-time effort to expand its Asian empire. Tsutsumi, for example, inherited his landholdings from his father; his half-brother Seiji (who is the legitimate son — Yoshiaki is the son of a mistress) inherited the Seibu department stores, and then marched on to create a group of over one hundred companies, including control of the Inter-Continental Hotels Corporation.

But does a list of the super rich have any wider relevance? After all, the rich are different from ordinary folks ('Yes, they have more money', as Hemingway answered Scott Fitzgerald). But while African dictators and South American drug barons — and Filipinos such as the late President Marcos — grow odiously rich at the expense of their societies, most of Asia's super-rich have become so by stimulating and encouraging the economies around them. The *Forbes* list merely outlines the summits of Asia's economic mountains: there are billionaires in Japan, Taiwan, South Korea, and Hong Kong because those economies have been the most flourishing in the world for at least the last decade. True, there are elements of exaggeration: the ludicrous price of land in Tokyo, for example, has created paper millionaires by the hundreds; so have the Taipei and Seoul stock exchanges, which operate more or less like rigged casinos. But even when those exaggerations are eliminated (a process that began in 1990), the 'real' economy will survive as strongly as ever. Japanese car and electronics exports will not falter because Tokyo land prices fall; Taiwan will not become poor because in 1990 its stock-market lost 80 per cent of its value. The great fortunes of Asia reflect more durable economic assets, such as heavy industry, banking, logging, transportation, and textiles. Those industries, in turn, represent a continuous surge of economic growth. In the past two decades, Asia's share of the world's gross domestic product has risen from around 14 per cent to over 21 per cent; by the end of this century, it will be perhaps 27 per cent. Since that growth means a bigger slice of a bigger cake, one certainty is that there will be many more fortunes, big and small, for Asians to enjoy.

A second certainty is that spending will become a habit for those who have no fortunes at all. Just as Americans and then Europeans became accustomed — indeed addicted — to credit cards and charge cards, so too will Asians get hooked on the habit of plastic money. Hong Kong's six million people now have over 400,000 American Express cards between them; in 1985 they had only 200,000, and in 1980 perhaps 100,000. Add in the cards from Diners' Club, Visa, MasterCard, and so on, and the same six million people have 1.5 million plastic cards in their wallets to feed their spending habit. Where Hong Kong leads, the rest of Asia will follow. The Taiwanese, for example, accumulated piles of cash during the 1980s — not least from playing the soaring stock-market — but were not allowed to have local-currency credit cards until 1989, fully five years behind their South Korean counterparts. Even the communist mainland of China will catch the habit: since 1989, foreign credit cards have been available for those who can prove they have access to hard currency — an invitation that China's corrupt will doubtless find irresistible.

All of which raises two questions: how will Asians enjoy their money, and how will that enjoyment change their attitudes? The two questions are clearly related, but the first is a lot easier to answer. Asians will start by defining the good life as the possession of material goods. Indeed, the definition is already well established: the Indians are switching from bicycles to motorbikes; the Taiwanese from motorbikes to motorcars; the Chinese from black-and-white to colour televisions; the Japanese from stills-cameras to movie-cameras.

This kind of consumerism can be indulged *ad infinitum*—as Americans are well aware. If the Japanese, for example, become sated with domestically produced cars and electronics goods, they can always spend their disposable income on BMW cars, Gucci shoes, and other brand-name imported luxuries — which is why in the second half of the 1980s such consumer goods tripled their share of imports to over 14 per cent. It is doubtful that any of the goods is markedly better than a Japanese equivalent (and they may be worse), but Japan has become a 'born to shop' society in which brand-names can command the premium of snobbery: hence the success in Japan of Scotch whisky and Jaguar cars. Indeed, Japan's super-rich go a little bit further, competing in the auction rooms of Sotheby's and Christie's for such designer labels as Van Gogh and Renoir (witness the $160 million bid in May 1990 by Ryoei Saito, a paper manufacturer, for *Portrait of Dr Gachet* and *Au Moulin de la Galette*).

Most of Asia, of course, will not reach Japan's heights — even foothills — of indulgence until the next century. Whereas virtually every household in Taiwan and Japan has a television set, most households in India and the Philippines do not. The same is true of refrigerators, washing machines, telephones, and cars — all the luxury items that developed nations now think of as necessities. A Hong Kong police-inspector needs to work only half a week to pay for a new television; his counterpart in Bangladesh will need several months, hence the temptation to hasten the process by taking bribes.

But it does not follow that this gap between Asia's rich and poor is an absolute measure. The fact is that while the rich may get richer, the poor are getting less poor — and so more able to equip themselves with the consumer goodies of their rich neighbours. India has an educated middle class which is perhaps an eighth of the population, but that adds up to 100 million people. By Western standards, their annual incomes are pitiful (households earning more than $6,500 a year are a rarity), but, over the second half of the 1980s, they probably bought more material goods in five years than their parents did in thirty. In 1983, India produced just 70,000 television sets; by 1989, the annual output was 1.2 million. In a survey sample with annual salaries of only $1,500, more than a third owned a refrigerator and one in eight owned a camera.

What is true of India will become true for even the poorest nations of Asia. Already, in near bankrupt Indochina, the consumer habit is fed by remittances from workers abroad, combined with smuggling and with a fall in the real price of consumer goods (a radio or TV today costs only a fraction of its price twenty years ago). The result is that Scotch whisky, Marlboro cigarettes, and Russian vodka (indeed caviar) are all available in the street markets of Vietnam's Ho Chi Minh City; Honda motorcycles can be bought in the Laotian capital of Vientiane, and a *jeunesse dorée*, with imported clothes, cars, and cigarettes, goes disco-dancing in Cambodia's Phnom Penh.

But the accumulation of material goods is only one way of enjoying money. Eventually, people want to enjoy time as well as objects. For Europeans, this point arrived in the 1960s: they had survived the privations of war and its aftermath — now they would travel. Ever since, the package holiday has been one definition of European popular leisure. Soon it will apply to Asia, too.

Japanese honeymooners cuddle on Honolulu's Waikiki beach; Taiwanese tour groups clog Hong Kong's Kai Tak airport; Singaporean families cautiously steer rented camper-vans through New Zealand's Southern Alps. Travel anywhere in Asia and the Pacific and where ten years, even five years ago the tourists were overwhelmingly Americans and Europeans, now they are as likely to be Asia's nouveaux riches. In Hawaii, the Japanese in 1990 accounted for a fifth of all tourists, and about half of the money they spent. In Australia, each day a Boeing 747 brings 400 or so Japanese tourists to the resort town of Cairns; by 1995, according to some Australians' estimates, Japanese visitors to Cairns will quadruple to 600,000 a year — which means that on any given day they could outnumber the town's Australian residents. The wry reality is that resource-rich Australia, which at the start of the century was the world's richest country per capita, is slipping down the wealth ladder (it was barely in the top 30 at the start of the 1990s) to become a convenient quarry, farm, beach, and hotel for the rich of Asia.

All this is the predictable outcome of Asia's affluence. Japanese honeymooners choose to sun themselves in Hawaii, or even Guam, because then they are 'in America', the country whose soldiers, films, and music have defined Asia's new materialism. The Taiwanese use Hong Kong as a shopping-filled transit point on their way to the mainland. The Singaporeans are venturing to Australasia partly because it is Anglophone, partly because Australians and New Zealanders are well known, as tourists and as visiting troops, to Singaporeans — and partly because Singaporeans have already explored the tourist spots of their South-east Asian neighbours.

What is equally predictable is that Asia's tourism will grow larger and faster. At the start of the 1990s only 6 per cent of Asia's three billion or so people made one or more air trips a year. By the end of the 1990s, with a conservative annual increase in travel of 7.5 per cent, the proportion of

Asian flyers will have doubled to 12 per cent — roughly half the level that applies in North America and Europe. More to the point, because the rich parts of Asia are surrounded by sea — witness Japan, Singapore, and Taiwan — almost all of this flying will be for the purpose of foreign travel. In 1985 just under five million Japanese travelled abroad; by 1989 there were just under 10 million. Extrapolate from that growth (risky, but in Japan's case plausible) and Japan's overseas travellers will number 20 million in 1995 and 40 million (out of a population of perhaps 130 million) by the end of the century. Yet still Japan's level will be modest compared with Europe, where 40 per cent of Britons, for example, travel abroad each year. Meanwhile, the poor masses of Asia—the Chinese, Indians, Pakistanis, Indonesians, Filipinos, Vietnamese, and so on — will barely merit a footnote in the statistics of international travel. The reason is that the poor, who travel abroad for work, not play, are a tiny minority in international air travel: at least 80 per cent of all international flying is for the purpose of straightforward tourism. It will be well into the next century before Asia's present poor attain the power to travel for pleasure.

Never mind that distant prospect. Consider, instead, the imminent impact of Asia's rich on the world around them. The most obvious will be physical: a shortage of aircraft, airports, hotels, and resorts. Airbus Industrie, the European aircraft-making consortium, reckons that by the mid-1990s the passenger traffic carried by Asia's airlines will exceed Europe's. America's Boeing puts the same point a different way: by the year 2000 the airlines of Asia and the Pacific will be carrying almost a quarter of the whole world's passenger traffic. Both agree that while North America will remain the world's biggest concentration of airline traffic, demand will grow faster to, from, and within Asia than anywhere else in the world.

Coping with that demand will stretch balance sheets and fill order books. Asia's airlines have the world's youngest fleets — which means that only rarely in the next decade will they have to buy new aircraft to replace worn out ones. Instead, they will have to buy new aircraft to carry new passengers. In 1989 Asia's airlines had just over 1,000 jet-powered aircraft out of a world total of 8,300 (America's airlines had about 4,000 planes). By the year 2000 Boeing reckons Asia's number will have grown to more than 2,000, and in another five years to more than 2,600. That adds up to a purchase cost of $167 billion (a heroic Boeing guesstimate) in a mere fifteen years — equivalent to spending Thailand's annual gross domestic product three times over.

The proof of the spending will be the latest in airliner technology: four-engined and three-engined jumbo jets that can carry over four hundred tourists non-stop from Tokyo to Sydney, or from Seoul to New York, or from Hong Kong to Los Angeles; smaller, twin-engined airliners that can fly the same distances and so profitably service less popular routes; and shorter range aircraft to shuttle between the cities and resorts of Thailand, Malaysia, and the rest of South-east Asia. Conceivably, by the end of this century there could even be a supersonic airliner, a new (and it is to be hoped profitable) version of Concorde, to contract Asia's huge distances into manageable time.

Such aircraft represent airline supply adjusting to passenger demand, and demand will be so great that new airlines will squabble to meet it. The Japanese carrier, All Nippon Airways (ANA), was originally a domestic airline, but by the late 1980s it had forced itself onto the international scene, competing with a disgruntled Japan Air Lines (JAL) for the travelling money of Japanese tourists. Similarly, Taiwan's Evergreen Airways — an offshoot of the island's Evergreen container shipping corporation — was formed in 1989 to go head-to-head with the state-owned China Air Lines. Why should Evergreen bother? Because martial law ended in Taiwan in 1987 and restrictions on travel were loosened: some 20 million people, therefore, are now rich enough and free enough to indulge a hitherto forbidden taste for foreign travel. So far, understandably eager to see the Chinese motherland (and their Chinese relatives), they go mainly to mainland China by way of Hong Kong, but soon they will take the same flight paths as the Japanese — especially to South-east Asia and Australia.

Unhappily, two problems will hamper everyone's plans: a lack of airports and a lack of hotels. At the start of the 1990s, Tokyo's Narita airport and Sydney's Kingsford Smith airport were both stretched to the limit — and Hong Kong's Kai Tak was stretched beyond most people's idea of a civilised limit. Meanwhile, the hotels of Singapore and Bangkok were full to the brim; resorts such as Phuket in south Thailand were becoming ecological disasters — there were too many tourists for the available infrastructure of roads, water, and sewage. In other words, if Asia's tourist industry, like Europe's before it, tries to pour quarts — even gallons — into pint pots, tourism will become as much a blight as a benefit.

Happily, there are remedies, or at least soothing prescriptions, for the problems. There will be new airports, as in Hong Kong (assuming co-operation, to give confidence to the airport's bankers, between the departing British administration and the government of China); or more terminals, as already at Singapore's Changi 'airtropolis' (a name coined to highlight the airport's futuristic excellence) and Bangkok's Don Muang; or extra runways, as are planned for Sydney.

There will, too, be new hotels, from Bali to Chiang Mai and from Bangkok to Jakarta. Inevitably, they will be planned, approved, and financed all together when demand is high — and when they are simultaneously finished, there will be an immediate glut. But just as inevitably, demand will increase in two or three years to absorb the new supply — which is why so many of Asia's billionaires, including the above-mentioned Yoshiaki Tsutsumi, are now in the resort business, purpose-building facilities from ski lodges at Sapporo in northern Japan to golf-courses and boating marinas in Thailand.

Lastly, there will be new areas to welcome tourists. The foreigners may be socially disruptive but they bring immediate injections of hard currency into an economy, as every street beggar, souvenir seller, and finance minister from India to Indonesia is well aware. When Thailand, the 'land of smiles', decreed 1987 as 'Visit Thailand Year', tourist arrivals soared by 24 per cent; just as importantly, tourist spending rose by almost 20 per cent. Imitation is the sincerest form of flattery: Malaysia named 1990 as 'Visit Malaysia Year', while 1991 was chosen as 'Visit Indonesia Year'. The lesson is easily learned by even the least likely student: Vietnam, for example, proclaimed 1990 its 'Year of Tourism', masking its greed for foreign exchange by saying the year was in honour of the 100th anniversary of the birth of Ho Chi Minh.

Yet Vietnam is hardly the first Marxist nation to solicit tourists' money: China has been hard-selling the Great Wall, the Bund waterfront in Shanghai, and the terracotta warriors of Xian since the mid-1980s — and, except when the bloodshed of Beijing's Tiananmen Square in June 1989 rendered China an unpopular place to visit, has been rewarded by droves of American, Japanese, and Taiwanese tourists willing to pay through the nose for inferior service because China is still an 'exotic' destination. No wonder, then, that Vietnam craves tourism; so, too, by the end of the century will Cambodia, Laos, and Burma.

Their ambitions may seem hopeless today. There is no infrastructure and, after years of war and communism, no tradition of welcoming outsiders. In 1989 there were only 77,000 foreign visitors, including overseas Vietnamese, to Vietnam. When they arrived there were only 1,200 or so hotel rooms in the whole country considered fit for tourists (some were in the Saigon Floating Hotel, doing a roaring trade moored in Ho Chi Minh City after being a commercial failure in an earlier spell moored by Australia's Great Barrier Reef). But what seems hopeless today will seem realistic tomorrow. The beaches of Vietnam are as unspoilt now as Thailand's were in the 1960s; their discovery by the outside world is inevitable, and probably imminent. Come the end of this century and Asia, especially South-east Asia and Indochina, and Australasia will be a vast playground for affluent Asians. But what games will they want to play?

Figure 8 *Major Orient-Connected Markets*

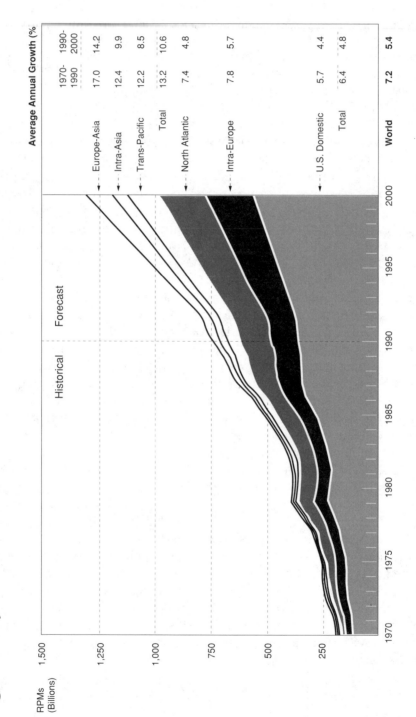

Source: 'Current Market Outlook', Boeing, February 1991.

Asia's biggest industry, by annual turnover and number of employees, is almost certainly sex (there are, of course, no proper statistics to prove this embarrassing fact). In Thailand, there are said to be 500,000 prostitutes. Indeed, one social-work group claimed in 1989 that there were 800,000 child prostitutes alone — an improbable assertion which provoked an official estimate of 30,000. In the Philippine capital of Manila there are 100,000 licensed 'hospitality workers', and perhaps another 200,000 who are unlicensed. In Taipei there are thousands of brothels and massage parlours that masquerade as barber's shops because, technically, prostitution is illegal. In Tokyo, there are perhaps 500,000 *naisu gyaru* (nice girls) at work in the hostess bars and 'soapland' massage parlours. Quite simply, sex as a saleable commodity exists in Asia on a scale far beyond its European and American equivalents.

Moreover, the industry is likely to get bigger, not smaller. One reason is that demand will increase as Asians get richer, and there will be an endless supply of poor Asians to meet that demand. In Tokyo, for example, many of the prostitutes are Filipinas who arrive either on tourist visas or with contracts to work as 'singers'. In Chinese cities such as Shanghai and Guangzhou prostitutes loiter around the big hotels — and the authorities complain that venereal disease has reappeared because of the economic re-opening to the outside world.

But another reason is that prostitution is woven into much of Asia's cultural fabric. It is a mistake to assume that the Asian sex industry exists to serve mainly Western demand. That may be true of a few specific areas, such as Patpong in Bangkok or the honky-tonk strips of Olongapo City and Angeles City that serve the American servicemen at Subic Bay and Clark Field in the Philippines. But Westerners often have less money now than Asians (which is why American servicemen in Seoul are no longer cock of the roost in the red-light area of Itaewon), and they are too few to subsidise on their own the vast Asian industry.

The truth is that Asia's sex industry pre-dates Western demand and exists independently of it, witness the quintessentially Japanese tradition of the geisha girl. Whereas the Protestant tradition of northern Europe and America associates pleasure, especially sexual pleasure, with sin and guilt, the Buddhism of Asia does not condemn man for indulging his desires. The result — incongruous and unacceptable to Western sensibilities — is that sexual favours are a relatively common business perk in Asia. This happens not only on the individual level, for executives who need to be wined, dined, and 'entertained' for the sake of the business relationship, but also for whole work-forces. A reward for productivity and profits in Japan, even in strait-laced Singapore, is a company-sponsored trip to the fleshpots of

Bangkok or Manila or Taipei. The pretext offered to the wives left at home
is that the trips are to play golf — which is why so many golf-bags are
deposited at the airport or the hotel lobby.

Some of this will change over time. One reason is that women will
become a more assertive part of society in general and the work-force in
particular. This will not only lessen the number of women for whom the
'hospitality' industry is the only feasible career, it will also modify what is
acceptable corporate behaviour. A second reason is that AIDS will strike
ever deeper into Asia's sex industry. So far, the penetration is shallow —
optimists claim Asians are somehow less susceptible to AIDS than Caucasians
and Negroes; pessimists say governments are reluctant to admit the spread
of AIDS for fear of discouraging tourists. Realists, of course, know that the
penetration is bound to go considerably deeper.

But not much will change. As other industries grow, so will the sex
industry: after all, cultures do not change their values quickly — and maybe
a cure or vaccine will render Asia's pleasures harmless. The truth is that
while sex as an industry will be restricted by social disapproval in Asia's
Muslim countries (especially Pakistan and tiny Brunei), in East Asia it will
flourish as an integral part of the overall culture.

So, too, will East Asia's other two passions, golf and gambling. The first,
by virtue of its cost, is often unrequited; the second is pursued with a zeal
that would shame even an Australian. Golfing enthusiasts in Japan, Hong
Kong, Taiwan, and Singapore will happily wait for an hour or more merely
to hit a bucket of balls at a driving range — and will wait for years to play
on a proper course. Gamblers in Hong Kong will bet over $100 million in
a single day's horse-racing, more than is wagered in a day at all of Britain's
racecourses. When there is no racing in Hong Kong, they will still go to the
Happy Valley or Shatin racecourses — to bet on satellite transmissions of
racing in Perth, Australia.

Hong Kong's gambling passion is shared by most of Asia east of India.
It may not always involve horses — although horse-racing has been revived
even in Ho Chi Minh City — but it will certainly involve all manner of dice
and card games, legal and illegal. One certainty is that when Hong Kong's
neighbour, Macao, reverts from Portugal's sovereignty to China's in 1999,
its casinos will continue to flourish and underpin the whole economy. It is
equally certain that ethnic-Chinese gamblers will pack the casinos of
Malaysia, the Philippines, Australia, and even Nevada.

Why should this be? The simple answer is that most people, regardless
of race and culture, would be happy to get rich quick. The less simple
answer is that East Asians, especially Chinese, have a faith in spirits and
supernatural forces that the West dismisses as rank superstition: belief in

fung shui, the 'wind and water' balance of natural forces, has persuaded many an individual or corporation — including the Hong Kong and Shanghai Banking Corporation — to alter concrete fixtures or architectural plans; and most numbers have some kind of luck or grief attached to them for reasons that defy logic. The result is that in Thailand, every house has a small 'spirit house', like a miniature temple, carefully positioned to appease the gods; in Singapore and Hong Kong, businessmen open new enterprises on the eighth day of the month. The phenomenon is not, in fact, confined to the peoples of East Asia — there are no people more convinced of fortune-telling and numerology than the Indians — but it is in East Asia that it most coincides with a mass passion for gambling.

Golf, however, will be a mass passion only for television viewers. Actual participation is for an élite, since demand is always outstripping supply. By 1990 Japan had some 1,650 golf courses, and another 250 were being planned or built, but that still left most would-be golfers confined to around 4,800 driving ranges, unable to afford the fees — ¥160 million ($1.2 million) for the very best — to join a club. The same élitism-by-price is at work in Taiwan, Hong Kong, and Singapore. Although Singapore's trade unions and an organisation for armed forces reservists are committed to providing affordable golf courses for their members, most Asian golfers cannot conceive of the situation that prevails in under-populated New Zealand, where public links and fairways abound and cost next to nothing to play on.

On the other hand, it is precisely the cost of playing golf that appeals to Asia's newly affluent. Just as European businessmen entertain each other in expensive restaurants, so Asian businessmen use expensive golf as a way of making the right impression and concluding the important deal. Ironically, this gives opportunities to the poor: Philippine golf clubs regularly cater to Japanese visitors, who find a weekend of golf (and, of course, 'hospitality') in the Philippines is cheaper, even after the air ticket, than playing in Japan. The same, minus the 'hospitality', is true in southern China, where one club near the Zhuhai Special Economic Zone is Japanese-financed and has an almost entirely Japanese membership. When Zhao Ziyang was general secretary of China's Communist Party, he became an avid golfer — with honorary membership of the best clubs.

But if golf remains the sport for an East Asian élite, then, by definition, the majority in Asia will have to find other leisure activities. For most, the activities will be passive — a contradiction in terms that exists because participation in a sport costs both money and time, and the poor have little of either. This is most true in the Indian subcontinent: cricket and, to a lesser extent, hockey are the games, derived from the British colonial past, that command mass support, but they cannot really command mass participation because most villagers cannot afford to buy the basic equipment. The result is that the Indian cricket team, for example, is dominated by players from 'good families', who play before huge, fanatical crowds of their social inferiors.

The sports that poor Asians actually practise are those which require virtually no equipment or money: Indonesian villagers play badminton because the sport does not require a large tract of flat space; Chinese peasants and workers play snooker with a flat metal 'cue-ball' on makeshift wooden tables set up by the roadside; Malaysians play *sepak tekraw*, a kind of aerial soccer in which the 'ball' is made of straw; Filipinos play basketball, a legacy from American colonialism that requires only one ball and a couple of hoops for a lot of players — and the small stature of Filipinos does not matter as long as they play each other (professional teams are allowed to import two foreign players each, as long as the combined heights of the two players does not exceed a set amount!). Across all of Asia, the single most popular sport is probably soccer: it needs only one ball — any size will do — for two teams (again any size will do) to enjoy themselves. And when people get richer, they can watch the world's best soccer on their television screens, which is why thousands of fans in Malaysia and Singapore stay awake until the dawn hours to watch important European matches broadcast live.

But leisure is not a static concept; its definition changes as people get richer, better travelled, more sophisticated. Westerners, with two generations of post-World War II affluence behind them, view leisure as the freedom to do things. Initially, that meant going to the pub, or to the nearest seaside resort. Next, it meant going abroad on cheap, organised tours abroad. Now, increasingly, it involves individually tailored holidays — to sail, play golf, visit art galleries, climb mountains, and so on.

Asians have still only inched along that curve of Western experience. Even the richest seldom venture outside the organised group tour. The tourist spots of the world are all subjected to the phenomenon of the Confucian package tour: the group of Japanese, or Koreans, or Hong Kongers, or Taiwanese who queue behind their flag-carrying guide and follow him or her from hotel to tourist spot to restaurant — even to the organised bathroom stop. The tour embraces the superlatives, such as the highest building or the longest bridge, but rarely does it offer the freedom to divert from the beaten path — indeed, Japanese tourists are sometimes warned not to venture in the streets of Hong Kong after dark, even though Hong Kong, like Tokyo, is one of the world's safest cities. Add to this docility a profound lack of interest in what makes a foreign culture tick, and a common Western reaction is to dismiss the Asian tourist as a robotic materialist (Asian tourists in Singapore, for example, love the Orchard Road shopping malls; Western tourists quickly tire of the shopping and look for 'exotic Asia', which the local tourist board tries, against the odds, to provide).

But the sneer is hard to justify in the absolute: Western tourists were, and sometimes are, just as narrow in their interests. The 'ugly Japanese', with his pockets full of cash, is a later version of the 'ugly American'. Moreover, Confucian societies do not breed the drunken teenage hooligans of the North European working class, and the crass behaviour of Japanese factory workers in the clubs of Taipei and Bangkok is nowhere near as crude as their British and German counterparts in the coastal resorts of Spain.

The fact is that Asian tourists in the 1990s will climb much the same curve of experience as Europeans did in the 1970s and '80s. Already, many Singaporeans are taking individual holidays of a kind that makes most other East Asians feel very uncomfortable. For example, they climb mountains in Sabah, or they take family — not group — trips to Europe, or Australia and New Zealand. A smidgeon of this may be because government policy now calls on Singaporeans to be more 'rugged' and 'spontaneous'; mostly it is because Singapore has a large middle class that has outgrown the protective cocoon of the guided group. Where Singapore's leisure-seekers lead, other rich Asians will soon follow.

It would, however, be wrong to conclude that Asians and Westerners have identical views of leisure simply because they will end up taking the same kind of foreign holidays. After all, leisure encompasses more than holidays; the way a nation plays depends, like the way a nation works, on its culture. The Japanese word for leisure is *yoka*, a combination of the character which means 'left over' and the character which means 'rest' — in other words the time left over after work, to be spent either recovering or indulging in mindless amusement.

That, of course, is probably how most Westerners view leisure, especially if they have hard, boring factory jobs. What is different in the East Asian attitude to leisure is how the Japanese and others view work. Whereas Westerners tend to see work as a means and leisure as the goal, Confucian countries think the opposite: leisure exists to help one resume the goal of work. The result is the world's most determined work ethic: the countries with the longest work hours and least free time are China, South Korea, and Japan, in that order. Japan's Leisure Development Center (formed to encourage less work and more play as a way of reducing Japan's politically embarrassing trade surplus) found that whereas two out of every three Japanese worked more than 45 hours a week, eight out of ten West Germans did not. The two-day weekend holiday is the norm throughout

the Western world; in China and the rest of East Asia it is virtually unknown
— the best a worker can hope for is to be free at lunch-time on Saturday.
Similarly with annual holidays: whereas Europeans have a month or more,
and Americans two or three weeks, the Chinese get only New Year's Day,
the three-day Spring Festival, International Labour Day on May 1st, and two
days, on October 1st and 2nd, to mark the communist revolution. The
Japanese do somewhat better, with thirteen days of public holidays and
perhaps a week of annual leave — but many employees, especially white-
collar workers, take less than two-thirds of their holiday entitlement, and
very few executives take a holiday as long as ten days.

One should not, of course, confuse this time spent at work with time
spent actually working. China's factories are monuments to sloth; office
workers in Osaka and Seoul are just as prone to idle paper-shuffling as civil
servants in Glasgow and Milan. But even if all workers everywhere were
equally lazy, more time at work will obviously also mean more time
working, which, in turn, is likely to elevate the importance of work in a
person's life. The evidence is the greater enthusiasm a Nissan or Hyundai
car worker displays when compared with his counterpart at Renault or
General Motors. China is perhaps a huge exception, but only because its
system — regardless of the economic reforms of the 1980s — still fails to
reward effort and penalise inefficiency. Elsewhere, the simple truth is that
Asians do work longer and harder than Westerners. In Japan the Economic
Council's Special Committee on Economic Restructuring found that in 1987
the average Japanese worker in the manufacturing sector spent 2,168 hours
a year at his job — which was over 200 hours more than his American and
British equivalents, and over 520 hours more than the typical French and
German worker. The Council's report, known as the Second Maekawa
Report, gravely recommended (again in the cause of cutting the trade
surplus) that the working year be cut by 300 hours by the end of this century.
In the same vein, in April 1988 government employees were given six days
off a month, by alternating between one- and two-day weekend holidays;
and in the following January it was decreed that government offices should
close on the second and fourth Saturdays of the month. Come the end of the
century and the working year should be 1,800 hours, with 104 weekend
days free from work, 15 national holidays, and 20 days' paid vacation.

What will the Japanese car worker or low-grade civil servant do with his
extra 300 hours of leisure? After all, the foreign holiday cannot be taken
every week; and the trip to the golf driving-range is not for everyone. One
weekend outlet for the whole family will doubtless be a trip to the theme
park: the Tokyo Disneyland, for example, opened in 1983, took in over 10
million visitors in its first year and has been setting admission records ever
since. The similar weekend outlet for young professionals could be the ski
resort or hot-springs centre.

But what of the evening hours after work? The immediate likelihood is that they will be whiled away in the work-forgetting ways of the post-war tradition: hard drinking in the bars; the mindless insertion of money into Japan's 3.6 million *pachinko*, or pin-ball, machines; the hilarious performance at the karaoke, the 'empty orchestra' machine that gives recorded backing music (and lyrics on a laser-disc video) to any amateur singer willing to take the microphone. Such habits may never die. Indeed, the karaoke machine has invaded bars, and now homes, from Seoul to Bangkok. But will the habits satisfy Japan's young, or their imitators in the rest of Asia?

Coin a word, and you invent a concept. This may be a mangling of linguistic theory, but it has a superficial truth. Teenagers used to be 'young people', or even 'children', until the new word defined them for the English-speaking world as a sociological phenomenon, a consumer market, and a parents' nightmare. The Japanese version of the theory is the *shinjinrui*—the new human race, or new breed.

There is some doubt as to who first used the term. One claim is that a weekly magazine, the *Asahi Journal*, invented it in an article in 1985, punning on different sets of Japanese characters that make the same sound: *shinjin-rui*, or new faces; and *shin-jinrui*, or new human race. Another claim is that it was an expression used to advertise a new whiskey aimed at young adults. If so, the whiskey, unlike the *shinjinrui*, has faded from Japan's consciousness.

Whatever the derivation, the definition is more or less accepted. The *shinjinrui* are the Japanese generation born after 1960 (some would say 1955). They are a generation that has known neither war nor privation, and they are the first in Japan to have absorbed much of their knowledge — and some of their values — from watching the television screen. They are therefore different from their parents: they believe more in play than work, more in pleasure than in sacrifice, more in spending than in saving. One Japanese account, penned for the instruction of puzzled foreigners by Tokyo's official Foreign Press Center, calls them the 'digital' generation. 'Members of the new breed dislike analogical thinking. They have no desire to contemplate their existence in the context of history . . . Today's young adults feel no solidarity with others. Uninterested in lofty matters, they are a narcissistic breed. They show no interest in what others think and live according to their own values. In this way, the *shinjinrui* generation is representative of the so-called age of the splintered masses. The new breed . . . seeks to live life as fully and comfortably as possible.'

Who are the other splinters? Try *kyujinrui* ('old human race', or 'old breed') for the generation that believes in work and responsibility. For pre-teens, reared on home computers instead of television, try *shin shinjinrui* (new 'new breed') or, more imaginatively, *daisan jinrui*— 'the third human race'.

How much substance these amusing definitions actually have is, of course, a matter of conjecture. The *shinjinrui* are really Japanese yuppies. The teenage version is more likely to dress up as leather-clad 'bikers', or as punks, and parade through the streets like their equivalents on King's Road, Chelsea. In Tokyo's Yoyogi Park, in a pattern that started in the mid-1970s, young trendies known as the Takenoka-zoku — the Bamboo Tribe — spend the afternoon jiving in the streets to old rock 'n roll records.

Put all this together, and you might assume that Japan is following America's lead — and that where Japan goes, the rest of Asia will follow. After all, American pop culture, or its English derivative, has already permeated the whole continent. Music stores in Manila, Bali, Bangkok, and Taipei are filled with the pirated tapes and compact discs of Western singers. The Beatles and Bruce Springsteen are heroes in Kathmandu and Goa. In the discothèques of southern China, youngsters try to 'moon-walk' like Michael Jackson. Only Hong Kongers, defiantly Cantonese, are unimpressed by Western pop-stars — and yet their 'Canto-rock' is heavily influenced by the American and British hit-parades. Meanwhile, the best-paid advertising models are those with quasi-Western and Eurasian (or 'pan-Asian', as the Malaysians and Singaporeans say) looks; they give a product an 'international' dimension, and therefore an aura of sophistication.

But the imitation goes only so far. Japan's *shinjinrui* are not egocentric materialists simply because they enjoy the life of a New York or London yuppie; the Malay youths in Kuala Lumpur are not teenage rebels, James Dean-style, simply because they have long side-burns and flared jeans. The fact is that Asia's youth remain part of the cultural continuum, merely modifying it as economic circumstances allow. The rock 'n rollers of the Tokyo streets are a Sunday phenomenon; for the rest of the week they put on ordinary clothes and go to work like everyone else. As for the *shinjinrui*, are their basic values really so different from their parents? After all, they share the same desire to work hard in a big, secure company, and the same lack of interest in politics.

If Asia's development is really a delayed carbon copy of the West's, then the 1990s will be a decade of drug addiction and inner-city riots. That prospect seems inherently unlikely. True, there will be a drugs problem in parts of Asia. Southern China already has thousands of opium- and heroin-users in the provinces adjacent to the 'Golden Triangle' of opium fields straddling Burma, Laos, and Thailand. Methamphetamine ('ice' to Americans, '*shabu*' to Japanese and Filipinos, '*hiroppon*' to Koreans) was invented in

Japan in 1893 and given as a stimulant in World War II to tired soldiers and factory workers; now, it is an addictive new prop to hundreds of thousands, from Seoul stockbrokers to Manila bar-girls. Meanwhile, hashish is the drug of relaxation for millions of Asian poor, from Afghanistan down to Sri Lanka.

But the problem should not be exaggerated; so far, even at its worst, it is slight in comparison with the situation in the United States, where drugs — from aspirin to cocaine — seem to be an integral part of the culture. When Mick Jagger sang before 47,000 adoring Tokyo-ites in 1988, a British journalist, Robert Cottrell, wrote an amusingly perceptive review: because Japan dates its calendar from the accession of the Emperor, and Hirohito ascended the chrysanthemum throne in 1925, the audience was really experiencing the Sixties, just as America and Britain had two decades earlier. The difference, however, is that 'unlike London in its day, the Japanese can genuinely afford to swing now on a lavish scale because they did things in the right order: they got rich before they started to get crazy.'

It is a fair point, and the implication is that the craziness will not get out of hand. There may have been political extremism in the 1960s and '70s, witness the Japanese Red Army, but it was the aberration of a tiny minority that will never appeal to a majority. The Confucian societies of East Asia are too disciplined and too consensual to produce the social melodramas that afflict the West; so, too, are the Muslim societies of Asia. The most likely breeding places for social unrest are the big cities of poor, un-Confucian Asia, such as Jakarta, Delhi, and Dhaka. But they have long had many more problems than Los Angeles or New York, and still — occasional bouts of racial rioting excepted — have remained immune from the despairing violence that characterises the decaying inner-city areas of the West.

The most likely future for Asia is that Japan, as its American influences fade, will assume its own identity in defining Asia outside the factory and office. Just as the Japanese vogue for black-and-white fashions and 'minimalist' design has invaded Taiwan, Hong Kong, and Singapore, so will the icons of Japanese playtime spread through Asia. Indeed, it has already started: the Walkman stereo, the passion for golf, the proliferation of karaoke.

What will change is the variety of the icons. Affluence brings choice, which is why the 1980s brought squash courts — just a handful — to the Taiwanese and windsurfing and ocean yacht-racing to the Japanese. True, the choice is available only to the few: in 1989, for example, a Japanese was likely to go surfing or windsurfing just once in a whole year. The same survey showed that an American would go 2.5 times a year, a Briton 3.7 and an Australian (living in what is, after all, 'Godzowne' country) 10 times. But the point is that the choice for Asians is increasing — and is being offered to an increasing number of people. Where there is little or no choice, as in the Indian subcontinent and Indochina, there is little or no money. Asia's obvious challenge, therefore, is to earn enough to enjoy itself.

Six

Pursuing a Profit

'The rich find favour in Heaven; the poor must find favour in the rich' — Chinese proverb

'Japanese are not fools' — Akio Morita, chairman of Sony

*T*hai multinationals compete to buy ailing American farm businesses . . .
The latest cellular telephone from Japan automatically translates between
English and Japanese . . . Taiwan companies may list on the Shanghai
stock exchange . . . India limits foreign investors to 10 per cent of the
shares in its new round of corporate privatisations . . . Vietnam bids to host
the biggest Japanese car and truck plant in South-east Asia . . .

(potential business prospects in Asia)

Japan's economic planners are fond of comparing Asia's development to the pattern of geese in flight: at the point of the V-shaped formation is Japan itself; close behind are the Newly Industrialising Economies (NIEs) of South Korea, Taiwan, Hong Kong, and Singapore; then the aspiring NIEs, such as Thailand, Malaysia, and the coast of China. The flight is an ordered migration to development and wealth. If the rest of Asia watches carefully, it, too, will eventually be fit to join the flight.

The analogy appeals to the Japanese sense of purpose — but it also reflects a sense of arrogant achievement. Japan, mighty in capital and vast in industrial bulk, is the leader who must be obeyed. Its foreign aid, overseas subsidiaries, and willingness to lend will define the happy embrace of Japan's technology with the rest of Asia's people and raw materials. One Japanese government study in 1988 was called 'Promoting Comprehensive Economic Co-operation in an International Economic Environment Undergoing Upheavals: Towards the Construction of an Asian Network'. No wonder Asians with long memories hear uncomfortable echoes of the 'Greater East Asia Co-Prosperity Sphere', the concept which persuaded Japanese soldiers to lay Asia cruelly to waste in World War II.

But will the geese keep in formation? The NIEs — they used to be called Newly Industrialising Countries until China objected to the independence that implied for Taiwan and Hong Kong — are so unlike each other it is easier to define them by what they are not. They are not, for example, dependent on agriculture or raw materials; they do not have a mass of people living at subsistence levels. Otherwise, the similarities are few. Korea, with 42 million people, strives to emulate Japan, its former coloniser; Taiwan's 20 million have carved a profitable, but uneasy, separation from the Chinese motherland.

The other two NIEs are little more than cities: Hong Kong, with 6 million residents, is an entrepôt for the Chinese hinterland — and will be part of

China by 1 July 1997. Singapore is an independent republic of a mere 2.7 million, dependent on the whims and economic fortunes of its larger, and poorer, neighbours. Yet, on a per capita basis, Singapore and Hong Kong are more than twice as rich as South Korea and over a third richer than Taiwan. Clearly, Asia's four 'dragons' or 'tigers' — the epithets given them by admiring, and slightly fearful, foreigners — have been progressing at different speeds. It would be rash, therefore, to assume a united advance behind Japan's lead into the next century.

Even if they could, they might not want to. Without a doubt, Japan will be the biggest economic force in Asia for at least the next decade. But it will not be the only one. At the start of the 1990s, the United States was the biggest single market for almost every Asian nation, from Pakistan, India, and Sri Lanka to Singapore, Taiwan, the Philippines — and, indeed, Japan. True, the relationship is fraught with tension. It cannot be otherwise while Japan and the NIEs account, as they did by the end of the 1980s, for roughly 70 per cent of America's enervating trade deficit. But, short of economic or social catastrophe, it is a relationship neither Americans nor Asians can quickly change. America's self-indulgent consumers have grown used to their cheap imported textiles, shoes, computers, and cars; Asia's work-force has grown used to exporting the goods Americans have long been too rich to make for themselves.

Moreover, just as America's fading power cannot be ignored, neither can the potential strength of China and India. They may account for only 4 per cent or so of the world economy, but they also account for two-fifths of the world's population — an enormous resource if properly employed. How to employ it is another matter. Japan may well see itself leading a formation of Asia's finest, but there are alternative visions. Why not consider a Greater China, linking the mainland's masses with the capital and expertise of Taiwan, Hong Kong, and Singapore? Or a South-east Asian crescent, running from Burma, Thailand, and Indochina down the Malaysian peninsula, through Singapore and Indonesia, and up to the Philippines? It would have all manner of natural resources, from rubber and copra to oil and gold; the population to be a self-sustaining market; and the technical skills, especially from Singapore, to manage itself. Or think beyond the NIEs, to an India grown expansionist, with the military clout to exploit Burma's untapped resources and to command the co-operation of South-east Asia. Or to an Indonesia exercising similar sway over its wealthy fellows — Brunei, Singapore, Thailand, Malaysia, and the Philippines — in the Association of South-East Asian Nations. Look, indeed, to a Russia using the resources of Siberia to forge an economic link with the capital and expertise of Japan and South Korea.

Figure 9   *World GDP by Region (percentage shares)*

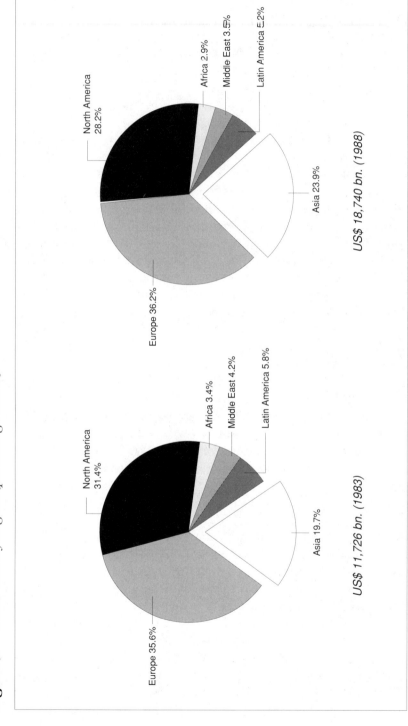

North America 28.2%

Africa 2.9%

Middle East 3.5%

Latin America 5.2%

Asia 23.9%

Europe 36.2%

US$ 18,740 bn. (1988)

North America 31.4%

Africa 3.4%

Middle East 4.2%

Latin America 5.8%

Asia 19.7%

Europe 35.6%

US$ 11,726 bn. (1983)

Source: Business International Global Forecasting Services

Figure 10 *Shares In World GDP by Region*

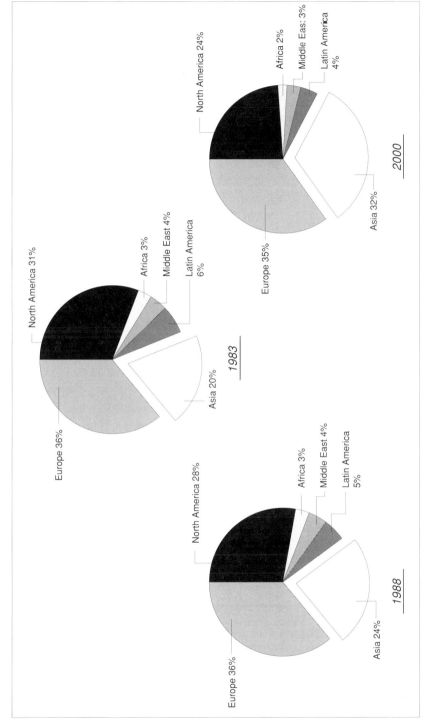

Source: Business International Global Forecasting Services

In practice, there will be no single concept, no clever image, to define Asia's economic future. The array of interests is too broad, the potential too diverse, and the starting point too fuzzy for any one country — including Japan — to impose its absolute will. Instead, Asia's development will depend on a series of questions with uncertain answers: will Japan sustain the momentum of its economic advance; will China recover its balance and continue on the quasi-capitalist path of reform; will America retreat into protectionism; will Asia, in consequence, become a *de facto* 'Yen Block'?

The past provides precious few clues to this uncertain future. In the 1950s, for example, the Philippines was the richest country in Asia next to Japan. It had timber, coconut, sugar, bananas, rubber, minerals; the output from its factories and workshops was increasing by an astounding 12 per cent a year; its people were growing richer at a pace that left the rest of South-east Asia gasping. While Singapore's per capita GDP was growing by a mere 1.3 per cent a year, and Malaysia's by just 1 per cent, the annual rate in the Philippines was 3.6 per cent. There was, it seemed, no cloud on the Philippine horizon.

But go fast forward to the 1980s, and the Philippines had fallen from grace. Under the corrupt President Marcos, the country was so deep in debt that it could not pay its bills to some 483 foreign banks — and 70 per cent of its people were below the official poverty line, struggling simply to survive. Incredibly, Marcos ordered the Central Bank to overstate the country's reserves by $600 million in the hope of getting more credit.

Meanwhile, the Philippines' Asian neighbours were going from strength to strength. By the end of the 1980s, the Chinese of Singapore and Hong Kong had graduated from their sweat-shops to become as rich as New Zealanders; Malaysians were three times richer than Filipinos; Thais were 50 per cent richer. In non-communist South-east Asia, only the teeming millions of Indonesia are now poorer than the Filipinos.

And what of Japan? Forty years ago it was a nation humiliated by defeat in war and dependent on the aid of its American conquerors. Its products were shoddy copies of Western originals; some of its companies, like Sharp and Citizen, even took Western names to hide their Japanese nationality. Until the early 1960s, Japan had a trade deficit with the United States that one American Congressional committee described as a 'crisis' — but for Japan, not the USA. Taiwan and South Korea were in the same decrepit boat — indigent countries dependent for their survival on the combination of America's financial largesse and its military protection. In short, in the 1960s only the recklessly brave or the clairvoyant would have predicted the situation at the start of the 1990s: Japan as the world's biggest economy after America; Taiwan in competition with Japan as the holder of the world's largest reserves of foreign exchange; South Korea as one of the world's most successful exporters (so successful, in fact, that the Japanese knitwear industry begged for protection from Korean imports). But even the clairvoyant would have had trouble seeing America as the world's biggest debtor, kept solvent only by the bankers and brokers of Tokyo.

Academic economists can explain it all. Most convincingly, they point to Asia's willingness to save, rather than consume. This means that a Japanese household salts away in bank and post-office savings accounts 15 per cent or more of its income — more than twice as much as an American household. Take in corporate and public sector savings and Japan's gross savings rate rises above 30 per cent of the country's gross domestic product — again twice as big as America's. The thriftiness is not Japan's alone. In the 1960s the NIEs saved around a fifth of their GDP; by the 1980s, the proportion was about a third. Indeed, Singapore, where two-fifths of a worker's wages are automatically siphoned off into a compulsory savings scheme known as the 'Central Provident Fund', was saving over 40 per cent of its GDP at the end of the 1980s — the highest proportion in the world (although, in a phenomenon that bodes well for its future, China also held that honour at other times in the 1980s). Scan the breadth of Asia, and, broadly speaking, Asia's least successful countries are those with relatively low savings rates: Bangladesh, for example, with a rate equivalent to just 3 per cent of its GDP in the 1970s and '80s, or Nepal, Pakistan and Sri Lanka with rates below 10 per cent at the end of the '80s.

The figures have no particular magic. What counts is that a country's savings do not accumulate idly under some government mattress — they provide the funds for a country's investment: in roads, schools, hospitals, housing, and factories. When they are surplus to domestic needs, they provide funds to invest abroad, in another country's companies and factories. Moreover, the greater the savings, the cheaper the funds — and so the easier the investment. The other side of the coin is the United States: because Americans save too little, investment has to be limited — or has to be paid for with money lent by foreigners at high interest rates. The result is the $100 billion-a-year American current account deficit in the 1980s, or the perennial federal budget deficit that in 1986 peaked at a daunting $213 billion: both are evidence of a nation living beyond its means on the charity of others, and especially on the charity of the Japanese. Put simply, American citizens refused to restrain their consumption, and the American government refused to increase its savings by raising taxes. Clearly, the unbalanced equation cannot last forever.

But the savings rate is only one (albeit extremely important) reason for the advance of Japan and the NIEs. The academics can find supporting explanations. One is land reform. Dispossess feudal families of their giant tracts of land and two things happen: the people who work on the land become the new owners, and hence happily productive; and the ex-landowners take their compensation to the cities and invest it in industry. In Japan, land reform happened a century ago, and so helped the nation become the first industrialised country in Asia. In South Korea, it was the American occupiers who imposed land reform — and also restructured the corporate sector and gave foreign aid. In Taiwan, it was the Kuomintang, fleeing under Generalissimo Chiang Kai-shek from the communist victory on the mainland, who forced land reform on the islanders — and the Americans, again, who provided the financial support and defence guarantees.

A second explanation is that when aid is withdrawn, it shocks a nation into high productivity. For example, when America's aid to Taiwan dried up at the end of the 1950s, the Taiwanese concentrated on building a textiles industry: it would need relatively little capital and would benefit from Taiwan's cheap labour and entrepreneurial instinct. Within a decade or so, Taiwan was the world's leading supplier of textiles. Singapore is another example of the positive approach: when Britain withdrew its naval presence in the 1960s, the naval base was swiftly turned into one of the world's most efficient ship-repair facilities.

A third explanation is a mercantilist streak among the economic planners — except in Singapore and laissez-faire Hong Kong — that decrees that imports are bad and exports are good. The consequence is a pattern of development common to most of Asia, from Japan to Indonesia. The first step is to industrialise in sectors whose output can replace imports. This move to 'import substitution' saves foreign exchange, creates employment, and upgrades skills — but it works only by erecting barriers to any more efficient foreign competitor. The next step, having achieved expertise and economies of scale in the protected home market, is to establish export-oriented industries based on the import-substituting factories. It is the process that built the car and steel industries of Japan and South Korea, or the petrochemical sector of Taiwan — and it enrages disadvantaged trading partners, who complain that they can buy as much as they want, but can sell very little in return.

Do not, however, assume the process works for everyone: the temptation, as in the Philippines, India, and (until the mid-1980s) Indonesia, is to stop at step number one. After all, if an industrialist, protected from outside competition, can make easy profits in his home market, why should he risk failure trying to sell abroad? Until Japan's Suzuki gained a manufacturing foothold in India in the early 1980s, the only new cars on sale in India were models that had ended their production life in Britain two decades earlier.

Figure 11 *Investment Approvals in South-east Asia, 1988*

To/ From	Thailand[a]		Philippines[b]		Malaysia[c]		Indonesia[d]	
	$ Million	% Change	$Million	% Change	$ Million	% Change	$ Million	$ Change
Japan	3063	217	95	229	214	134	225	-56
Hong Kong	446	266	27	-3	50	350	232	90
Korea	106	742	2	100	9	1013	209	1249
Singapore	275	330	2	166	66	22	255	1876
Taiwan	850	184	109	1109	147	212	923	11584
Asia Total	5019	221	253	222	508	134	1844	175
WORLD	6225	220	452	171	768	158	4426	257

Notes:
a   Total foreign investment in projects receiving Board of Investment privileges.
b   Equity investments approved by the Board of Investments.
c   Foreign equity in manufacturing projects approved by the Malaysian Industrial Development Authority.
d   Total foreign capital in projects approved by BKPM; excludes investment in oil, financial sectors.

Source: The Asian Development Outlook, 1990.
        Printed by permission of The Asian Development Bank, Manila.

All these factors have helped to keep the geese flying in formation for the past quarter century: while South America, Africa and, despite its period of surplus petrodollars, the Middle East fluffed their potential or lost their momentum, the NIEs increased their share of world trade from under 2 per cent to over 8 per cent, and Japan doubled its share to 10 per cent. It is an economic feat that really has no precedent: in 1983 Asia's trade with America across the Pacific became bigger than America's trade across the Atlantic; soon, Asia's trade with itself will be worth more than its trade with America — which means that Asian families will have become rich enough to begin elbowing Americans aside in the global marketplace.

But there is one other reason for the success of Japan and the NIEs: they are all Confucian societies that have known poverty and still fear — despite all indications to the contrary — its return. Why has the Philippines fallen from grace? Perhaps because its land reform has been a failure, or because America did not impose a post-war pattern. But perhaps also because it is a country — Latin and Malay in manner, American in aspiration — that is all too ready to relax in the good fortune of its natural resources. By contrast, the Confucians — Chinese, Japanese, and Koreans — work hard and save hard. One of the biggest questions for the future is when, or whether, they will change their habits.

Japan is an easy target for envy. The world's most successful car maker (Toyota) is Japanese. So, too, is the biggest bank (Dai-Ichi Kangyo), second biggest securities house (Nomura), largest transportation company (NYK), biggest life-insurance company (Nippon Life), and the biggest travel agency (Japan Travel Bureau). Indeed, the world's first company by market value, NTT, is Japanese — and, in mid-1990, was worth twice as much as the second biggest, America's IBM.

These companies stand out only as first among Japanese equals. Toyota has to compete with Nissan and Honda; Nomura trades with and against Daiwa, Yamaichi, and Nikko. NTT, or Nippon Telegraph and Telephone, is exceptionally large — but is one of six Japanese companies in the world's top ten by value. And of the world's top ten banks by assets, in early 1990 Dai-Ichi Kangyo was the first of seven Japanese (there were only two Japanese in the 1982 top ten, including Dai-Ichi Kangyo at number eight). The lone American bank, Citicorp, was at number ten.

Do such rankings have any meaning? Arguably, not as much as one might suppose. Bank assets, for example, consist mainly of the loans a bank makes, and since Japan has only about 150 commercial banks compared with America's 14,000, a Japanese bank is bound to have more loans on its books than its American equivalent. Similarly, Japanese market values make sense more in terms of speculative froth than underlying worth. At the market's peak in 1989 (some sense began returning in 1990), punters bought shares at prices that would, in theory, take several hundred years to be paid back by company earnings — which means the profit-seeking punter was buying in the expectation of later finding another punter willing to pay an even higher price. Just as bizarre was the price of land, especially in central Tokyo: this was inflated, by both scarcity and speculation, to levels that arithmetically made metropolitan Tokyo worth the whole of the United States. If the emperor were so minded, he could theoretically buy all of Canada by selling off the Imperial Palace.

What the rankings do mean is that the Japanese, buoyed (thanks, in large part, to the high savings rate) on a wave of surplus capital, are the most powerful actors in the global economy since the Arabs in their OPEC heyday. Japan's securities houses have been the biggest buyers of American Treasury bonds since 1984 — and so have been responsible for allowing Americans to continue to live beyond their means. Japan's manufacturers have set up factories from Thailand to Britain. Its retail chains now spread from Hong Kong to Bangkok. In the heart of Manhattan, the Rockefeller Center and the Mobil, Exxon, and ABC buildings all now belong to Japanese owners. So, following Sony's purchase in 1989 of Columbia Pictures and Matsushita's acquisition a year later of MCA, does most of Hollywood. And so does over 75 per cent of the equity in the hotels along Hawaii's Waikiki beach.

Not surprisingly, the foreigners' envy can turn stupidly violent — especially in America, which imports from Japan double the amount it exports back. American steelworkers, because they are losing their jobs, bash Japanese cars bought by their fellow Americans. Best-selling books talk of a repeat of the Japanese attack on Pearl Harbor, but this time with Japanese businessmen and bankers taking the role of the Zero fighter-pilots. Congressional legislators in Washington DC, all eyes on re-election, smash a Toshiba hi-fi set before the waiting cameramen. And the American government, determined to make Japan provide a 'level playing field' for bi-lateral trade, waves the big stick of 'Super 301', a section of the 1988 Omnibus Trade and Competitiveness Act that threatens to block imports if a trading partner accused of unfair practices does not mend his ways. Most Americans do not realise that Japan, for all its barriers — real and imagined — to imports, is their country's biggest export market after Canada. They know only that Japanese exporters sell more to America than anywhere else.

But if the envy is natural, are the resentment and fear that accompany it justified? Is Japan preparing to buy the world and enslave its inhabitants according to some master plan produced by the bureaucrats of the Ministry of International Trade and Industry (MITI) and the Ministry of Finance? Only if the Japanese can somehow suspend the laws of economics and human nature. Only if the Japanese really are different.

Those propositions seem inherently ridiculous. Put the Japanese 'economic miracle' in context, and it becomes explicable by the human traits of hard work and good planning. Japan had been an industrial country for half a century before America's atomic bombs were dropped on Hiroshima and Nagasaki in 1945. That defeat had the accidental virtue of destroying both Japan's still-feudal class system and its military and colonial aspirations. The consequence was that a well-educated, and extremely cheap, work-force was free to concentrate on rebuilding the civilian economy, guided by the strategists of MITI and the Ministry of Finance.

At the beginning, this meant investment in coal, steel, and chemical fertilisers; later it meant shipbuilding; then automobiles and consumer electronics. In the process, the Korean war of 1950–53 was an unexpected boon, demanding huge purchases of Japanese chemicals and heavy industrial goods. By contrast, the OPEC oil crises of the mid- and late-1970s were sudden challenges, plunging the country into recessions from which it quickly emerged through hard work and energy conservation — and by exporting to the newly rich oil producers. Along the way, import substitution was succeeded by exports, targeted to grab market share in sectors where the incumbent Western companies were too lazy, inefficient, or careless to resist. By the start of the 1980s, Japan dominated the world in an array of industries, from motorcycles, steel, and shipbuilding to the production of watches and televisions. MITI and the Ministry of Finance were becoming less and less influential because their 'think tanks' were less and less needed. Industry could now make its own strategic decisions, to cede shipbuilding to the lower-cost South Koreans or to circumvent the rising yen and trade barriers abroad by directly investing in overseas factories.

But again, put this in context. It is tempting to see Japan as poised to take on the mantle of economic leadership worn in this century first by Britain and then by the United States. The temptation should be resisted for a while yet. At the start of the 1990s, Japan's economy was just over half the size of America's. Even with optimistic assumptions of high Japanese economic growth and low American growth, Japan's economy is unlikely to be more than 70 per cent of America's by the end of the century, and perhaps 80 per cent by 2010. And if Japan did overtake America, how much difference would it really make? The United States surpassed Britain in economic size in 1913 — but did not assume effective economic and political leadership for another forty years or so.

The real likelihood of the 1990s is not that Japan will mould the world to its ways — the prerogative of all economic superpowers — but that it will begin to change its ways. Part of this will be the result of outside pressure, not least America's cutely named 'Structural Impediments Initiative'. This was begun in 1990 to persuade Japan to 'level the playing field' by action on some 200 items, such as by saving less, investing more in infrastructure (in order to lessen the emphasis on exports), and allowing large retail stores to set up in competition with the long-protected 'mom and pop' stores (the consequent freeing of the distribution system would supposedly help foreigners to penetrate the market).

The popular American conception is that the Japanese are determined to resist such persuasion. The facts suggest otherwise. Ever since the era of Prime Minister Yasuhiro Nakasone in the mid-1980s, Japanese governments have realised the need to re-balance Japan's trading relations by opening up the domestic market. Their economists' rule of thumb is that when the current account surplus is more than 2 per cent of GDP — the case in Japan in the early 1980s and again in the second half of the '80s — trade friction heats up. To cool it down, Japanese negotiators agreed at a meeting in New York's Plaza Hotel in September 1985 to let the yen appreciate against the dollar. The idea was that a weaker dollar would increase America's exports by making them cheaper; likewise, a stronger yen would reduce Japan's exports and increase its imports. In response, an American dollar that was worth over 250 yen at the start of 1985 was worth only 123 yen by the end of 1987.

The Japanese called this phenomenon of the strengthening yen *endaka*, and ordinary people worried that it would provoke high unemployment and recession. In fact, the nation shrugged off the danger thanks to a mixture of increased efficiency, upgraded exports — and America's failure to take its opportunity. No wonder foreigners think the Japanese are 'different': two oil crises — Japan imports 90 per cent of its energy requirements — and one *endaka* have made only temporary dents in the smooth upward progress of the Japanese economy.

But never mind. The far-sighted with political and bureaucratic power in Japan keep trying, by deregulating Japan's financial markets (for example by removing the ceiling on interest rates for large deposits) and opening them to foreigners; by initiating huge infrastructure projects (in which the Americans are determined to get their share); and by telling the populace to save less, work less — and spend more. There is even talk, albeit *sotto voce*, of taking on the farmers, whose political clout with the Liberal Democratic Party stops imports and makes Japanese consumers pay outrageously high prices for domestic beef and rice.

Those efforts will eventually bear fruit. Foreigners tend to think of Japan's infrastructure in terms of gleaming *shinkansen* 'bullet trains'. Reality is inadequate airports and narrow roads; only a third of the population live in houses connected to a main sewer; two-fifths of the population do not have access to flushing toilets; and too many of the houses, in the scathing (if somewhat unfair) phrase of one European Community official in the late 1970s, are 'little more than rabbit hutches'. As more and more Japanese travel, they will inevitably demand a better quality of life at home, both through personal spending (the savings rate is already falling) and government investment. That demand will automatically spur more imports, of consumer goods from elsewhere in Asia, of American agricultural products, and of American construction expertise (Japanese and Korean companies are not the only ones that can build roads, bridges, harbours, and airports). In short, the edge of foreign envy will be dulled as domestic demand, not exports, drives the Japanese economy.

But one other factor will dull that envy: Japan's jealousy-stirring boom will fade in the 1990s — and probably quite fast. The basic reason is simple: all speculative bubbles eventually burst. The stratospheric rise in the Tokyo and Osaka stock exchanges during the 1980s was a classic example of too much money chasing too few stocks — too few because, to guard against takeover bids, between half and three-quarters of all Japanese shares are held in 'friendly' hands and are never traded. The result is that stock-market activity sometimes becomes a deliberate exercise in 'ramping', with a chain of buyers trading only to bid up the price. The same process applies to land prices. Because the tax system militates against land transfers, the underlying scarcity is exaggerated and the price of land and real estate soars. The problem is that the system feeds upon itself: land, property, and shares become the collateral with which to borrow more money in order to buy more land, property, and shares. As the yen strengthened and cut into their traditional profits, quite ordinary manufacturing companies became hooked on the system of *zaitek*, a word formed from the character for finance and the English-sounding suffix tek. *Zaitek* means wheeling and dealing in all manner of financial instruments, from shares and index-futures to bonds and currency options. By the late 1980s, companies on the Tokyo stock exchange were making as much from their *zaitek* investments as from their normal operations.

Believe that the Japanese are 'different', and you believe that the bubbles can keep inflating. They surely cannot — and, as proof, stock and land prices started tumbling in 1990. New internationally agreed laws (from the Bank for International Settlements in Basle) on prudent banking mean that by March 1993 Japan's banks will have to have capital equal to at least 8 per cent of their assets. This coincides with a deregulation of the financial markets that is raising interest rates and so making Japanese equities, with their minuscule dividends, less attractive and so less valuable. Because their huge share portfolios (or rather the unrealised gains on the portfolios) are part of the banks' capital, their capital is constantly being reduced in proportion to their assets — and so the assets, too, have to be squeezed. Since many of these assets are loans, secured by shares and land already held, taken out in order for the borrower to buy more shares and land, the credit squeeze only makes market values drop still further. The result is that the upward spiral of the market abruptly turns down as investors rush to sell their depreciating holdings.

But that is not the end of the horror story. In the meantime, to bolster their capital at home, Japan's banks are having to reduce their assets abroad. Because they expanded their assets overseas at an annual rate of almost 25 per cent for the whole of the 1980s, the implications are frightening — and not just for the American government selling its Treasury bills. In 1989, Japan's banks were responsible for at least 10 per cent of Britain's outstanding property loans; and the California subsidiary of Dai-Ichi Kangyo had a fifth of its assets in construction and land development, traditionally the riskiest of all property lending.

Put all that together, and it is easy to paint a nightmare vision of collapsing markets and recessions on both sides of the Pacific. With luck, the nightmare will be avoided. Japan's bureaucrats, both within government and outside it, are used to consensus: they will certainly co-operate in an effort to manage a 'soft landing' for the markets and all who play them — and they may succeed. Yet, win or lose, the rescue attempt will point up the obvious: the bubble has burst and Japan can no longer flood the world with cheap money, or grab market share in international banking by accepting the thinnest of margins. Instead, Japan will have to concentrate on what it does best — manufacturing. And there, too, it will change its habits.

The most important adaptation Japanese companies will have to make is to go still further 'up-market'. As Japanese labour becomes ever more expensive in comparison with the workers of Korea and South-east Asia, so it will have to add more value to its work. The process is already underway, hence the relative decline of Japanese shipbuilding and the willingness to let other countries make colour televisions. The aim is to reach for the technological heights; aerospace, satellites, advanced telecommunications, biotechnology; advanced robotics; opto-electronics; and so on. Some heights have already been scaled: by 1990, for example, high-definition television (HDTV), which mimics natural sight, was on the brink of commercial reality. Other heights will take longer to conquer. In the 1980s MITI began sponsoring a 'fifth generation' project in artificial intelligence; now there is a 'sixth generation' in the works, with the idea of imitating the human brain on a microchip.

The problem is finding the right people to do the intellectual mountaineering. Japan's rote-learning excellence at school is followed by indolence at university, which means that creative scientific study happens only when graduates are snapped up by industry — universities cannot compete for the best brains — and begin their work in company laboratories. This work is perhaps the best in the world, but it is geared to application rather than pure discovery. As one of my colleagues, Nick Valery, perceptively observed in a 1989 survey of Japanese technology, Japan has traditionally opted for the 'hardware', not the 'software', in its technological advance: 'Thus it made the video recorder not the movie, the hi-fi not the record, the camera not the film, the computer not the program.' It did so by applying manufacturing genius to other people's bright ideas. The first video-tape recorder, for example, was built by America's Ampex in 1956 for use in television studios. But it used two-inch tape, which meant a machine far too bulky for use in the home. Sony's solution: use a half-inch tape but set the recording head at an angle in order to record the picture along a long, diagonal line. The same story applies in almost every part of consumer electronics, from the transistor radio to the compact disc — invented in the West, developed in Japan.

That approach cannot last much longer: a dozen countries, from Singapore to Mexico, can now make hardware which is just as good and costs much less. The challenge, therefore, is to produce the 'software'. It will be difficult, but not impossible. Japanese culture and education is certainly not as individually creative as America's or Britain's. As Susumu Tonegawa, the America-based 1987 Nobel Laureate for Medicine, said: 'Had I stayed in a Japanese university, I may not have been able to do this kind of work.' But this does not mean there is no creativity at all. In fact, quite the reverse — Japanese companies are now responsible for almost half of the patents being filed around the world; in America, where Japan accounts for almost a third of patents, the top three recipients in 1987 were Canon, Hitachi, and Toshiba, all of them Japanese. Moreover, the attitude to intellectual investment is changing. Japan has remarkably little government-funded research and development (the government pays for a fifth of the country's R&D, compared with the half paid for by the American taxpayer), and, historically, Japanese companies have strictly geared their R&D spending to commercially immediate applications. Now, however, Japanese high-tech companies are pouring money into research. In 1985, for example, the 68 leading industrial companies spent 30 per cent more on capital expenditure — new machinery and the like — than on R&D; by 1988 they were spending 8 per cent less. Indeed, the high-tech companies were spending 80 per cent more on research and development than on plants and equipment. From that wave of spending, results are bound to flow, in faster and smarter computers, in vacuum microelectronics, even, perhaps, in civilian aerospace — the one area in which Japan has consistently failed to catch America's lead.

But the results will take time. At the end of the 1980s, the government reckoned Japan needed an extra 50,000 computer programmers; by the end of the 1990s, the shortage could be as great as 900,000. Whereas America graduates nine scientists and a dozen engineers for every 100,000 people, and Britain ten scientists and seven engineers, Japan's universities produce only two scientists and nine engineers. That kind of imbalance cannot change until the educational system lower down changes — and until society wants it to change. In the meantime, to maintain their competitive margin, Japan's manufacturers will increasingly invest in operations overseas.

All economic powers acquire foreign possessions. Britain had an empire that spanned the globe; the Americans, with companies such as Ford, Exxon, and IBM, virtually invented the multinational company (or MNC, as the business school acronym has it). Inevitably, it is now Japan's turn to plant factories in the home ground of its trading partners. Through the 1990s the Japanese MNC will be as obvious to the world as its American forebears were in the 1950s and '60s.

Yet Japan has invested overseas with considerable reluctance. Until the 1980s, there were only a handful of Japanese companies, mainly in minerals and timber (of which Japan has little), that made and sold goods abroad. For the majority, there was no reason to set up overseas — it was cheaper to export from Japanese factories, where the work-force was cheap enough and where its quality could be closely monitored. Toyota, for example, did not have an overseas plant until 1984.

Two developments of the 1980s changed this collective reluctance. Foreign countries, blaming Japanese imports for their lurch into trade deficits, threatened to erect barriers to Japanese goods. The British and French, for example, persuaded Japan's car makers to adopt 'voluntary export restraints' (VERs), in order to limit their share of the United Kingdom and French markets (the perverse effect was that the Japanese were able to charge higher prices to the British consumer). Similarly, the French also decided in the early 1980s that imports of Japanese video-cassette recorders would all have to go through customs in Poitiers, well inland and miles from any convenient port or airport. (Not that the Japanese could complain too much; they used to limit foreign car imports to Japan by insisting on all manner of trivia, from paperwork to the shape of the stop lights.) The other factor, especially after 1985, was the rise of the yen. Suddenly, it had become expensive, even with productivity improvements, to manufacture mass production items such as cars, televisions, and basic semiconductors in Japan.

The consequence was — and is — an exponential growth of Japan's direct investment (as opposed to the indirect investment of buying Treasury bonds and the like) overseas. In 1982, Japan made direct investments abroad of just under $8 billion; in 1986 the figure just over $22 billion; and in 1989, some $67.5 billion. Some of this is big-ticket stuff: Toyota's joint venture plant with General Motors in California cost $500 million, and its wholly owned plant in Kentucky another $800 million. Toshiba announced in 1990 plans for a $500 million semiconductor plant in northern California. But there will still be plenty of small-ticket items to add on: one 1990 survey of 9,000 small Japanese companies found that 2,500 of them were planning to invest abroad, mainly in South-east Asia. At that time, Japan's direct investment overseas over a period of four decades already amounted to $254 billion — over half of which was committed in the second half of the 1980s.

But so what? The populist tendency, especially in North America, which has accounted for roughly 40 per cent of Japan's direct overseas investment, is to see the trend as a mix of conquest and theft. And yet Japan's overseas investments are much less than America's or Britain's — and in its favourite investment spot, the United States, at the end of the 1980s it still lagged behind Britain and Holland in terms of annual spending as well as cumulative investment. Over time, the Japanese factory in America's Tennessee or Britain's Teesside will become like the IBM subsidiary in Japan or the Exxon subsidiary, Esso, in Britain — it will become an accepted part of the industrial landscape, its national origins forgotten. The truth is that objections are always more jingoistic than economic. After all, foreign investment is not a threat but a blessing: it provides jobs, the transfer of technology, and the spur of competition; it lessens a country's need to burden itself with foreign debt, which must later be repaid out of export earnings; it gives investors a healthy interest in opposing protectionist barriers, regardless of which country is erecting them. It also goes where it can be best used.

The proof lies with the NIEs and the countries of South-east Asia. They have been the world's most vibrant economies for the past decade — and, after North America, the most popular recipients of foreign investment, especially from Japan. Moreover, the trend will continue. Foreign companies which once invested in the 'dragons' for their cheap labour, will increasingly do so in the future for their skilled labour — and to take advantage of the growing market they represent. The same is true for aspiring dragons, such as Malaysia and Thailand. At the end of the 1980s personal spending in

South Korea, Singapore, Thailand, Malaysia, and Taiwan was rising at an annual rate of between 7 and 14 per cent. Translate that into products, and it becomes millions of television sets, portable radios and, yes, McDonald's hamburgers.

Arguably, it is possible to exaggerate the role of direct foreign investment in the improving fortunes of East and South-east Asia: the spending by MNCs constitutes only a relatively small part, less than 10 per cent, of total investment. But the modesty is misleading, since invariably foreign investment increases the dynamism of key sectors.

The country most aware of this is Singapore, which goes out of its way to entice foreign companies to set up their regional manufacturing and administrative bases in the island republic. What it offers them, apart from tax concessions in many cases, is extremely efficient communications, a completely open trading environment, and an absence of corruption. What it gets in return, apart from jobs, is the spin-off of technology and of expertise in industrial management — the only way a country with no natural resources apart from its people and its sheltered harbour can keep ahead of its rivals. Philip Yeo, the chairman of the Economic Development Board, explains in typically high-tech Singaporean jargon: 'The decision was to plug the nation into the global economic system . . . by promoting foreign investment in Singapore [and] by adopting a free trade policy that would enable liberal import and export of goods and services. This would ensure that goods and services produced in Singapore will be internationally competitive.'

The decision has served Singapore brilliantly well. In just twenty-five years the per capita income has gone from $800 to over $10,000. Apart from a sudden, small recession in 1985, economic growth has surged, frequently reaching rates of 10 per cent a year. The corollary is the hundreds of foreign companies using Singapore as a regional centre — for example British Petroleum; Philips of Holland; Apple of America; Sony of Japan and its subsidiary Aiwa; the financial information networks of Reuters and Telerate; America's Union Carbide. Most recent foreign investment has been from Japan, which by 1988 had committed to Singapore $3.8 billion, twice as much as the amount invested in neighbouring Malaysia — and a fifth more than the figure for Japan's former colony, South Korea. By 1986, foreign affiliates were responsible for three-quarters of Singapore's exports; in South Korea and Taiwan, which both have large domestic markets to attract MNCs, the equivalent proportions of the export totals were between a fifth and a quarter.

As with Singapore, so with Hong Kong. Just as Singapore provides a hub for trade with South-east Asia, so the British colony is a base for thousands of foreign manufacturers, banks, and brokers to do business with mainland

China (and, for many, South-east Asia). Its container port rivals Singapore's; and its people earn marginally more per head than Singaporeans. It is also attracting almost twice as much direct investment from Japan. The reason is that while many foreign companies see the reversion of sovereignty to China in 1997 as a threat of instability and so as an incentive to move elsewhere (normally to Singapore), Japanese companies see 1997 as confirmation that Hong Kong's umbilical tie to the mainland will never be severed — in which case, the sensible thing is to establish a presence in Hong Kong in time to benefit from closer links with an increasingly prosperous China. So far, that idea has enticed more than 1,500 Japanese companies to Hong Kong, from builders such as Kumagai Gumi to banks such as Sanwa. The most intriguing arrival is the provincial Japanese retail chain, Yaohan. Impatient at the obstacles to expansion that all retail groups face in Japan, Yaohan's chairman, Kazuo Wada, decided in 1989 to move himself and his corporate headquarters to Hong Kong. With his department stores already operating in America, Costa Rica, Taiwan, and throughout South-east Asia, Wada's aim is simple: to grow, as Sony did, by succeeding outside Japan.

But it is a mistake to see Singapore and Hong Kong as identical twins, however much they share a belief in open trade and the benefits of foreign investment. What distinguishes one twin from the other is that Hong Kong is truly a laissez-faire economy, with minimal government intervention. By contrast, Singapore's élite civil servants plan economic development, target areas for investment, and then build strong companies as a core around which others can cluster. Eventually, the core companies — Jurong Shipyard, DBS Bank, Neptune Orient Lines, Singapore Airlines, and the like — are ready to be privatised, but usually in part rather than whole and with an ex-civil servant as chief executive.

Singapore is not a paradigm for the rest of its region. How could it be, given its puny size and dependence on the world around it? That very dependence demands a belief in free and open trade, since Singapore's internal economy is too small even to pretend to a separate existence. But the ability of its government to push and pull the levers of a capitalist, 'free' market is precisely the quality that has helped both Japan and two dragons, South Korea and Taiwan, to achieve their feats of economic growth. Put that ability together with the Confucian work ethic, add in an undervalued currency (as for most of the 1970s and '80s in Japan, Taiwan, and Korea) and success, it seems, is assured. Failure happens when governments decide to pull the levers of a planned economy, under the illusion that bureaucrats can do more than target areas for investment — they can also decide how many tractors need to be made, who should buy them, and what price they should pay. The result is the economic mess of China, and more especially of Vietnam, a country with precisely the same human and natural resources as prospering Thailand.

A second type of failure is that of the Philippines. The forces of a free market are there in theory — but in practice are constantly thwarted by corruption and political interference. The result is that the Philippines is the laggard of non-communist South-east Asia, likely in the 1990s to be overtaken in per capita income by Indonesia. What would accelerate progress is a substantial increase in foreign investment — but this will not happen while politicians, with an eye on the presidential and congressional elections of 1992, stir up opposition. Their jingoistic nonsense argument is: 'Why should a foreigner profit instead of a Filipino?' — heedless of the reality that the foreigner has created the profit and in the process benefited the Filipino. Ironically, the emerging reformists of Vietnam are more eager than some Filipinos to attract venturesome dollars and yens.

The adventurers, however, will not be just the American and Japanese. The 1990s will see the growth in Asia of non-Japanese multinationals. Many will be companies from Hong Kong and Singapore that have grown too big to find new opportunities within their home economies. In Hong Kong, for example, the New World group has already taken on huge hotel and real estate investments in America; Hutchison Whampoa has oil and real estate interests in Canada. A Singaporean food company, Yeo Hiap Seng, has acquired an American counterpart; Singapore Press Holdings has publishing and printing interests in Britain. But companies outside the 'city states' will begin to flex their wings. At the start of the 1990s, Taiwan's accumulated cash — the result of its perennial trade surplus and consequent huge current account surplus — was flowing almost as fast as Japan's, in fact sometimes faster, into America (the world's biggest market, and so always a favourite), Indonesia, Thailand, and Malaysia. Korean companies like Daewoo and Samsung were following suit. But the 1990s will see development beyond Japan and the dragons. Already, Thailand's agribusiness giant, Charoen Pokphand, has established subsidiaries and affiliates in China, Hong Kong, and Indonesia; other Thai companies will soon go into Vietnam, Cambodia, Laos, and Burma, establishing what then Thai prime minister, Chatichai Choonhaven, described in 1989 as a *Suwannaphume*, a 'Golden Land' to realise his ambition of changing Indochina from a 'battleground into a marketplace'.

What will all this add up to? Obviously a much more integrated Asia: the geese that fly behind Japan used to send her petroleum, minerals, and other raw materials — now, more than 60 per cent of Asian exports to Japan are manufactured goods, including the output of Japan's overseas subsidiaries. Japan will not be a substitute for America as a market, but it will lessen Asia's perilous dependence on the United States.

It will also be a more balanced Asia. Japan, and to a lesser extent South Korea and Taiwan, will be driven by domestic consumption, which will cool some of the trans-Pacific trade friction. Together with Hong Kong and Singapore, they will provide Asia's poorer nations with capital, technology, and managerial expertise. Meanwhile, Thailand, Indonesia, the Philippines, and Malaysia will provide willing workers and a surfeit of raw materials, from oil and gas to rubber and timber. Singapore, for example, talks of 'growth triangles', marrying its own technology and management to the land and people of Indonesia and Malaysia (the first triangle is being formed with Batam, an Indonesian island right next to Singapore, and the neighbouring Malaysian town of Johor Bahru). In essence, the Singaporeans are defining in jargon a development that will happen in much of Asia — think, for example, of South Korea's technology, China's work-force, and Siberia's raw materials. Or a triangle linking Thailand with Vietnam and Burma. It hardly matters what the geometrical shape is, the result will be an integration and momentum to sustain Asia's economic growth well into the next century. But the balance will not be perfect. That can only happen if two billion Chinese and Indians can join in, too.

Dreamers see China as the world's next economic giant: a market of over a billion consumers; a work-force of half a billion; a commercial instinct that has survived four decades of communism; a network of overseas Chinese, from Singapore and Hong Kong to Vancouver and Los Angeles, who are ever ready to lend their help to a motherland for which all Chinese, regardless of politics, feel an affinity. True, a country as vast and populous as China will not achieve uniform prosperity, but think of the great cities — Beijing, Shanghai, Tianjin — and, of course, the coastal regions of the south, envious neighbours of the capitalist citadels of Hong Kong and Taiwan. Surely, they are destined to match the wealth already achieved by Asia's dragons.

Probably so, but not within the decade ahead on which this book is concentrating. Instead, three factors will hinder China's progress. The first is the obvious distraction of population growth. If China's economy grows by 8 per cent a year through the 1990s (not impossible given its double-digit rates through most of the 1980s) it will be almost twice the size of Britain's — but the average Chinese will still be desperately poor in comparison with his British equivalent.

The second factor is the less obvious, but equally real, distraction of the struggle for leadership. Through China's 2,000 years of cultural and political union (there were at least another 2,000 years of less united history before then), there has always been a tension between the centre and the provinces — and there has always been an emperor attempting to maintain the power of the centre. Mao Zedong, whatever his ostensible doctrine, was just such an emperor; so, too, Deng Xiaoping. But, just as it took Deng two years to emerge as Mao's successor, so will Deng's successor also need time to consolidate a hold on power. Time spent on politics is bound to be time spent away from economic reform — and the difficulty of effecting, even deciding, that reform is the third factor that will slow China's advance.

Deng's insight was to realise that central planning could never raise China's living standards above the barely adequate. His goal was that China should enjoy a 'middle income' status, with a GDP per head of around $1,000, by the end of the 20th century. His solution was to give increasing freedom to market forces: at the end of 1978 he inaugurated the 'open door' policy to foreign investors and gave the nation's peasants the right to sell produce for their own profit once they had met the quota due to the state. Six years later, the reforms were spread to China's towns and cities. Once a factory had fulfilled its quota, it could make profits for its own managers and workers to share as bonuses. In the countryside, the system of 'household responsibility' meant that the family replaced the People's Commune as the unit to farm the land and reap the reward. In the towns and cities, 'contract responsibility' meant that an individual manager or, indeed, a whole factory would bid against others to meet output targets, and would enjoy profits or suffer losses in consequence. Along China's coastline, Deng's reform-minded protégé, Communist Party general secretary Zhao Ziyang, established fourteen 'open' cities and five 'Special Economic Zones'. They offered foreign investors tax privileges, cheap labour, and even the right to lease land, sometimes for up to seventy-five years. In many cases, the lease itself could be sold on to another investor, making the system virtually equivalent to land use in the West.

How could this be reconciled with China's Maoist past and continued profession of Marxism? Deng's answer was to call it 'socialism with Chinese characteristics': the colour of the cat, he said, does not matter as long as it catches the mice. Anyway, such capitalist behaviour was, according to Marx's dogmata, the 'primary stage of socialism' — and, as such, it could last for a hundred years.

In fact, it cannot if the present characteristics remain in place. The Deng reforms wrought minor miracles: urban incomes doubled, rural incomes tripled, and China turned from being one of the world's biggest grain importers into being, on occasion, a net exporter. Foreigners rushed to join Deng's dream, investing more than $15 billion (and promising as much again) in over 21,000 different projects. Foreign trade grew so fast that by 1990 it accounted for around a third of China's gross national product, an enormous proportion for a vast land mass like China. All this was, and is, an amazing achievement. Peasants who a generation ago literally scratched a living from the soil, now have tractors and four-storey houses. Factory workers have colour televisions, even the occasional video-recorder.

But where next? The ultimate logic of Deng's reforms should have been total liberalisation — in other words, the abandonment of communism. Understandably, that is a step neither Deng nor his colleagues have been able to make, and the chaos of Eastern Europe, where communism committed suicide in 1989, is no incentive to try. But the status quo is inherently unhealthy: some prices remain fixed, while others float free; workers receive their bonuses even if they are lazy, and no State enterprise — however inefficient and unprofitable — is allowed to go properly bankrupt.

In this co-existence of the 'free' market with the planned economy, corruption is inevitable. The well-connected buy grain, pigs, steel — virtually anything — at low, State-controlled prices, and sell at higher free-market (and black-market) prices. Since the well-connected have Party connections, the Party's credibility is automatically corroded. In retrospect, the tragedy of 4 June 1989, when troops with tanks swept peaceful student protesters from Beijing's Tiananmen Square, was not political in its origins, but economic: the call for democracy was a by-product of 'open door' economic liberalism; so was the corruption against which the students demonstrated. The problem for the nation's leaders is that renewed economic liberalisation is bound to create pressure for political liberalisation — and for the end of the communist party's monopoly on power.

Will India, echoing with the dissenting voices of democracy for all its post-colonial life, offer China a solution? Probably not. The nation's mind-set is an introspective socialism, worsened by a corruption that is China's equal and a bureaucracy that has no equal. Add in a birth rate that is a third higher than China's, and the result is a country that struggles in China's wake. After all, China's economy, even with Maoist madnesses such as the Great Leap Forward and the Cultural Revolution, still grew by over 5 per cent a year between 1950 and 1980. India managed only three and a bit per cent, a level some cynics called the 'Hindu rate of growth'. State controls were ubiquitous, on imports, exports, and even what sort of vehicles a car plant could make. Established industrialists saw no reason to upgrade their factories since they had a captive home market, protected by tariff barriers from foreign competition. Corporations such as the Tata and Birla groups are big by any standards — and yet are virtually unknown outside India. The unintended result has been a colossal waste of the entrepreneurial talent that has surfaced as the millionaires of the Indian diaspora.

Yet India is not a hopeless case to be consigned to economic oblivion. It used to have famines; now it exports food. It has a ramshackle transport system, but can put satellites in space. Most of its people use firewood as fuel, yet there is a nuclear power industry that should provide a tenth of India's energy by the end of the century. Moreover, just as China had the reforms of Deng, so India in the 1980s had the reforms of Rajiv Gandhi: less bureaucracy, fewer tariffs, more incentives to export, special deals to attract investment from Indians abroad. Their effect was to boost India's average rate of economic growth in the 1980s to a more respectable five and a bit per cent a year. Unfortunately, come 1990, and the reforms were losing momentum, slowed down by political upheavals, 'vested interests', and, of course, the mind-set of a nation intellectually reared on socialism and profoundly mistrustful of foreign investors.

In which case, the challenge for both China and India is really the same act of political daring: to give the forces of the market-place freedom to inspire greater productivity in search of greater reward. The lesson from the prospering Asian dragons is that foreign investment is the easiest catalyst for the process. So far it is China, not India, that has learned that lesson — and China has the ethnic advantage of capital pouring in from Taiwan and Hong Kong. Moreover, China has gone too far to turn back: its Special Economic Zones and southern provinces will be too rich and powerful to be reined in by any doctrinaire Marxists emerging in Beijing. Instead, the likelihood is that more parts of China, led by Shanghai, will demand to follow the liberal trend. Shanghai has already announced a $10 billion scheme to build a high-technology industrial zone, the Pudong New Area, to help the city recover its pre-communist glory. Put 'greater China' together — by 1990, Taiwan had invested more than $1 billion in the mainland, and Hong Kong companies were employing over two million workers in China's Guangdong Province — and it would make a mighty big bird to join Japan's formation of flying geese sometime next century.

In the meantime, just how closely the formation will stick together is a matter of conjecture. But all its members will have some characteristics in common: companies that are owned abroad and local companies that invest abroad; increasingly open financial markets; vigorous stock-markets that become better regulated; economies that upgrade themselves as workers become richer and so more expensive. The question is how to ensure the geese fly smoothly.

Seven

Questions of Class

'Labour without reward does nothing except make a man feel tired' — Chinese proverb

*F*oreign workers on Singapore's construction sites strike for better
housing . . . The Islamic Conference demands police protection for India's
Muslim minority . . . China's State-run media praise the new class of
independent entrepreneurs . . . The Japanese Diet approves an amnesty for
the country's illegal foreign workers . . .

(social possibilities for Asia's future)

All Asians may be born equal — but
some, to borrow George Orwell's ironic observation, are more equal than
others. Usually, the 'most equal' are those with the whitest skins: in India,
the lighter her skin, the better a teenage girl's prospects of marriage; in the
Philippines, the *mestizo* élite, with their colonial mix of Spanish blood, are
waited on by brown-skinned 'Indios'. If the distinction by colour is unclear,
it can always be made by some atavistic appeal to the bloodline. The Han
Chinese find it culturally impossible — whatever the official dogma of
egalitarian Marxism — to consider Tibetans (or anyone else, for that matter)
as their equals. The Japanese consider themselves a superior, entirely
homogeneous race, heedless of a genetic past that mixes in large dashes of
Mongol, Korean, and Chinese blood. Of all the surprises that greet Westerners
new to Asia, perhaps the biggest is Asia's racism — not just because it is so
pervasive but also because it is so accepted. Indeed, in India, discrimination,
social rather than racial, is institutionalised in the Hindu caste system.

Yet there is no real mystery in the prejudices that are so clearly exhibited:
they simply reflect relative economic strengths, be they actual or historic.
One American diplomat, posted from China to the Philippines, once told
me how odd it felt to have moved from a culture whose people assume they
are the world's best to one where people suspect they are the world's worst.
Actually, it is not odd. Whatever their present poverty, the Chinese have an
arrogant memory of past glories and a consciousness of a continuing
civilisation; by contrast, the Filipinos have no recorded history before the
arrival of Spanish colonisers — and the Spanish were followed by Americans
who, in the condescending words of President Taft, thought of the Filipinos
as their 'little brown brothers'.

Economists, of course, can use a mass of statistics to chart Asia's present
strengths and weaknesses: the different growth rates of Japan and the
Philippines, or the contrast in personal incomes between Singaporeans and
Indians. But the most obvious evidence is visible to the casual observer
almost anywhere in Asia: it is the constant procession of poor Asians hoping
to work for other, richer Asians. Every Sunday in and around Hong Kong's
Chater Gardens thousands of Filipina maids gather to gossip in Tagalog; in

Singapore, the Filipinas congregate by the shopping malls of Orchard Road and Scotts Road. Board an oil tanker on its way from the Gulf and, as likely as not, the crew will be from the Philippines, Thailand, and Indonesia. Behind the high-rise buildings that line the Creek, the back streets of Dubai could pass for sections of Karachi, Dhaka, or Bombay. The construction sites of Taipei are manned by illegal immigrants from mainland China, Malaysia, and Indonesia. In Japan, the 'hospitality' industry increasingly relies on Filipinas who arrive on tourist visas to become recruits — sometimes gullible, sometimes not—of the *yakuza* gangs who control vice in Japan. In Hong Kong the labour shortage provides a constant incentive to employers to give jobs to the stream of illegal immigrants from China; when plans to build a new airport for Hong Kong gather physical momentum, the stream will become legal.

The phenomenon is hardly new. Rich countries have always attracted labour from poor ones: the Irish have been fleeing to the United States for over a century; so have South Americans, Europeans, West Indians, Africans, and Asians. And if not the United States, there was always Australia — or, especially in their final years of empire, Britain and France. In the days when the sun never set on their empire, the British imported Tamils and Chinese to work the plantations and mines of what was then Malaya; Indians built the railroads of East Africa, or cut the sugar cane of South Africa. In the 1960s, South Korea, just recovering from war with the North, sent first coal miners and then nurses to work in booming West Germany. In the 1970s and early '80s, the magnets were the sparsely populated oil-producing states of the Middle East. In the Arabian peninsula, at least four million migrants — Arab and Asian — provided the essential labour for the grand ambitions of the OPEC era. The citizens of Kuwait, the United Arab Emirates, and Qatar were (and are) privileged minorities in their own countries.

Moreover, the phenomenon endures. As the oil states of Arabia and the Gulf have become less wealthy, or, with grand infrastructure schemes complete, less in need of foreign workers, so the slack since the mid-1980s has been taken up by the prospering nations of East Asia. The Japanese talk of 'three Ks' in the workplace — *kitsui, kitanai*, and *kiken*, or hard, dirty, and dangerous. It is the work the Japanese no longer want to do for themselves, and so immigrants take their place regardless of the near-total ban on the legal entry of foreign workers.

What will happen in the 1990s is more of the same: the migration of the poor to the lands of the rich. South Korea will stop sending contract labourers abroad, and, instead, will become a host to growing numbers of workers from China, the Philippines, and Indonesia. Thailand and Malaysia will still export workers to Singapore — but will also import workers, from

Burma, India, Indonesia, Sri Lanka, and the Philippines. And all the time impoverished Vietnam will be desperately seeking new destinations for the workers it used to send to the Soviet Union and Eastern Europe. When it does so, it will be competing with equally cheap labour from China. At the start of 1991, there were already about 66,000 Chinese labourers working abroad — with an immense reservoir of available workers in reserve, since, according to one Chinese estimate, by the end of the century the country will have an astounding 240 million labourers surplus to its own requirements. In short, Asia will remain the largest market for migrant labour that the world has ever seen. Pick any day between now and the end of the century, and some five million Asians — from Filipina maids and Bangladeshi labourers to Indian doctors and Vietnamese miners — will be working outside their own countries.

The question is what the effects will be, economic and social, of the phenomenon. If a perfect deal is one with a willing seller and a willing buyer, then the transactions of the Asian labour market could surely be cited as textbook examples. The country exporting its labour gets foreign exchange, in the form of the remittances from its overseas workers, and lessens its domestic unemployment. The country importing the labour gets muscle and skills to make economic progress that would otherwise falter for lack of manpower. During the 'OPEC decade', from the mid-1970s to the mid-1980s, Pakistani workers abroad sent home more than $16 billion; the remittances of Bangladesh's overseas workers in some years paid for a quarter of the country's imports; Philippine governments rely on remittances of around $1 billion a year to help service the country's near-crippling load of foreign debt. Moreover, these figures understate the workers' importance to their home economies: add in the black-market transactions that most sensible workers use when they send money to their families (the black market avoids tax and gets a better exchange rate), and in some cases the estimates could well be doubled.

What is true of Pakistan, Bangladesh, and the Philippines is also true — in varying degrees — in all Asia's poor countries. In Indian states such as Kerala and Gujarat, whole villages depend on money sent home from workers in the Gulf. Probably the most critical problem facing the finance minister of Vietnam is not how to attract foreign investment (vital though that is), but how to find work for a labour force being swollen by workers returning from Eastern Europe and by soldiers being demobilised from a shrinking army. The obvious short-term solution is to find them jobs abroad. If Vietnam, like the Indian subcontinent or Indonesia or the Philippines, stays poor, then the solution goes from being a short-term remedy to becoming a seemingly permanent — and inherently vulnerable — dependence on the employment needs of others. Among Asia's traditional exporters of labour, only South Korea can contemplate with equanimity an end to the inward flow of remittances. The reason is simple arithmetic: as their country has become richer so Korean workers have become more expensive. The days are going when companies like Hyundai will ship thousands of Korean workers (some of them as an alternative to military service) to build refineries, petrochemical plants, and roads in the Middle East. There are still thousands of South Koreans working abroad, especially in Japan and Germany, but there are also thousands of non-Koreans attempting to find work (usually illegally) in South Korea. And why not? Since a Pakistani will happily work in a Seoul factory for a third of a South Korean's wages, there is plenty of opportunity.

Some, of course, argue that this movement of labour is detrimental, especially to the labour exporters. After all, the very language of the process — the 'brain drain' or the 'skills drain' — is implicitly critical. Just think, the argument goes, how advanced India could be if its scientists and doctors stayed at home. Or just think of the commercial advance the Philippines could make if only its thousands of computer graduates stayed on in Manila, or if its bankers and managers gave up the 'green cards' that allow them to live, work, and prosper in the United States. Why should rich countries exploit poor ones by bribing the most talented to serve foreign masters?

Superficially, it may seem a strong argument. But fundamentally, it is flawed. The skilled, the talented, and the adventurous emigrate for work because they are surplus not to their countries' requirements but to their countries' abilities to use them. There is no point in Filipino computer programmers staying on in Manila or Mindanao if there are no computers for them to program. It makes more sense for them to go abroad and send back as much money as they can — until the country, thanks indirectly to their remittances, does have enough computers. If they return having learned new skills, it is an added bonus. One of the mainstays of Vietnam's economy in the 1990s will be the remittances from the hundreds of thousands who left as 'boat people'; many of them will also return as investors — in small factories or hotels or whatever — and bring with them the capitalist skills learned in the West.

The real criticism of Asia's constant flow of labour is not economic, but social. Migrant workers, both men and women, work in conditions—social or financial — that the nationals of their host countries find, by definition, unattractive. To get their jobs they often have to borrow money, pay agents, and bribe officials. The result is a debt that takes months to work off. A Filipina from 'the province', as the country outside Manila is colloquially termed, will have to borrow perhaps $1,000 to get herself to a job as a maid in Singapore or Hong Kong: she has to pay to get a passport; have her papers processed by a government-approved agent; take a medical test to check against pregnancy, tuberculosis, and venereal disease; go through a course on rudiments such as how to iron shirts or use a vacuum cleaner; and provide the 'placement fee' for the recruitment agent, who will use part of it to buy a cheap air-ticket. All of this will take time, and several costly trips to Manila.

And what next? The answer for her and almost all of Asia's migrant workers is a contract that reduces the worker to virtual serfdom and to a separation from relatives and friends that will last for months or even years.

Amazingly, some academics believe the harm done to family relations is nonetheless slight. The extended family — the bedrock of the Third World that in the West has been eroded away — supposedly provides support when it is needed. According to one study in the Philippines, cases of infidelity among wives whose husbands are working abroad are 'few and far between'. Other studies argue that women in developing countries gain added status and power from the independence and responsibility they must assume when their husbands leave for work abroad.

Doubtless, some of that is true — but it is easier to be sceptical. Separation for months on end cannot be a recipe for marital happiness. In the Philippines there are countless anecdotes of the extra-marital jinks of the 'Arabiana' — the woman whose husband has gone to work in Saudi Arabia. In Pakistan, psychiatrists at one hospital have treated so many wives of migrant workers that they now talk of the 'Dubai syndrome'. And it surely cannot be ideal for children to be reared in the absence of their parents (although the British upper class, with its fondness for boarding schools, has perversely persisted in the habit for centuries).

But whatever the human qualms one may have, sheer economic need makes travel enthusiasts of most migrants. The challenge is for their governments to ensure that their foreign employers do not abuse them. That, of course, is much easier for politicians to proclaim than to deliver. The basic truth is that the buyers are more powerful than the sellers in Asia's labour market: Filipina and Sri Lankan maids are frequent victims of sexual abuse, especially in the Middle East, but rarely receive legal or financial redress; construction workers from the Indian subcontinent are often paid late, or below the agreed rate — and yet they fear instant deportation if they begin to complain. Only South Korea, with economic clout in its own right, has been able to specify, and enforce, precise conditions that foreign employers must meet if they want Korean contract workers — even down to one newspaper and one flush lavatory for every 20 workers, and at least two videotape recorders for every 200.

When weaker countries try to emulate South Korea, they are doomed to fail. In 1988 the Philippines, for example, banned the export of its maids until agreements to protect their rights could be concluded with foreign governments (for diplomatic reasons, Arab nations were not singled out). The ban was ill-conceived from the outset. In Hong Kong, Filipina maids demonstrated against President Aquino, complaining that if they went home for a holiday they would not be able to leave the Philippines again to resume their jobs. In Manila, cynics observed that a ban designed to protect the virtue of Filipinas would force many young women who might find honourable employment abroad to stay, instead, in the Philippines — where there was almost no work for them except as prostitutes. And lastly, while the ban lasted, the flow of remittances — vital to the Philippine economy — would slow. Predictably enough, virtually no new agreements were signed and the ban was quietly forgotten. Filipina maids are still ill-protected around the world, and yet they still compete to go abroad to join, for example, the 50,000 and more Filipinas in Hong Kong (where they vie with Vietnamese boat people as the largest expatriate community) or the 20,000 or so in Singapore. There is many a Filipina college graduate who chooses to give up being a schoolteacher in Manila in order to get ten times more money as a maid in the Gulf or in one of the Asian dragon economies.

But if Asia's traffic in human beings exacts a social and emotional cost, it also provides some benefit in return. At the most basic, this is money. The 150,000 foreigners thought to be working illegally in Japan get precious few yen compared with Japanese workers for doing the *kitsui*, *kitanai*, and *kiken* jobs that the Japanese now shirk — but however few the yen may be in a Japanese context, once sent to the Philippines, Bangladesh, Pakistan, and China, they will feed, house, and clothe whole families. If, at some point in the 1990s, Japan bows to economic reality and legalises its foreign work-force in order to expand it, wage rates will rise and those foreign families will be all the better fed, housed, and clothed — and will get still more of the radios, televisions, and other electronic goodies that define success for the migrant worker.

If that were the total benefit, then perhaps the rewards would be too temporary to justify the costs. After all, what happens when the migrant returns and the remittances stop? But, in fact, the benefit is more lasting. Families with a migrant as the breadwinner tend to buy a piece of land, build their own house, and put their children through as much schooling as they can cope with — precisely what our Filipina *amah* did with the money my wife and I paid her in Singapore and Hong Kong. That sort of investment raises both expectations and achievements. With luck, it can drag a single family from feudal servitude to middle-class pride in one generation. Extrapolate from a single family to thousands of families, and a country's whole social structure can change.

That degree of extrapolated luck, however, will depend on much more than the efforts of migrant workers. The rich, industrialised countries of Asia all share a certain social uniformity, and hence cohesion: the gap between rich and poor is not enormous, and most people fall somewhere in the middle. In Taiwan, for example, the richest fifth of the population has an income only five times greater than the poorest fifth — the government became genuinely alarmed in the late 1980s when the soaring stock-market threatened to increase the multiple. Likewise, in South Korea, it is 'not done' for rich industrialists (of whom there are now many) to flaunt their wealth with extravagant mansions.

By contrast, the poor countries of Asia are usually (but not invariably) marked by social extremes. A score of families supposedly controls Pakistan's economy; in the Philippines, the top fifth of the population gets half the country's income, and the top tenth a third; in India, the 'middle class' of over 100 million people is huge in absolute terms, but is just a fraction of a nation numerically dominated by the relatively poor and the abjectly poor. Such countries are trapped in a feudalism which becomes oppressive simply because of a growing population on the same amount of land. But — short of revolution, or of land reform imposed, as we have seen in Taiwan and South Korea, from outside — this feudalism is hard to change. After all, why should any cosseted élite willingly give up power? The optimistic answer is that feudal societies are agricultural ones; once the feudal élites see the opportunities offered by industrialisation, the societies will become more urbanised and the élites, whose power rests really on land ownership, will lose much of their control. The obvious question for the optimists is how long will the process take. In the special case of caste-riven India, the trite answer is 'for ever'.

Most nations have some form of enduring class system. In Britain, the 'old school tie' denotes not just a person's background but also his future. Only the rich or well-connected will normally go to the 'best' schools — and their graduates are disproportionately numerous in the senior ranks of government, politics and business. The same is true of France, with its *grandes écoles*, and even of equal-opportunity America, with its Ivy League universities. And the same, of course, is true of Asia: from Pakistan to the Philippines, people talk of 'good families' and 'good schools', where contemporaries form alliances that promote successful careers in politics, the armed services, or business. Even China has its class structure, with obvious preferment given to the children of the political élite.

The drawback of such systems is their failure to tap a nation's full potential: bright children born into poor families get inferior educations and fewer chances to exploit their brains. Yet, over time, the systems become less powerful. Economic development spreads not only wealth but also opportunity. Just as regional accents have crept into Britain's hitherto élitist foreign service, so will 'ordinary' Asians gain more power as their countries prosper. This is already evident in Japan and the Asian dragons; soon, it will happen in aspiring dragons, like Thailand and Malaysia.

But how can it happen in India? Asia's second biggest country not only has the class system of the old British Raj (upper-class Indians pigeon-hole each other by accent just as quickly and finely as their British equivalents), it also has the institutionalised caste system of the Hindu religion. Quite simply, Hindu Indians — which means at least 700 million Indians — are not born equal; nor do they stand any chance of becoming equal. Instead, they are trapped in their castes. Originally, some 3,000 or more years ago, Hinduism had a mere four categories — the Brahmins, or priestly caste, followed by warriors, farmers and traders, and finally servants. But the centuries have multiplied the divisions: there are now almost 3,000 castes and subcastes. At the very bottom are the 'outcastes', or scheduled castes as they are now known (although many consider they are so low as to be properly outside the caste system). They do all the dirty jobs that higher castes will not touch: sweeping roads, collecting garbage, tanning leather hides. Because they do untouchable work, they themselves are 'untouchables', to be carefully avoided by their social superiors.

Arguably, the caste system ensures a stable society in India, rather as Confucian hierarchies do in East Asia. Traditionally, castes provide for each other — an exchange of labour and services in return for grain and fodder. Because your caste depends on the karmic balance of good and bad accumulated in your last incarnation, you cannot hope to climb the caste ladder until your next incarnation. The result, therefore, is a rigid social matrix, which can be escaped only by converting to other religions (many Indian Muslims and Christians are descended from low-caste Hindus) or, in the case of women, by marrying 'upwards'. True, the class system of education and wealth can operate separately from the castes, but not to the extent of ignoring castes: a Brahmin does not marry an untouchable even if both are graduates of Cambridge (inherently unlikely in the case of the untouchable).

But the presumed stability is, in fact, an illusion. Modern Indian history is scarred not just by sectarian strife — between Hindus and Muslims or Hindus and Sikhs — but also by conflict between the castes. In his peaceful struggle for Indian independence, Mahatma Gandhi (from the traders' caste) attempted to elevate the position of the untouchables by terming them *Harijan*, or 'children of God'. But it was a term that the untouchable leader B.R. Ambedkar refused to use: he preferred the more pugnacious *dalit*, or 'downtrodden'. Ambedkar was right. In the pyramid of Indian wealth, the untouchables are the disproportionately wide base, mainly landless peasants working as bonded labourers — in effect as slaves for the higher-caste landowners. The theory of the constitution is that discrimination on the basis of caste is illegal. The reality is that it is both ingrained and pervasive — which is why the constitution also states that the scheduled castes and the 600 or so tribal minorities should hold seats in both the national and the state parliaments equivalent to their numbers in the overall population. It is also why successive Indian governments have practised what the Americans call 'affirmative action', reserving school places for untouchables and tribals and giving them scholarships and even extra examination marks.

The question is just how affirmative a government can be before it offends those it decides not to favour. In August 1990, India's then prime minister, V.P. Singh, decided to reserve 22 per cent of government jobs for 'backward' castes. This was in addition to the 27 per cent quota already reserved for untouchables and tribals. Mr Singh's minister of labour, Ram Vilas Paswan, grandly declared that the move, accompanied by a plan to create up to 120,000 new civil service openings, would 'generate awareness that the ordinary people are also masters of this country'. Perhaps so, but a more likely motive was that Messrs Singh and Paswan were playing politics on behalf of their Janata Dal Party, seeking to entice the untouchables and lower castes away from their traditional allegiance to the Congress Party.

But if they were playing politics, they were also playing with social fire. In a country with high unemployment and a burgeoning population, government jobs — as a lowly clerk in a rural railway station or a high-flying entrant to the prestigious foreign service — are highly prized. The higher castes, who of course are in general better educated than 'untouchable' and other 'backward' castes, were enraged at this departure from meritocracy (although Tamil Nadu and Karnataka states long ago reserved almost 70 per cent of government jobs for the backward castes). Their reaction was a two-month spate of rioting, vandalism, effigy-burning, killing, and horrific self-immolation. The awful irony is that giving privileges on the basis of castes will not help to reduce the importance of the caste system, but will serve only to emphasise it.

Unhappily, the caste system is not the only social curse India will have to endure into the next century. Just as certain is the curse of sectarian conflict, pitting the Hindu majority against Muslims and Sikhs; just as enduring will be ethnic strife that has nothing to do with religion. Both are in their way more dangerous for India's future than strife between the castes: inter-religious violence threatens India's identity as a secular state; ethnic insurrections threaten the integrity of the whole state. Sometimes, both elements come into play — the Kashmiris, for example, are overwhelmingly Muslim and have been trying, by war as much as by words, to secede from the Indian union ever since India's declaration of independence in 1947. But if Kashmir were to gain independence, or to unite with Muslim Pakistan, what would stop the secessionist fire from burning still more fiercely among the tribes of Assam, an oil-producing state the union can scarcely afford to lose, or among the Sikhs of Punjab, who bloodily seek to establish an independent state of 'Khalistan', or among the Maoist-minded Naxalites in heartland states such as Orissa and Andhra Pradesh? And as minorities become more violent, what is there to restrain the countervailing force of Hindu chauvinism? In the autumn of 1990, for example, Hindu extremists, stirred up by the Hindu revivalist Bharatiya Janata Party, attempted to seize the site of a 16th-century mosque in Ayodhya, in Uttar Pradesh state, in order to establish a temple marking the supposed birthplace of the Hindu god-hero Ram. By the time the dispute had simmered down, scores had died in confessional strife across the nation. But inevitably this or similar sores will erupt again to threaten India's fragile social peace.

Such a prospect is, of course, a warning to many Asian governments, not just India. The simple fact is that there are minorities dotted over most of Asia. When minorities are tiny, they can be discriminated against with impunity. The Japanese, for example, make few apologies for their prejudice against the 620,000 or so ethnic Koreans who were born in Japan (often from parents brought over as forced labour during World War II) but have no right of citizenship. In looks and accent, they are indistinguishable from their Japanese contemporaries—but until 1991, when Japan finally bowed to diplomatic pressure from South Korea, they had to register their fingerprints with the state. The same inured discrimination faces the *burakumin*, some two million Japanese 'untouchables' stigmatised by their dirty work as tanners and butchers in the pre-Meiji era more than a century ago. Meanwhile, Indonesia's Chinese, a mere 3.5 million in a nation of more than 180 million, accept that their business dominance (by one estimate, they account for 75 per cent of the nation's private capital) will provoke the occasional street riot, burnt factory, or stone thrown through the window.

The real problems come when minorities are too big to be pushed around without retaliation. One obvious example is Sri Lanka, bathed in bloodshed since 1983 because its Tamils — one in every five of the population — want independence from the Sinhalese majority. What stirs the emotions of the mainly Hindu Tamils goes back as far as 1956 when the Sri Lanka Freedom Party came to power on a platform of Sinhalese as the official language and Buddhism as the predominant religion. Another example is Fiji: in 1987, the ethnic Fijians, now outnumbered by the descendants of the 19th-century immigrants from India, mounted a military coup to preserve their political control over 'their' country. A third example, now part of South-east Asian folklore, is the race riots in Malaysia in May 1969, which left several hundred dead: angry Malays, representing half the population, ran amok in the capital Kuala Lumpur as the Chinese minority — roughly a third of the population — celebrated its election victories with provocative chants of 'Death to Malays, aborigines go back to the jungle, this country does not belong to Malays' and so on.

The question is how to deal with the problems. The trite answer is that governments should do whatever is necessary to promote economic growth, since prosperous people tend to be happier and less restive than poor people. True enough in the abstract; the particular is rather different. When some sections of society prosper at a faster rate than others, the laggards grow jealous, resentful, and even violent — which is why the tax systems of the developed world are 'progressive' rather than 'regressive'. The idea is simple and, to most people, compelling: the richer you are, the more you can — and should — pay for the benefit of the community.

But what may work well enough in the cohesive societies of industrialised Europe and America is not automatically sufficient in developing Asia. For one thing, the average Asian tax net covers only a few taxpayers; for another, the net is so inexpertly thrown that many of these few still manage to swim free. The Philippine élite, for example, regularly receive a comfortable income by renting their Hollywood-style homes in Manila's Forbes Park development to foreign diplomats and businessmen. Yet when tax-return time comes, virtually all the houses in Forbes Park turn out to be 'owner-occupied', with no rental income to be seen. Similarly, why should a Chinese businessman in Jakarta or Bangkok pay his tax when he can more cheaply bribe the collector — or simply hide his profits in accounts that would baffle any auditor?

A better answer, according to some Asian governments, is to engineer social harmony through 'affirmative action' (shades, again, of India) and legislation. Malaysia's race riots of 1969 prompted a worried government to introduce in the following year the New Economic Policy. The thinking behind the NEP was simple, perhaps excessively so: poverty must be eradicated and the Malays had to be brought simultaneously into the economic mainstream — or there would always be the risk of friction with a Chinese community that was economically powerful beyond its numbers. Accordingly, the NEP directed that the Malay ownership of shares in the corporate sector should rise from less than 3 per cent (the Chinese had around 34 per cent, and foreigners most of the rest) at the plan's start to 30 per cent by its end in 1990. By then, the non-Malay Malaysian (in effect Chinese) share could rise to 40 per cent, while foreigners were to be restricted to 30 per cent. It was social engineering on a grand scale, and was made more complex by other measures to favour the Malay *bumiputras*, or 'sons of the soil' — for example, scholarships and preferential admission to college and university, and guaranteed access to jobs in both the public and private sector.

It was also social engineering with some obvious flaws. Interestingly, its neglect of Malaysia's Indians was not one of them: the Indians, who are Malaysia's poorest community, comprise only a tenth of the population, so they have no choice but to ally themselves with a more powerful party — which, by virtue of the constitution, is politically the ruling Malays. The real mistake was to imagine that Malays needed only the spur of legislation to become commercially astute, and that non-*bumiputras* (anyone who is neither Malay nor an aborigine, no matter how many generations his family has spent in the country) would happily concur in this pro-Malay bias.

Life is not like that. The simple truth is that the Chinese culture has a commercial instinct that to most Malays is irrelevant or even slightly distasteful. By the time the NEP ended, the Malay share of corporate ownership had risen only to about 21 per cent — and most of that was achieved not by breeding a new class of Malay capitalists, but by placing shares with State-established Malay pension funds and similar institutions. Meanwhile, foreign investors bemoaned the need to employ people by race rather than merit, and the Chinese became resigned and resentful — and, in many cases, inclined to emigrate to more egalitarian climes, especially Australia.

But one should not dismiss the NEP out of hand. Nor should one criticise too quickly the race-based politics that spawned it. Malaysia's racial balance, or imbalance, means the country is bound to be nearer than most to the brink of violent upheaval — but the fact is that during the NEP there was no such upheaval, and foreign investors, whatever their grumbles, continued to put their money and factories in Malaysia. Ergo, some would say, the NEP was a success. Certainly, some form of economic favouritism — less precise, but still real — will continue for the *bumiputras* until at least the end of this century. Indeed, it will have the backing of mainstream Chinese political leaders; they will see privileges for the Malays as a small price to pay for continuing prosperity and inter-racial calm.

That same pragmatism will hold sway in neighbouring Singapore, too. By all measures, Singapore's 410,000 or so Malays — just over 15 per cent of the island's population — are on the bottom rungs of the country's economic and educational ladder. They lag behind the dominant Chinese, some 76 per cent of the population, and the Indians, whose share is around 6.5 per cent. As Goh Chok Tong, the country's prime minister since November 1990, told the Singapore Malay Teachers' Union in 1987, 'It is extremely difficult to build a harmonious nation out of a multiracial and multireligious population. Difficult, because differences between races and religions are real and abiding.' Goh went on to recall that in 1965 Malaysia's prime minister, Tunku Abdul Rahman, had expelled Singapore from the Malaysian Federation precisely because of those difficulties. Singapore's Lee Kuan Yew was campaigning for a 'Malaysian Malaysia', one in which the Chinese half of the federation's people had as much right to political power as the Malays. The Tunku, however, realised that the Malays would never accept Lee as their prime minister and his Chinese-dominated People's Action Party as their government. In consequence, 'he cut Singapore loose.' As Goh explained: 'Whether they liked it or not, the Malays, Chinese and Indians in Singapore found themselves adrift in the same boat. They had to row together, or sink together.' Hence the concept of the Singaporean identity: 'We are committed to building a multiracial nation, based on shared destiny, shared benefits, and respect and tolerance for each other's language, culture and religion.'

Commitment is one thing, achievement another. Goh is a pleasant man, not the sort to rile his audience. Accordingly, he did not mention what is obvious to all Singaporeans — that their republic is a Chinese-run island surrounded by the Malay ocean of Malaysia and Indonesia. The clear implication is that in times of regional tension Singapore's Malay minority may have divided loyalties — which is why Malays in the Singapore Armed Forces are not allowed to pilot fighter aircraft or perform other sensitive functions (an embarrassing fact later blurted out, deliberately or otherwise, by Brigadier-General Lee Hsien Loong, the son of Kuan Yew and by nature more abrasive and assertive than Goh). What increases that possibility is that Malays, practically by definition, are Muslim: not surprisingly, Singapore's Malays have always felt uneasy about the close relationship between their country and Israel. Similarly, when the Gulf war broke out in January 1991 the Malays tended to sympathise with Iraq's Saddam Hussein, even though the country officially opposed his invasion of Kuwait.

Yet, whatever the potential pitfalls, Singapore has so far been remarkably adept at keeping its racial balance. The secret is a mix of careful planning and ruthless control. When the Housing and Development Board began its building programme in 1960, thousands of Malays were moved out of their traditional *kampongs*, or villages, into new public housing. They would have liked to stay together, to preserve communities that had grown over generations. Instead, the HDB insisted that they be dispersed among the new apartment blocks. The idea was simple: to prevent the rash of racial ghettoes that scars cities such as New York, London, and Paris. The policy worked then, and it works now: nine out of every ten Singaporeans live in an HDB apartment, and — thanks to the HDB's 'Home Ownership Scheme'

— eight out of every ten own their apartment. But the 'Big Brother' HDB makes sure that Malays will never be more than 25 per cent of the residents of a single apartment block, or 22 per cent of the residents of a single neighbourhood. The equivalent proportions for Chinese are 87 per cent and 84 per cent; for 'Indians and others', 13 per cent and 10 per cent. All this is bluntly known as the Ethnic Integration Policy. It goes together with other measures: financial aid to Malay schoolchildren; constant, often condescending, exhortations to the Malay community to strive for excellence lest Malays lag too far behind the Chinese and Indians; and recognition of Malay as the 'national' language (although English is the language of administration).

There is one other device that the government brings to bear — control over foreign newspapers and magazines (the domestic press is already tame). 'The Singapore government's position is straightforward,' Lee Kuan Yew told the Commonwealth Press Union in October 1990. 'It will not allow interference by foreigners in its domestic debate.' Why not? Because, according to Lee and his colleagues, Singapore's political institutions are too fragile and its racial and religious feelings too sensitive to withstand Western-style reporting and adversarial argument. Maybe he is right — although that assumes Singaporeans are more vulnerable and less sophisticated and mature than they appear. For example, in 1987 Singapore used the Draconian Internal Security Act (a legacy of Britain's colonial war against communism in the Malayan peninsula) to imprison without trial a group of alleged 'Marxist conspirators'. To most foreigners, they looked perfectly innocuous. Indeed, one minister admitted to me that the arrests had been made not because the conspirators were at all dangerous, but to ensure that they did not become so in the future. He did not say how Marxism would manage to flourish in a country that is one of Asia's richest and most middle-class.

An alternative explanation for controlling the foreign press is that after three decades in power, Lee himself had become sensitive — and overly so — to outside reporting and comment, hence the bombardment of letters by Singapore officials to foreign publications. Either way, *Time* magazine, its sister publication *Asiaweek*, and the Dow Jones-owned *Asian Wall Street Journal* and *Far Eastern Economic Review* were all at various times in the late 1980s 'gazetted'. This meant that their circulations were restricted but the publications were not actually banned. In other words, the publications' advertising revenue would fall, but Singapore could smugly maintain that it was not censoring the free flow of information.

Had the publications 'interfered in Singapore's domestic debate'? Not by the definition of most outside observers, and certainly not according to the publications themselves. The *Asian Wall Street Journal's* offence stemmed

from an article on a new secondary market for the stock exchange, hardly
a subject likely to stir social unrest. *Time*'s offence was not to print a
government letter following an article on one of Singapore's two opposition
members of parliament. Is it really true, as Lee alleges, that the *Asian Wall
Street Journal* and other regional publications based in Hong Kong 'are no
longer the foreign press. They have become a domestic Singapore press,
based offshore. Their correspondents act like journalists do in America,
taking sides to determine the outcome of issues under debate.'? That again
seems unlikely, although Lee does make the point that Singapore's electorate
is the only one in Asia to use English as its common, and often first, language
— and it is certainly true that the gazetted publications had had large
circulations in Singapore (over 9,000 copies sold each week of the *Far Eastern
Economic Review*, and over 5,000 copies daily of the *Asian Wall Street
Journal*).

Doubtless, at some point in the 1990s the feud between Singapore and
the foreign press will fade away. For one thing, Lee is no longer prime
minister; for another, Singaporean politicians are pragmatic enough to
realise that their country's position as a regional hub will be enhanced by
the unhindered presence of foreign publications and reporters — and
lessened by their absence. Lastly, of course, the foreign press will tread very
carefully in their coverage of Singapore.

But put aside the conflicting charges of Singaporean paranoia and
foreign arrogance, and what remains is Singapore's concern to create an
enduring national identity when the country's natural elements — its
people — are divided by race and culture. The Malaysian solution is to
impose Malay political supremacy. The Singaporean solution is to encourage
different groups to cherish their differing cultural heritages, while
simultaneously sharing in a common 'National Ideology' (Singaporeans
love to make slogans in capital letters). This will be a set of 'Shared Values'
— Nation before community and society above self; Family as the basic unit
of society; Regard and community support for the individual; Consensus
instead of contention; Racial and religious harmony. It sounds a little like
Indonesia's *pancasila*, a formula that no one can take offence at, but which
can be used to justify the suppression of all manner of anti-social behaviour,
from communism to the proselytising of fundamentalist Christians.

How well this set of Shared Values will work is a matter of conjecture.
Sceptics will argue that Singaporeans are getting tired of slogans, spoon-fed
to them by a 'mummy knows best' government: Speak Mandarin, Courtesy
Begins With Me, Excellence for Singapore, and so on. Thousands of
talented Singaporeans emigrate each year. Thousands more search for their
values by adopting a new religious faith. Between 1980 and 1988 the
proportion of Singapore's Muslims and Hindus remained constant, but the

proportion of Singaporeans who are Christian rose from 10.3 per cent to 18.7 per cent. Because Muslims are almost always Malay, and because Hindus are all Indian, the obvious conclusion is that the new Christians are almost always Chinese, departing from the Buddhism and Taoism of their forefathers. Moreover, the growth of Christianity is strongest among the best educated. Since the most appealing forms of Christianity are of the fundamentalist and charismatic variety, the government understandably fears that Singaporeans, not foreigners, may start to make religion — and by extension race — an issue in Singapore.

But if scepticism implies pessimism, it is probably a false sequence. The truth is that Singapore is a small laboratory in which social experiments can be tried — and controlled. Because problems are seen well in advance, they can be solved, or at least minimised. Asia's intractable problems are those of poor, agrarian societies in the Indian subcontinent, or the Philippines: feudalism, corruption, and the huge gaps between rich and poor. In the Philippines, for example, the surprise is not that there should be a communist insurgency but that it shows no signs of succeeding. By contrast, the worries of Singapore and the rest of rich Asia are trivial: how should prosperous middle-class societies, with full employment and good services, become still more prosperous and middle-class?

A general truth of Asia's trade unions is that they are not on one side of a class struggle. There are, of course, exceptions, especially where land reform is yet to be properly accomplished. For example, the sugar-workers' union on the Philippine island of Negros is avowedly left-wing, locked in perpetual conflict with land-owning *hacienderos* who pay their workers, including women and young children, pittances that are well below the official minimum wage. Victory for the union would amount to a social revolution — which is hardly likely to happen given the private armies of the landlords and the feudal deference ingrained in most of the workers. In Manila, there are dozens of strikes at any one time (few are effective), called by a plethora of workers' groups and tacitly supported by the Communist Party of the Philippines. But look beyond the Philippines, or the communist pockets of India, and the picture in industrialised Asia is remarkably harmonious: workers and their bosses share much the same values, background, and goals. There is no parallel with the 'them and us' mentality that sours the shop-floor air in Britain or Australia.

There are several reasons why this should be. The most obvious is the influence of Confucianism: east of the Indian subcontinent, cultures prefer consensus to confrontation everywhere, including in the workplace. But that alone cannot always keep the industrial peace. What helps in Japan and Asia's dragon economies is that as the economic pie has expanded, the workers' slice has grown, too. What helps also is that some governments keep trade unions on a tight leash that comes close to strangulation. In Singapore, the leader of the trades union congress is also a deputy prime minister; the pay-fixing National Wages Council is a tripartite grouping of employers, unions, and government that does not believe in challenging the cabinet. In Malaysia, the government can ban a strike before it happens by obtaining a court order. In Indonesia, the union movement is under the thumb of the ruling Golkar party, and is in any case constrained by 'Pancasila Industrial Relations'. In China, the Communist Party absolutely controls the approved unions (although workers sometimes strike in defiance of their unions). Put culture, material progress, and political control together, and it becomes a sound formula for industrial peace (strikes are virtually unknown in Singapore, a leading proponent of a formula which has given Singaporean workers material benefits their fathers could scarcely have dreamed of).

The problems come when the values of the formula are changed. Until 1987, South Korea's economic advance was achieved at the expense of its workers: their wages rose, but not as fast as their productivity; their unions were controlled by their managers, in co-operation with the state; and their attempts to strike were repressed both quickly and brutally. In other words, the workers' slice of the economic cake was getting proportionately smaller, with no means of redress. Come the emergence of presidential candidate Roh Tae Woo in 1987 and the consequent political liberalisation, and it was as though the floodgates opened for the workers' grievances. In the second half of that year, each day brought twenty new strikes; in December 1988, Hyundai Heavy Industries, the world's largest shipbuilder, was shut by striking workers for nearly four months (the strikers were finally routed by a sea-borne invasion of 10,000 riot police). In 1989, car makers Hyundai, Daewoo, and Kia Motors were all held to ransom by workers who went on strike or mounted other forms of industrial inaction. By the following year, the inflamed passions in the workplace had cooled to more manageable levels, helped by a slowing economy for which the government took delight in blaming the workers.

The blame is not, of course, entirely that of the workers. The underlying fault is that a mercantilist government, believing in exports above everything, had relied for too long on a cheap labour force paid in an undervalued currency. The result is a correction that was bound to hurt: a doubling of labour costs in just three years for the car makers; a slump in exports; a cut in staff by foreign banks who by 1991 had been blackmailed into raising wages by their workers by 50 per cent a year for four years. But the pain will be only temporary. In the rest of the 1990s, Korea will follow the labour pattern of Japan before it: it will pay high wages in return for higher productivity in areas which increasingly depend on brain and capital rather than brawn. In short, it will enjoy industrial peace.

But while Korea is copying Japan, Japan itself will be changing. One of the great myths of Japan is that its workers have 'jobs for life'. In fact, probably only one in five of Japanese workers has such security of tenure, since only the biggest companies have the financial resources to give such a guarantee as they ride the business cycle — and even these companies cushion themselves by hiring many temporary workers. Moreover, the figure will get smaller as Japan's living standards rise and its business costs increase. But the myth is important for the paternal care it symbolises, rather than for its vanishing reality. The fact is that Japanese employers do care for their workers. The majority may not offer a job for life, but they do their utmost to ensure that a laid-off worker is re-employed by a friendly company.

In return, the companies get co-operative unions. The Shunto, or Spring Wage Offensive, is a ritual that rarely leads to warfare. Peace prevails even though, in a perennially tight labour market, the unions have considerable bargaining strength (after all, unemployment, always below 3 per cent of the work-force, for practical purposes hardly exists). One reason for the peace is that only a few workers, such as the seamen and teachers, are organised on an industry-wide basis. Most workers belong to in-house, company unions, formed with the approval of the management. Their natural tendency is to identify their own interests with those of the company and its management — hardly a good basis for bargaining for higher wages. On the other hand, Japanese management is not like American management. There is no pressure on Japanese managers to perform well for quarterly results, or to increase profit margins above a sectoral average. Instead, the Japanese manager is expected to look to the long term by gaining market share and by protecting his workers. The unions bid for wage rises which they know the company can easily afford; the company then awards additional bonuses according to its profits — knowing that the bonuses can go down as well as up, and do not feed through into additional pension obligations.

All this reflects a community of interest within the company: it exists not for the benefit of its shareholders — the Western concept — but for and because of its employees. Western companies reward high flyers with faster promotion; in Japanese companies, even the brightest must wait his turn — promotion and salary increases come with age and seniority, not talent. It is a system that has served Japan well: economic growth and full employment has continued from the 1960s through two oil shocks to the

1990s. Of the major industrial nations, only Germany has had a better record on days lost to strikes.

Nonetheless, this system will change — and not just with a lessening of the 'job for life' phenomenon. One reason is that the industrial landscape is changing. Manufacturing is declining, services are rising, and more and more women and part-timers are taking jobs. The result is that unions are seen by more and more workers as irrelevant to their needs. In 1950, for example, 56 per cent of Japanese workers were union members; by 1989, the figure was down to 26 per cent; and by the year 2000, fewer than one in every five Japanese workers will be a union member. A second reason is that for all their preference for consensus, Japanese are becoming more individually motivated as they become more internationally aware. It is no longer rare for a talented Japanese to ignore a Japanese company's offer in favour of working for a foreign company for more money; and it is becoming accepted that an employee may work for more than one company in his lifetime, or that he may want to take his full holiday entitlement. A third reason is that the internationalisation of the economy, including Japan's stock exchanges, will inevitably bring in Western methods of assessing performance.

But the system will not change so much that it loses its identity and imitates the 'hire and fire' mentality of free-wheeling America. That may work for America, but the essence of Japan's success is ingrained in a different cultural tradition: its people work together for the collective good. Since nothing succeeds like success, it is the Japanese model that will influence the rest of Asia, not the American one. The theoretical prospect then is an Asia that becomes both more prosperous and less marked by social extremes. The question is: once this happens, how will it be protected?

Figure 12 *Growth Rate of GDP (per cent per annum)*

	Average 1971–80	1981	1982	1983	1984	1985	1986	1987	1988	1989	*1990	*1991
Newly Industrialising Economies	9.2	7.3	5.4	9.6	9.7	4.5	11.3	12.1	9.4	6.4	6.2	6.8
Hong Kong	9.5	9.4	3.0	6.5	9.5	-0.1	11.9	13.8	7.3	3.6	3.0	5.5
South Korea	8.7	6.7	7.3	11.8	9.4	6.9	12.4	11.8	11.3	5.9	6.3	6.7
Singapore	9.0	9.6	6.9	8.2	8.3	-1.6	1.8	8.8	11.0	9.2	7.5	7.7
Taiwan	9.7	6.2	3.6	8.4	10.6	5.0	11.6	12.3	7.3	7.7	7.2	7.4
South-east Asia	7.9	6.6	3.2	4.6	4.9	0.9	4.0	5.8	8.0	7.8	7.2	7.3
Indonesia	7.9	7.9	2.2	4.2	6.7	2.5	5.9	4.8	5.7	6.5	6.4	6.5
Laos	...	...	7.1	4.7	6.4	9.1	7.1	-2.4	2.1	4.0	5.2	5.5
Malaysia	8.0	6.9	5.9	6.3	7.8	-1.0	1.2	5.3	8.7	7.6	7.0	7.5
Philippines	6.2	3.9	2.9	0.9	-6.0	-4.3	1.4	4.7	6.2	6.0	5.0	6.2
Thailand	9.9	6.3	4.1	7.3	7.1	3.5	4.5	8.4	12.0	10.8	9.9	9.2
Vietnam	...	...	...	...	8.4	5.6	3.4	2.6	5.9	8.2	8.1	8.1
South Asia	3.7	6.6	4.3	7.9	3.9	6.5	4.5	4.3	8.5	4.4	5.3	5.2
Bangladesh	5.9	6.8	3.7	3.8	5.5	4.1	4.0	4.0	2.6	2.4	5.9	5.1
India	3.3	6.6	4.0	8.6	3.4	6.6	4.6	4.4	9.5	4.5	5.4	5.2
Burma	4.3	6.4	5.6	4.4	5.6	3.2	-1.1	-4.2	0.2	3.4	3.6	3.8
Nepal	2.3	8.3	3.8	-3.0	9.7	6.1	4.3	2.7	9.7	1.5	-3.5	1.0
Pakistan	4.8	6.9	6.5	6.8	5.1	7.6	5.5	6.5	7.0	5.6	5.5	6.0
Sri Lanka	5.5	4.7	6.0	4.8	5.1	5.0	4.3	1.6	2.8	2.0	3.2	3.4
China	6.5	4.5	8.7	10.3	14.6	12.7	8.3	11.0	10.9	4.0	5.5	6.5

* 1990 and 1991 figures are estimates.

Source: The Asian Development Outlook, 1990.
Printed by permission of The Asian Development Bank, Manila.

Figure 13 *Growth Rate of Per Capita GDP (per cent per annum)*

	1981	1982	1983	1984	1985	1986	1987	1988	1989	*1990	*1991	Per Capita GNP (US$) 1988
Newly Industrialising Economies	5.4	3.7	8.0	8.2	3.4	10.2	11.0	8.3	5.2	4.5	5.1	
Hong Kong	6.9	1.5	4.7	8.5	-1.2	10.5	12.2	6.0	2.3	0.5	2.9	9230
South Korea	5.1	5.6	10.1	7.8	6.1	11.4	10.7	10.2	4.9	4.8	5.2	3530
Singapore	8.3	5.6	6.9	7.0	-2.8	0.7	8.0	9.4	7.6	6.3	6.5	9100
Taiwan	4.2	1.7	6.8	9.1	3.5	10.3	11.2	6.3	6.3	5.5	5.7	6070
South-east Asia	4.3	0.8	2.2	2.6	-1.2	1.7	3.5	5.7	5.6	4.7	4.8	
Indonesia	5.6	0.0	1.9	4.4	0.6	3.8	2.6	3.5	4.7	4.0	4.1	430
Laos	...	4.8	1.9	3.8	6.4	4.2	-5.2	-0.8	1.2	2.9	3.3	180
Malaysia	4.4	2.8	3.5	5.1	-3.6	-1.5	2.6	6.2	4.9	4.1	4.6	1870
Philippines	1.3	0.4	-1.6	-8.3	-6.6	-1.0	2.2	3.6	3.3	2.4	3.6	630
Thailand	4.1	1.9	5.1	5.1	1.6	2.6	6.4	10.0	8.9	7.6	6.9	1000
Vietnam	...	1.9	...	6.0	3.5	-0.6	2.4	3.8	6.8	6.1	6.2	200
South Asia	4.2	2.0	5.5	1.6	4.2	2.3	2.1	6.3	2.3	2.9	2.8	
Bangladesh	4.7	0.8	1.3	2.9	1.5	1.4	1.6	0.2	0.1	3.4	2.6	170
India	4.3	1.8	6.3	1.3	4.4	2.5	2.4	7.4	2.5	3.2	3.0	330
Burma	4.2	3.5	2.3	2.0	1.2	-1.0	-6.1	-1.7	1.4	1.5	1.7	200 [1]
Nepal	5.5	1.1	-5.5	6.8	3.3	1.6	0.2	7.1	-1.0	-6.3	-1.9	170
Pakistan	3.7	3.3	3.6	1.9	4.4	2.3	3.2	3.8	2.4	2.3	2.8	350
Sri Lanka	2.9	4.8	3.2	3.8	3.4	2.5	-0.1	1.1	0.3	1.5	1.7	420
China	3.2	7.0	9.0	13.5	11.6	7.2	9.1	9.0	3.4	4.3	5.3	330

* 1990 and 1991 figures are estimates.
[1] 1986 estimate.

Source: The Asian Development Outlook, 1990.
Printed by permission of The Asian Development Bank, Manila.

Eight

On Guard

'Political power grows out of the barrel of a gun' — Mao Zedong

'To subdue the enemy without fighting is the acme of skill' — Sun Tzu, The Art of War

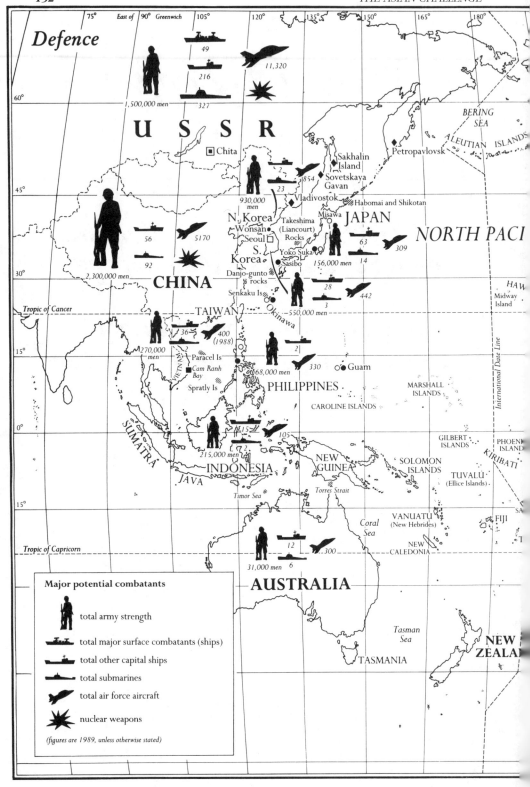

Defence

49

11,320

216

327

1,500,000 men

U S S R

☐ Chita

◆ Petropavlovsk

ALEUTIAN ISLANDS

BERING SEA

Sakhalin Island

2

1854

23

930,000 men

◆ Sovetskaya Gavan

◆ Vladivostok

Habomai and Shikotan

N. Korea

Wonsan ●

Seoul ☐

S. Korea

Takeshima (Liancourt) Rocks

● Misawa

JAPAN

63

309

NORTH PACI

156,000 men

14

5170

Yoko Suka

● Sasibo

56

92

2,300,000 men

CHINA

Danjo-gunto rocks

Senkaku Is

28

442

3

550,000 men

HA

Midway Island

Tropic of Cancer

TAIWAN

Okinawa

36

400 (1988)

270,000 men

2

Paracel Is

Cam Ranh Bay

Spratly Is

68,000 men

2

330

○○ Guam

MARSHALL ISLANDS

International Date Line

PHILIPPINES

CAROLINE ISLANDS

15

105

0°

215,000 men

2

INDONESIA

JAVA

NEW GUINEA

SOLOMON ISLANDS

GILBERT ISLANDS

KIRIBATI

PHOEN ISLAND

TUVALU (Ellice Islands)

Timor Sea

15°

Torres Strait

VANUATU (New Hebrides)

Coral Sea

FIJI

NEW CALEDONIA

SA

T

SUMATRA

Tropic of Capricorn

12

2,300

31,000 men

6

AUSTRALIA

Tasman Sea

NEW ZEALAL

TASMANIA

Major potential combatants

total army strength

total major surface combatants (ships)

total other capital ships

total submarines

total air force aircraft

nuclear weapons

(figures are 1989, unless otherwise stated)

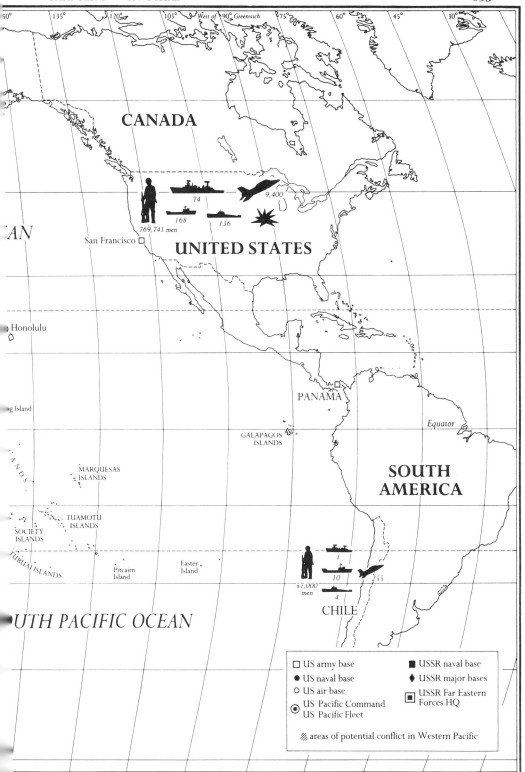

CANADA

UNITED STATES

San Francisco □

74

168

136

9,400

769,741 men

Honolulu

'g Island

PANAMA

GALAPAGOS
ISLANDS

Equator

SOUTH
AMERICA

MARQUESAS
ISLANDS

TUAMOTU
ISLANDS

SOCIETY
ISLANDS

TUBUAI ISLANDS

Pitcairn
Island

Easter
Island

57,000
men

1

10

4

255

CHILE

UTH PACIFIC OCEAN

□ US army base	■ USSR naval base
● US naval base	♦ USSR major bases
○ US air base	▣ USSR Far Eastern Forces HQ
◉ US Pacific Command US Pacific Fleet	

▨ areas of potential conflict in Western Pacific

Source: Simon Winchester, The Pacific © 1991 p474-5.
Printed by permission of Hutchinson/Random Century Group Ltd, London.

C hinese and Indian troops exchange artillery fire in the Himalayas . . . The
Vietnamese government says it will send troops into Cambodia to protect
the elected government . . . Malaysia appeals to the United Nations to stop
the naval clashes around the Spratly Islands . . . The Diet affirms that
Japan's navy has the constitutional right to use force to protect the sea
lanes off Sumatra . . . Thailand says it will come to Rangoon's rescue if the
Indian army fails to withdraw from northern Burma . . .

(some warlike possibilities for Asia 2000)

W hen it touches Asia, the Pacific
spurns the name it received, over four centuries ago, from Ferdinand
Magellan. Each year, typhoons sweep destructively across the Philippines
and on to China; monsoon weather along the coast changes from winter to
summer, and makes life for millions of East Asians either bitterly cold or
ennervatingly humid; and every once in a thankfully long while, an
underground eruption will send a tidal wave, the *tsunami*, to race terrifyingly
across the ocean's surface. In 1960, a *tsunami* which began with an eruption
in Chile hit the coast of Japan twenty-four hours later travelling at a speed
of 400 miles an hour.
But it is not just in meteorology that the Pacific is misnamed. Listen to
Mikhail Sergeyevitch Gorbachev, the leader of the Soviet Union:

On the whole the Pacific region has not as yet been militarised to the
extent Europe has. But the potentialities of its militarisation are truly
immense, and the consequences are extremely dangerous. One only
needs to look at a map to be convinced of this. Major nuclear powers are
situated here. Large land armies, navies and air forces have been
established. The scientific, technological and industrial potential of
many countries — from the western to the eastern fringes of the ocean
— makes it possible to step up any arms race. The situation is being
exacerbated by the preservation of conflict situations. Let us not forget:
it is in Asia that American imperialism waged the two biggest wars since
1945 — the war in Korea and the war in Indochina. In the last four
decades there is hardly a period of even just a few years when the flames
of war did not blaze in one or another part of the Asian and Pacific
region . . .

That is just a small part of the speech Gorbachev made on 28 July 1986,
in the Siberian port of Vladivostok, home for the Soviet's Pacific fleet and
for the nuclear submarines that prowl south into the neighbouring waters
of Japan and South Korea. Looking at his map and at history, Gorbachev

declared: 'The Soviet Union is also an Asian and Pacific country . . . Our interest is in the pooling of efforts and in co-operation, with full respect for the right of each nation to live as it chooses and resolve its problems on its own in conditions of peace.'

This single speech was intended to alert the world to the Gorbachev dream: a world at peace, with the rich nations of East Asia happy to accept a friendly Soviet Union among them — which would encourage them to rescue the Soviet economy from impending collapse. At the time the speech went almost unnoticed (to the annoyance of the Russians, whose embassies around the world then told everyone to notice it). Only when Gorbachev reduced the Soviet Union's defences on its western borders, so allowing the collapse of East European communism, did the world accept that he was serious about Asia, too.

But dreams are easier stated than realised. The irony of the Vladivostok speech is that it gave momentum to a process that in the 1990s will make Asia less, rather than more, secure. If the Soviet Union is offering peace and reducing its military presence in Asia and the Pacific, then why should America, now the world's biggest debtor, continue to hold an expensive military umbrella over its Asian allies? Following his Vladivostok speech, Gorbachev ordered the withdrawal of Soviet troops from Afghanistan, in February 1989; their partial withdrawal from Vietnam's Cam Ranh Bay naval base in January 1990; and the withdrawal, by 1991, of troops from Mongolia. To those visible measures should be added the political initiatives of the thrusting Mr Gorbachev: the summit meeting in May 1989 with an initially hesitant China; the arm-twisting of Vietnam to take its troops out of Cambodia in September 1989 (although some probably stayed on as 'advisers'); the normalisation of relations with South Korea in September 1990. And all the while the Soviet Union was surprising the United States with its proposals for partial nuclear disarmament and the reduction of conventional forces. Clearly, Gorbachev was being serious — even sincere.

The American reaction was at first cautious, and then enthusiastic. By the end of the Reagan administration, in 1988, talk had faded of the American president's wondrous Strategic Defense Initiative — colloquially known as 'Star Wars' because of its images of missile shields and laser swords in space. In its place came talk of the 'peace dividend': defence spending could now be cut without risk, and so help America escape from under its budget deficit. In 1990, the Department of Defense grandly announced that in the following two years 15,000 American troops — more than a tenth of the total in the region — would be withdrawn: some 7,000 from South Korea, 6,000 from Japan, and 2,000 from the Philippines. At the start of 1991, the same American negotiators who, two years earlier, had insisted that America's military facilities in the Philippines were essential to regional, indeed world, security, had a different tale to tell the Philippine government: the Clark air force base was no longer vital to America's interests; four small facilities could be given up immediately; and the 6,000 or more military personnel at the vast Subic naval base could be happily withdrawn after a suitable (they suggested ten or twelve years) phasing-out period. The Pacific, it seemed, was becoming so pacific it no longer needed Uncle Sam to hold quite such a big umbrella over its nations. To quote the 1990 Defense Department report, A Strategic Framework for the Asian Pacific Rim:

> Within the East Asian and Pacific region, traditional threat perceptions are changing. In Asia, unlike NATO, a region-wide consensus has never existed about the threat posed by the Soviet Union or about other sources of regional instability. However, since our forward deployments have been most commonly justified as a deterrent to Soviet expansionism, our presence in the region is now seen as less relevant in light of domestic changes within the USSR and prospects for US–Soviet arms control negotiations. Moreover, nationalist sentiment is on the rise in a number of prosperous Asian nations. Leaders in these countries must contend with influential public opinion that views continued US military presence on their soil as an affront to their sovereignty.

And then came the financial factor, which no American administration can any longer take lightly:

> Clearly, important US domestic considerations also must be taken into account. Significant reductions in the defense budget, generated by domestic perceptions of a diminished Soviet threat as well as by fiscal pressures, are probable. At the same time, it is appropriate to expect our prosperous Asian allies — Japan and Korea — to assume greater responsibility for their own defense and, by so doing, to contribute more directly to the stability of the region.

In other words, Asia can start looking after itself because America is no longer needed to keep the peace.

Unhappily, the confidence may have more to do with wishful thinking than sober assessment. A 'pax Americana' has more or less held in the Pacific ever since the end, with the 1975 fall of Saigon, of the Vietnam war (a defeat for America which did precious little good for a united Vietnam). But America's naval might in the Pacific has not existed in a vacuum: it has been part of a superpower balance which, just as in Europe, kept the peace in Asia and the Pacific through mutual deterrence — only much less effectively. Mikhail Gorbachev was right to recall 'the flames of war': between 1950 and 1953 they burned in Korea; communist guerrillas operated in the Malayan pensinsula until the 1960s (and, in some cases, beyond); Indonesian communists allegedly led a 1965 coup attempt that resulted in perhaps 500,000 deaths (mainly of communists); Vietnam's communists under Ho Chi Minh fought the French in the 1950s, the Americans in the 1960s and early '70s, and the Chinese — for just seventeen days — at the end of the 1970s. Meanwhile, India fought brief wars with China and Pakistan in the 1960s and with Pakistan again in the early '70s; and in the 1980s both Afghanistan and Sri Lanka plunged into civil war. In all these confrontations, the participants had the backing, with money, or men or weaponry, of outside powers. American and other United Nations troops saved South Korea from the North, which in turn was saved by Chinese troops and Russian arms. North Vietnam's ally was the Soviet Union; South Vietnam's was America. Delhi has always been on good terms with Moscow, which means that Washington felt an automatic sympathy for Islamabad — increasingly so after Soviet troops invaded Afghanistan in December 1979.

Arguably, the superpowers, playing politics in the background, are responsible for much of the misery these conflicts represent. They supply the weapons, the ammunition, the money, and sometimes the manpower that allow the combatants to sustain their violence. But just as arguably, the superpowers are the referees who restrain their clients from excess. After all, the conflicts are not the original work of outside forces — they are an expression of indigenous political, social, and economic forces. Take away the referees, and who knows to what extremes the players will go.

The question naturally alarms the smaller players more than the bigger ones. In the 1960s and '70s the advance of communism from its bastion in North Vietnam seemed inexorable. The vulnerable countries of South-east Asia would topple, in the image of the times, like dominoes — first Thailand, then Malaysia and Singapore, and finally the great prize of Indonesia. But the dominoes did not fall, and all those countries know the reason: it was the military and political commitment of America, notwithstanding its failure in Vietnam, to prevent the spread of communism. That commitment allowed America's allies not just security but also the bonus of economic development: while the vigour of Vietnam has been exhausted by decades of continuous warfare, the countries that are now in the Association of South-East Asian Nations (ASEAN) — Thailand, Malaysia, Singapore, Indonesia, the Philippines, and Brunei — have prospered in peace. Instead of reading Marx and Mao, the leaders of Vietnam should have read Sun Tzu. As the great Chinese strategist pointed out two and a half thousand years ago: 'There has never been a protracted war from which a country has benefited.' The implicit corollary is that every country benefits from protracted peace.

Yet it is politically difficult for many of Asia's beneficiaries to acknowledge their debt to the United States. Malaysia, for example, prides itself on membership in the Non-Aligned Movement; moreover, as an officially Muslim country, it is reluctant to appear too indebted to the country that is Israel's constant support. Indonesia has similar sensitivities. Only Singapore, tiny and — despite its heavy defence spending — essentially defenceless, is prepared to spell out what all believe: that America's diminishing role in Asia is a threat to the region's peace of mind. In 1989, the republic's foreign minister, Wong Kan Seng, emphasised that if ASEAN wanted America's support — which was well worth having — it had to lighten America's burden. 'The Singapore government,' he explained,

> has thought very carefully about the consequences of a sudden US withdrawal. We have come to the conclusion that even though the ASEAN states have grown in strength and confidence and even though the other major powers want to concentrate on economic development, it would not be wise for us to encourage a rapid withdrawal of US forces from Southeast Asia. The reason is simple. For the non-communist countries of Southeast Asia, the presence of the other major powers has been destabilising. Either they supported the communist parties of the region or they supported Vietnamese aggression in Cambodia. By contrast, the presence of the US has been stabilising. Why should we encourage the stabilising force to leave before the forces that have destabilised the region have done so? Furthermore, what guarantees do we have that the withdrawal of the US presence will not lead to the entry of other major powers waiting on the sidelines? . . . History has also taught us that when one major power withdraws from an area, another major power or powers always try to fill the vacuum.

Hence, Singapore's offer — quickly accepted — to increase its facilities for the American armed services. One purpose of the offer was to lessen the Philippines' sense of isolation as the sole ASEAN host of the American military; a second was to enhance the region's defence; a third, cynics allege, was to assure Singapore of American protection should the ASEAN region become troubled from within. One thing, however, is for sure: Singapore cannot replace the Philippines as America's military home-from-home in South-east Asia — if only because Singapore in area is smaller than America's Philippine bases.

All Mr Wong's concerns, of course, are understood by the Americans. They appreciate that 'our security presence moderates the actions of second-tier states with expansionist regional aspirations', as the inimitable language of the American Defense Department puts it. But their calculation is that America's presence in the region will still be enough to preserve the peace. There will still be thousands of American servicemen in Japan, South Korea, and the Philippines, manning hundreds of aircraft and dozens of ships. They will spend their dollars in the bars and brothels of Okinawa, Itaewon, and Olongapo, and be alternately loved and loathed by the local people around them. They and their military compatriots based in Hawaii, Guam, Saipan, and other dots in the Pacific will be the human proof of America's pledge that 'over the next decade, as a new global order takes shape, our forward presence will continue to be the region's irreplaceable balancing wheel.' The question, in that case, is where and when the wheel will wobble.

It does not follow that large armies make war more likely — but there is an uncomfortable correlation in Asia between its biggest armies and its points of actual or potential conflict. India's armed forces, their officers as *pukka* as the colonial British before them, have over 1.25 million men (half as many as America's). Pakistan has over half a million men under arms. China's People Liberation Army, which includes its navy and air force, has three million men in active service — down from an astounding four million before the military reforms of the late 1980s. North Korea has armed forces of 1.1 million, which means that almost one in twenty of the country's people is serving under arms; South Korea, with a population of around 44 million, has a 'mere' 750,000 in its armed forces — but supplemented by 4.5 million in the reserves. Vietnam, with a population of perhaps 70 million, has a million people on active service, and four or five million in the 'Strategic Reserve Force'. Look around parts of Asia and it is as though every able-bodied young male adult is in uniform.

Some will say that the bellicose image is exaggerated. China's PLA, clad in surely the scruffiest uniforms of any army in the world, is as much an instrument of national welfare as of national defence. Its spotty-faced recruits are the men who are building the green barrier of trees the length of China to stop the erosive power of the desert winds sweeping in from the west. Its plump-bellied officers are the men who sell arms around the world and invest in businesses — one is the Palace Hotel in Beijing — in order to supplement a budget that is deliberately insufficient for the PLA's basic needs. (It is somewhat ironic that the world's largest communist nation should have such a capitalist-minded military.) Other nations may not encourage entrepreneurial instincts in the military but they, too, use their armies to build roads, dig dykes, and construct dams. Clearly, most of Asia's men under arms will never hear a shot fired in anger.

Yet a look at just one part of Asia's map should discourage complacency. In the Himalayas (literally 'Snow Dwellings' in Sanskrit), where China, India, Pakistan, and Afghanistan jostle aside Nepal and Bhutan, nationalism and militarism are a perennially dangerous combination. The Indian and Chinese armies, for example, bristle at each other across their frozen Himalayan frontier. At issue is the Aksai Chin, where the high plateau of Jammu and Kashmir nestles against Tibet. India insists that its territory goes up to a line drawn on the map by the British in 1914; China believes the border should reflect its sovereignty (much disputed by the subjects involved) over Tibet. The result was a war in 1962 that left Chinese troops in complete control of the Aksai Chin — and rendered meaningless the Sino-Indian treaty, signed eight years earlier as an affirmation of the friendship of two newly liberated nations. This treaty, no longer worth the paper it was written on, was known as the Panchshul, or the 'Five Principles of Peaceful Co-existence'. Perhaps the 1990s will resolve the dispute: China proclaims its readiness to abandon claims to land east of Nepal if India recognises China's control of the Aksai Chin. But, even though in the late 1980s the two countries exchanged prime ministerial visits for the first time in three decades, resolution of the argument is a possibility rather than a probability. There are simply too many emotions at stake: the jingoistic calls from Indian politicians not to sacrifice 'one square inch of Indian territory' and the conviction in Beijing that Tibet is China's and that India should not harbour the Dalai Lama and other Tibetan exiles.

Meanwhile, as armies wait on permanent alert on the Indian-Chinese border, there remains a similar military tension between India and Pakistan. Their quarrel over Kashmir will not simply go away — its roots are too deeply embedded in the two countries' history and political rhetoric. When British India gained independence in 1947 and was swiftly partitioned into Muslim Pakistan and mainly Hindu India, Kashmir was an awkward anomaly: a Muslim populace ruled by a Hindu maharajah. The anomaly has frequently led to war — most notably immediately after partition, when both Pakistan and India seized as much of Kashmir as they could (India won the lion's share); again in 1965; and finally in 1971, when war spread to Kashmir after India intervened to help Bangladesh in its war of secession from Pakistan. Can there be a solution? Naive outsiders might suggest a plebiscite — promised by India's first prime minister, Jawaharlal Nehru, but never implemented — to let the people of Kashmir decide their own fate. Realists doubt it will happen. India officially incorporated Jammu and Kashmir as a fully fledged state in the Union of India as long ago as 1963. Since India is the stronger power, with a scarcely concealed nuclear capability, why should it turn back the clock of history for the sake of weaker Pakistan? Yet how can Pakistan, a Muslim state both by birth and by profession, be seen to abandon other Muslims? There will be no reason at all while both countries' parliaments and peoples are all too easily prone to the chauvinistic interpretation of their interests.

Meanwhile, for all these nationalist differences, there is a certain irony in the affinities of class and background that link the Pakistani and Indian élites. When Benazir Bhutto came to power in Pakistan in 1988, India's Rajiv Gandhi welcomed her election with a personal letter and paid the first visit to Pakistan by an Indian prime minister in three decades: they greeted each other almost as old friends, both of them the educated heirs to political dynasties. In the same vein, I remember my amused surprise when attending a prisoner of war exchange between Pakistan and India in 1973: while ordinary Pakistani POWs came across the border and kissed the soil of their homeland, the watching Pakistani officers chatted with their Indian counterparts in the clipped English tones that spoke of expensive boarding schools and a spell together at Britain's Sandhurst military college.

Unhappily that harmony of background is not enough to make a proper peace (both Bhutto and Gandhi were out of office within two years of their meeting). Instead, discord will continue to mar Indo-Pakistan relations. The underlying truth is that Pakistan is doomed by geography to be a buffer state wedged between larger and more powerful neighbours — the Soviet Union (which, even in disunion, remains a military power) to the north, just beyond a Soviet-influenced Afghanistan, and India to the south. Comfort is difficult to achieve: cosying up to China and the United States is one way; indulging military obsessions is another (Pakistan is thought, after much domestic effort and the smuggling in of foreign parts, to be on the brink of a 'nuclear capability' to match that which is assumed for India). But this is not the same as having the weight to create regional policy.

That role belongs to India, not just by the obvious virtue of size and weight of numbers, but also by a willingness to flex the military and political muscles that come with size. That willingness translates into an interventionist policy that marks the circumference of the Indian subcontinent. Consider just the last years of the 1980s: Indian peace-keeping troops over-stayed their welcome in Sri Lanka; Indian paratroopers flew out over the Indian Ocean to crush a coup attempt in the Maldives; Indian customs officials virtually blockaded Nepal after the kingdom, hitherto supplied with arms solely by India, accepted anti-aircraft guns and other weapons from China; and the Indian government bullied Bangladesh over river control, irrigation, and the countries' maritime borders. In the South Asian Association for Regional Cooperation (SAARC), which groups seven nations of the subcontinent and the Indian Ocean (Pakistan, India, Nepal, Bhutan,

Bangladesh, Sri Lanka, and the Maldives), it is India that calls the tune — and it is India that will call the tune still more loudly in the future.

What sort of tune is another matter. Ostensibly, India is a stalwart of the Non-Aligned Movement: the idea of independence from the great powers goes back in the political culture to the pre-independence days of Gandhi; it became official policy when Nehru attended the Bandung Conference on anti-colonialism in 1955, and the Belgrade meeting of non-aligned nations six years later. But in practice, India's governments have always sat on the edge of what could be called the 'Soviet camp', supporting Moscow at the United Nations, buying most of India's weapons from the Soviet arms industry, and signing a 'treaty of friendship' with the Soviet Union in 1971. Whether such a policy ever made much sense is a matter of debate (it helped drag down the Indian economy with Soviet-style planning and inefficiency) — but it can hardly make sense in the 1990s, when the Soviet Union is so clearly undergoing a crisis of identity, even existence.

Instead, India must now adjust to a world that no longer rests on the post-World War II assumption of a balance between two superpowers. In the jargon of geopolitics, the bipolar is being replaced by the monopolar: the power of the Soviet Union is waning, leaving the United States to command the world alone — perhaps, as George Bush was wont to say at the start of the 1990s, to create a 'New World Order'. If America, fresh from victory in the Gulf War of early 1991, emerges as the world's policeman, a sensible India will treat the policeman with a certain degree of respect — which will mean all sorts of things, from liberalising its economy according to free-market recipes to toeing an American line forbidding war with Pakistan.

But how long will a monopolar world survive? To compound our metaphors, the American policeman, for all his dramatic success in the Gulf War of early 1991, has feet of clay. The basic fact of America's huge indebtedness means that the surviving superpower is fundamentally weaker than Britain was when it, too, was the world's policeman. That weakness will have two effects: it will encourage isolationist tendencies within America — witness the lowering of the military profile in Asia — and it will encourage smaller powers to chance their arm, reasonably confident that a policeman intent on retirement will not be too zealous in stopping them. The result then will be a multipolar world of regional powers, the very development so much dreaded by Singapore — and foremost in the ranks of the world's regional powers will be India. It has weight of population, a large army, a military tradition, and a nuclear capability (albeit unadmitted). But most of all it has a powerful navy, manned by more than 50,000 servicemen and equipped with aircraft carriers, combat aircraft, helicopters, and a score of submarines. In other words, India has the means — and, after its interventions in Sri Lanka and the Maldives, the proven willingness — to project its power not just within the land mass of the subcontinent but also across the waves of the Indian Ocean. If, or perhaps as, America's naval presence diminishes through the 1990s, those facts of Indian power will make themselves felt in South-east Asia from Burma down to Indonesia. If South-east Asian nations are sensible, they will get themselves on good terms with their Indian big brother: more trading links, more access for India's migrant labour, more co-operation in all things, from the military to the financial.

All that, of course, is hypothesis. The immediate reality for South-east Asia is the struggle for Cambodia's future — which stems from a past that is the tragic overspill of great power rivalry. In a less harsh world, the smiling Khmer people of Cambodia (or Kampuchea, as it was known from the mid-1970s through the 1980s) would have been immune from the horrors of the Vietnam war. Instead, the neutrality espoused by Norodom Sihanouk, the ruler installed by the French colonial power in 1941 and the man who, a dozen years later, won Cambodia's independence from France, began to fail as soon as he was deposed by the pro-American General Lon Nol in 1970. For all his support from America, Lon Nol was unable to resist the Soviet-backed Vietnamese communists in his country and their Khmer communist allies. The result, in 1976, was the republic of Democratic Kampuchea, governed by the now infamous communist Khmers Rouges, led by Pol Pot and backed by China. Almost immediately, Pol Pot began his campaign to rid Cambodia of its bourgeois tendencies by returning the country to 'Year Zero': the people of the capital, Phnom Penh, were forced out into the countryside, to work the *padi* fields alongside the peasantry. The regime's enemies, real or alleged, were butchered in mass executions; others were made to work until they dropped. Perhaps a million Cambodians died of hunger, disease, and exhaustion, and meanwhile the Khmers Rouges were crossing the border to attack their former allies in Vietnam. Salvation for ordinary Cambodians came only in December 1978, when the Vietnamese army swept westwards to occupy the whole country and install a puppet regime (ironically dominated by ex-Khmers Rouges). And yet the Vietnamese, traditional foes of the Cambodians, were never likely to win popularity among the people they had saved.

Confused? Who wouldn't be. But the situation since 1978 has been even more confusing: the government of the 'People's Republic of Kampuchea' ruled courtesy of an occupying Vietnamese army which, in turn, was supplied and financed by the Soviet Union. Opposing this government was a guerrilla coalition made up of the communist Khmers Rouges; the anti-communist Khmer People's National Liberation Front under a former prime minister, Son Sann; and the Armée Nationale Sihanoukiste under the mercurial Prince Sihanouk. Of these three resistance groups, by far the most powerful was (and is) the Khmers Rouges, armed and financed, in opposition just as in power, by China. Yet the whole coalition, headed by Sihanouk as a symbol of the respect he commands among all Cambodians, was supported by most of the non-communist world, from ASEAN to America. The only explanation that makes sense of this tangle is that 'my enemy's enemy is my friend'.

The difficulty is to unravel the tangle. In a world of superpower rivalry there was little chance: the Soviet Union could not 'let down' its client state of Vietnam, which in turn could not abandon its Cambodian client; the United States could neither let down ASEAN, implacably opposed to rewarding Vietnam for its 1978 invasion of foreign territory, nor hand a prize to the Soviet Union — and so it found itself indirectly backing, in the form of the Khmers Rouges, one of the most vile political movements of the 20th century. Meanwhile, this deadlock suited the Khmers Rouges' direct backer, China, perfectly: the Chinese have never trusted the Vietnamese, and so they were quite content to see Vietnam distracted and exhausted by its involvement in Cambodia.

But this situation, for all its apparent painful and bloody intractability, will probably not survive the 1990s. The reason is that the superpower balance is a fading memory for South-east Asia and Indochina. The military spending of America during the Reagan years was so great that it forced Gorbachev's Russia out of the arms race — and therefore into a quest for economic improvement. The first victim of this development was Vietnam: by the late 1980s the Soviet Union was cutting aid to its client (it simply could not afford to keep bailing out the shambolic economy inflicted on Vietnam by its aging warrior-leaders) and forcing it to make peaceful overtures to China — not least because progress over Cambodia was a Chinese pre-condition for the 1989 summit meeting between Deng Xiaoping and Mikhail Gorbachev. Meanwhile, the then-prime minister of Thailand, Chatichai Choonhaven (a self-confessed former playboy with a proud reputation for past indulgence in wine, women, and song) was breaking ASEAN unity by inviting Hun Sen, the leader of the puppet Cambodian regime, on three occasions in 1989 to Bangkok. It was all part of Chatichai's dream of turning Indochina's battlefields into market-places dominated by Thai traders. With such pressures at work, change is inevitable: the Vietnamese withdrew from Cambodia in September 1989 and made a self-abasing rapprochement with China in 1990. Meanwhile, on 18 July 1990, the United States shocked everyone by announcing that instead of following ASEAN's lead on the Cambodian issue it would not support the presence of the Khmers Rouges in the Cambodian delegation to the United Nations; moreover, it would begin direct talks with Vietnam over a Cambodian solution and would give 'humanitarian assistance' to Cambodia (where, in the absence of the Vietnamese, the regime could no longer be classified as a 'puppet' of Vietnam).

Just how all this will lead to a peaceful settlement of Cambodia's agony remains to be seen. The momentum is there and some sort of settlement will surely happen eventually, if only because the outside powers who have practised politics by proxy in Cambodia no longer want the agony prolonged. Ideally, it will be a settlement, supervised by the United Nations and helped by free elections, that will reconcile the non-communist guerrillas with the regime of Hun Sen — and leave the Khmers Rouges out in the cold. Reality may be less than ideal, especially if China refuses to stop all its aid to the Khmers Rouges. The likelihood then is that the reconciled forces of Hun Sen, Son Sann, and Sihanouk will have to fight a civil war against the Khmers Rouges into the next century. Moreover, it could be a long and bloody war: the Khmers Rouges may be monsters to the outside world, with its television memories of human skulls piled high from Cambodia's 'killing fields', but to simple villagers in the Cambodian countryside they often appear as much less corrupt than the forces of Hun Sen's government and, indeed, of the other guerrilla groups. It may be true that only peace, as Israel's Abba Eban once said in a different context, is inevitable — but in Cambodia's case the inevitable is not necessarily imminent.

The same caution must attach to the problem — equally intractable, it seems — of the two Koreas. Their peninsula was liberated from Japanese colonialism at the end of the second world war — and immediately divided into a communist North and capitalist South by the mutual antipathy of the Russian and American victors. That Cold War antipathy soon became a real war by proxy, with the North in 1950 launching an attack on the South in pursuit of reunification. Three years and 500,000 deaths (including 54,000 Americans) later, with Chinese troops fighting for the North and American and other United Nations troops fighting for the South, reunification had become for both sides a mirage of Korean nationalism — always to be seen, yet never to be grasped.

While the mirage persists, reality over the past four decades has been an ever-widening gap between the Stalinist North and the economically ebullient South. In 1953, when the Korean war ended, all Koreans were poor; by the end of the 1980s, only Northerners were — with their per capita income barely a fifth that of South Koreans. And while South Koreans, after years of military dictatorships, were finally enjoying the freedoms of democracy as well as the comfort of national wealth, the North Koreans were locked in joyless obeisance to the 'Great Leader' Kim Il Sung and his son, the 'Dear Leader' Kim Jong Il. How could such unequal parts unite into a single nation?

Yet, paradoxically, the inequality may soon be a help, not a hindrance. Just as rich West Germany could in 1990 absorb the relatively poor (although by communist standards rich) East Germany, so South Korea may in the 1990s be able to embrace the North — and receive a vast pool of cheap Northern labour with which to power the Korean economy into the 21st century. What stands in the way is political egotism: the unwillingness of the Great and Dear Leaders to confess the folly of a personality cult that has failed to provide little more than basic material needs. But as the 1990s began the Great Leader was already 78 and the Dear Leader was becoming ever less popular with the North Korean military. It is surely, therefore, impossible for a Kim dynasty to take root — and if there is no Kim dynasty acting as a deterrent, the lure of the South becomes irresistible. What will speed the process is that the North's dearest allies are already succumbing to temptation: in June 1990, for example, Russia's Mr Gorbachev shook hands with South Korea's President Roh Tae Woo in San Francisco, and by September that handshake had led to full diplomatic relations. Just one month later, China likewise ignored North Korean sensitivities by opening a trade office in Seoul — recognition that China's trade with the South, roughly $3 billion a year, was running at six times the level of its trade with the North.

Such developments, along with the collapse of communism among the North's East European allies of old, had their effect: in the same September of 1990 the prime minister of the North paid a visit to Seoul, and in October President Roh travelled to Pyongyang — the first such high-level trips since the country's division in 1945. By 1991, the North and the South were even able to field joint sports teams. If people can play together, they surely can live together — which means that, with time, the South will no longer need the expensive military umbrella of Uncle Sam.

But it would be foolish to assume that Asia east of the Indian subcontinent will be lastingly at peace with itself . . . if only the Cambodian conflict can be settled, and if only the Korean peninsula can be reunited. Stripped of the hypotheses, reality will remain tense and potentially (even actually) explosive. One reason is the existence of territorial disputes that defy easy diplomatic solution: in the South China Sea the Spratly Islands and the nearby Paracels — permanently inhabited only by turtles and seagulls — are variously claimed by Vietnam, Malaysia, the Philippines, and, whether articulated by Taipei or by Beijing, by China too. What adds force to the claims of patriotism is the prospect that the sea around the islands may well be hiding commercially attractive fields of oil and gas. Twice, in 1974 in the Paracels and in 1988 in the Spratlys, communist China's navy has asserted Chinese claims by firing in anger against Vietnamese troops. Further north, between Taiwan and Japan, the two Chinas contest with Japan (so far using words rather than weapons) the rights of sovereignty over a God-forsaken, guano-encrusted clump of islands known to Japan as the Senkaku Islands and to the Chinese as the Diaoyutai Islands. Yet another, more significant, dispute pits the Soviet Union against Japan: both countries claim four islands at the southern end of the Kurile chain which were seized by Moscow at the end of the second world war (Japan insists that these 'Northern Territories' were never meant to be included with the northern part of the Kurile chain, which, along with the island of Sakhalin, was ceded to the Soviet Union in the San Francisco Peace Treaty of 1951).

What complicates the issue of nationalism in the case of the Kuriles is geography: the chain of islands stretches north-east from Japan to Russia's Kamchatka peninsula, home of Soviet missiles and early-warning systems. Moscow's military planners have always worried that to surrender the Kuriles in exchange for Japanese aid would be strategic madness: Japan and its Western allies would not just be dangerously close to the Kamchatka peninsula, the island of Sakhalin, and the important town of Khabarovsk, but they would also be able to pen into the Sea of Okhotsk and the Sea of Japan the whole of the Soviet Pacific Fleet.

Territorial squabbles, however, are only one reason to doubt a pacific future for Pacific Asia. Equally important, as noted earlier, is the presence of armed forces so huge that their slightest movements make the world around them shudder. The armed giants are the Soviet Union and the People's Republic of China, with their millions of men under arms. But even Japan, avowedly anti-militarist in sentiment ever since the atom bombs of Hiroshima and Nagasaki pulverised the nation's pernicious military pride, is potentially a power to be reckoned with: its 'Self-Defence Force' consists of a quarter of a million men and a lot of sophisticated technology. To the nervous military tadpoles of South-east Asia, or indeed to China, an armed Japan can never be a completely trustworthy trading partner — the memories of Japanese occupation before and during the second world war are simply too horrible to allow for trust. Likewise, there can be little lasting trust between China and the Soviet Union. For all their common espousal of communism and for all the help that the Soviet Union of Stalin and Khrushchev gave Mao's China in its early years, there is a fundamental tension — ethnic, cultural, territorial, and military — in the relationship between Moscow and Beijing. The tension showed itself in the past in the calculated rudeness of those masters of the personal snub, Mao, Stalin, and

Khrushchev. In 1956, when Khrushchev criticised Stalin's memory, the Chinese accused the Russians of revisionism. In 1959, Khrushchev withdrew Russia's promise to give China a 'sample' atom bomb (so driving the Chinese to develop their own). In 1960, all 1,300 Soviet technicians in China were withdrawn. In 1966 rampaging Red Guards besieged the Soviet embassy in Beijing. In 1969, Chinese and Soviet soldiers clashed along the frontier. In 1979, China invaded Russia's client state, Vietnam, to 'teach a lesson' after Vietnam's invasion of China's client state, Cambodia (it was, however, the teacher whose nose was bloodied). In 1980, China joined the international boycott of the Moscow Olympics in protest at the Soviet occupation of Afghanistan.

Those memories are part of the thinking of the men who now run China and Russia. It is, of course, true that relations during the second half of the 1980s — the Gorbachev era at its most convincing — did improve: there were trade agreements, border talks, bilateral talks on Cambodia, and the removal of Soviet troops from Mongolia. By May 1989 there was enough warmth in the political atmosphere to allow Gorbachev to meet Deng Xiaoping in Beijing — the first Sino-Soviet summit since Khrushchev's visit to Beijing in October 1959. But one summit in three decades will not change night into day — indeed, the subsequent political and economic tensions within the Soviet Union are likely to bolster, not diminish, the inherent wariness that China feels for the Soviet Union. One basic question that will hang over the last years of this century and the first few of the next is whether this North Asian trio of China, the Soviet Union, and Japan can live at peace with each other and with other neighbours.

So far, the signs are confusing. It is tempting to think that China, so introspective by culture, will be reluctant by nature to intervene beyond its frontiers. Indeed, after the great sea voyages of Admiral Cheng Ho in the 15th century, China lapsed into a national insularity so deep that travel abroad was an offence punishable by death — as was the teaching of Chinese to foreigners. But times change: first, the Western powers prised open China's borders to trade opium for tea and silk; then the Western philosophy of communism prised open Chinese minds; and finally the 'open door' policy of Deng Xiaoping opened China's economy to international markets. The parallel development is that China, for all its rhetoric of non-intervention, has a military policy that frequently reaches out into others' affairs. The classic examples are the war in Korea and the 1959 annexation of Tibet (which is therefore no longer, according to the Chinese, 'others' affairs'). But the smaller examples — the exporting of revolution during the Maoist era, the border clashes with India and Vietnam, the aggressive presence of the Chinese navy around the Spratlys — are just as indicative of China's willingness to advance its interests beyond its frontiers, and just as worrying therefore to the vulnerable nations of South-east Asia.

What adds to those worries is the weight of China's military clout. In terms of manpower, this weight is possibly over-rated. The Gulf War of 1991 has proved that 'human wave' tactics, used by Mao in the Korean war and by both Iraq and Iran in their war of the 1980s, are a form of futile suicide against modern weapons of high technology. Yet the counter argument is that the Third World countries with whom China might find a quarrel do not possess such weaponry of high technology. And meanwhile, China has a proven nuclear capability, both short- and long-range missiles, and a modernising navy. By regional standards, China is already a genuine military power. By world standards she is not — but if the economy grows as fast in the 1990s as it did in the 1980s, the subsequent military improvements will change many of today's disparaging assessments. For the moment, few would disparage China's success as an avid exporter of arms: by American reckoning, China at the end of the 1980s was the world's fifth largest exporter of military hardware, from the secret sales of intermediate-range ballistic missiles to Saudi Arabia in the mid-'80s to the provision of Silkworm anti-ship missiles to both sides in the Iraq-Iran war.

But worry is not confined to China's neighbours in Asia; China, too, has its fears for the future. In the past, because Chinese policy has always been to prevent any power exercising a 'hegemony' over East Asia, China inserted itself into a 'strategic triangle' between the Soviet Union and the United States — both of them much more powerful than China. In the 1950s, therefore, China balanced the triangle by allying itself with Moscow against the 'imperialist ambitions' of the powerful USA; in the 1970s and '80s, as Soviet military power increased, China shifted its weight and played the 'Russia card' to entice America into friendship. But what of the 1990s? Because of the collapse of the Soviet economy and the accompanying disunion of the Soviet Union, the triangle has fallen apart. There is no 'Russia card' for China to play in a world where America is now so clearly the only military superpower. Some ideologues in China believe that after the Gulf War a triumphant America will create its own quasi-empire in Asia, the very 'hegemonism' that China fears, and they argue that China must fight American dominance at all costs.

Perhaps so — but how? Deng Xiaoping, ever the pragmatist, warned the ideologues: 'Do not harbour unrealistic illusions of China's might.' Realism should dictate Chinese moderation in all things: co-operation with the United States, because it is now a confident superpower and is also the main market for China's exports; co-operation with Moscow, because Russia can be a supplier of arms (as in the 1950s) to supplement China's own output, because Russia can be, through barter, an important trading partner, and because, in resisting an American hegemony, two countries together — however weak — are better than two countries apart. But that sort of realism is dealing with the known or reasonably certain. The question that as yet has no certain answer is the future military role of Japan.

The reason for the uncertainty is Japan's own ambivalence on the subject. Other Asians, past victims of Japanese colonial cruelty, fear a resurgence of Japan's *bushido* mentality — the 'way of the warrior' which is marked by a fanatical devotion to the emperor. But most Japanese share the very same fear, aware that their military past has caused immense harm to themselves, as well as to *gaijin* foreigners. Why else is Japan the only country ever to have suffered nuclear attack? The blasts from the atom bombs on Hiroshima and Nagasaki have converted the *samurai* tradition into a semi-pacifism. Under article 9 of the 'peace constitution' imposed on defeated Japan by America's General MacArthur, Japan has renounced war, the potential to make war, and the right to be belligerent. All that is left is the right of self-defence, hence the title of 'Self-Defence Forces' for Japan's men in uniform (a title shared, with somewhat dubious accuracy, by Israeli soldiers). But the right of self-defence naturally begs a definition of self-defence.

For successive Japanese governments, the meaning has been simple: Japan will not possess intercontinental ballistic missiles or long-range bombers or nuclear weapons, since their only purpose would be to strike beyond Japan's borders; Japan will not exercise what article 51 of the United Nations Charter calls the 'right of collective self-defence', since this could involve sending Japanese troops to help allies abroad; and Japan will limit its defence spending, in accordance with a 1976 decision by the cabinet of Takeo Miki, to just 1 per cent of gross national product (most Western nations spend about 4 per cent of their GNP on defence). Meanwhile, 50,000 American troops (or rather 44,000, once the Department of Defense's planned cuts are carried out) will keep Japan additionally secure by threatening the force that will keep the peace beyond Japan's coastal horizons.

The instant conclusion is that Japan is both having its cake and eating it — that its economy prospers and its exports rise because it leaves the defence of its interests to Uncle Sam. There is clearly something to the argument, but how much is a matter of opinion and prejudice. When America sent half a million troops to the Gulf to liberate Kuwait, a lot of American Congressmen noted that Japan was not among the allies who rushed to help — even though imported oil, most of it from the Gulf, meets over half of Japan's energy needs. The excuse was a good one: the constitutional ban on sending troops to foreign wars. But the Japanese Diet applied the ban, against the government's wishes, to troops in noncombatant roles, and was embarrassingly slow to approve the government's decision to provide first $4 billion and then another $9 billion to help pay for their allies' 'Desert Storm'. Clearly, Japan's reluctance to get involved in the Gulf conflict will add to the economic strains already present in its relationship with the United States.

But the idea that a deliberately defenceless Japan is a cynical free-loader on the American taxpayer distorts reality. The truth is that because of Japan's economic success, 1 per cent of its GNP is a great deal of money (and by creative accounting the limit has sometimes, in practice, been breached). In 1990, for example, the defence budget was over $28 billion, within a few missiles and bombs of the amount spent by Britain or France or Germany. Moreover, Japan's concept of self-defence is flexible enough to allow its ships to patrol the sea lanes a thousand nautical miles from Japan's shores, while the Japanese Air Self-Defence Force — with over 360 jet fighters, scores of radar surveillance aircraft and a hundred anti-submarine helicopters — is the most potent air force in the region apart from those of America and the Soviet Union. With weapons like those, who needs intercontinental ballistic missiles and long-range bombers? Is it not better to promote long-range friendships by giving financial aid — a policy that over the 1980s tripled Japan's official development assistance and leapfrogged the country ahead of America as the world's biggest aid donor?

The answer is that a lot of Japanese strategists think that an ability to project military deterrence beyond the horizon — an ability Japan's own forces do not have — is still essential to Japan's defence. They point out that the region around Japan is fraught with problems that cannot be bought off with sack-loads of yen. The Korean peninsula is an armed camp in a permanent state of high alert, and the North Koreans have a frightening record of unpredictability and extremism, from building tunnels underneath the De-Militarised Zone to the 1983 terrorist attack in Rangoon, Burma, on South Korean government ministers and officials. Meanwhile, as its leadership changes generations, China will spend the 1990s in a state of political fragility — and if that fragility should turn into disintegration and chaos, Japan's Asian investments and trading links will not escape some painful repercussions. But the greatest threat will remain the Soviet Union. One Japanese pessimist, Osamu Kaihara, a former secretary-general of the Defence Council, says Soviet bombers could neutralise Japan's air power in just 20 minutes by destroying the country's radar sites. He claims: 'The meagre military power we maintain is wholly inadequate to our defence needs. The Self-Defence Force is actually nothing more than a garrison troop.' Arguably, the Soviet threat has been diminishing ever since Gorbachev's speech in Vladivostok — but who is to say that the Gorbachev era will not be succeeded by an era of renascent Soviet militarism, with

Soviet generals determined to use military power to gain economic success? Those generals will not have been impressed by Japan's stand-offish refusal in the late 1980s to aid the Soviet Union with investments in joint ventures to exploit the enormous natural resources of Siberia.

In other words, when Japanese look at their nation's security needs in the 1990s, they will inevitably want to continue sheltering under the American military umbrella — and will happily pay for the privilege. That is why America's demands for 'burden sharing' get such a sympathetic hearing from a Japan which, in the trade arena, is beginning to resent America's demands. At the start of the 1990s, Japan was paying about $3 billion, anywhere from 35 per cent to 40 per cent of the total cost, to keep America troops and equipment on its soil — by the mid-1990s its contribution will rise by $1.7 billion to cover 73 per cent of the whole cost of America's presence, minus American military and civilian salaries (the Pentagon realised its independence of action would be jeopardised if Japan became the paymaster of American citizens). A similar increase in generosity will come from South Korea: in 1990 it provided $70 million in 'host nation support' for America's bases; by 1991 the figure was $150 million, and American politicians were telling their Korean counterparts that it should soon rise to $350 million.

Carried to an extreme, these developments will make modern mercenaries of the American forces that patrol Asia. In fact, the extreme will not be reached even in the unlikely event that Japan and South Korea pick up the whole tab for their American bases. One reason is that in return for allowing Philippine land to be occupied by American troops, the impoverished Philippines will continue to receive, rather than give, 'host nation support'. Once 'off-base spending' — a phrase that covers everything from car repairs to bar-girls — is included, this American support will add up to over $1 billion a year, enough to soften for a while, but not to mute, the voices of Filipino nationalism. Another reason is that America's patrols in Asia are for its own interests, as well as those of its allies. Since America's trans-Pacific trade is now worth one and a half times its trade with Europe, it matters intensely to America that about 50 per cent of East Asia's oil requirements and 80 per cent of its other strategic materials must pass through South-east Asian 'choke points' — the narrow straits around Indonesia of Malacca or Lombok or Sunda. If those supplies do not arrive safely, how will the economies of Japan, Taiwan, South Korea, Hong Kong, and Singapore survive? Yet because of the volume and value of trans-Pacific trade, the health of these Asian economies is crucial to America's own economic health.

The consequence of this is that the web of security treaties crisscrossing the Pacific will stay in place, and perhaps bind even tighter. The United

States has been linked to the Philippines with a mutual defence treaty signed in 1952, and to Thailand ever since the Manila Pact of 1954 set up the now extinct South-East Asia Treaty Organisation. It has been linked to Australia and New Zealand since the ANZUS Treaty of 1952 (although America suspended its security obligations to New Zealand in the late 1980s after the government of David Lange in 1985 adopted an anti-nuclear defence policy). And the two Antipodean nations are linked to Malaysia, Singapore, and Britain through the Five-Power Defence Arrangement of 1971. Meanwhile, Malaysia and Singapore join Thailand, Indonesia, the Philippines, and Brunei in the Association of South-East Asian Nations — a body whose diplomatic co-operation automatically leads to military co-operation. When the American treaties with Japan and South Korea, and America's *sotto voce* guarantee to sustain Taiwan militarily, are additional strands, it is hard to see the web unravelling fast.

But that does not mean the strands will not be tested. Today's security web was spun in the aftermath of the second world war, when the world was easily divided between good and bad, friend and foe. Defining the division was the task of an Anglo-Saxon clique — America, Britain, Australia, and New Zealand — whose military, economic, and political power could not be challenged. What is different now is that the clique's power is permanently diminished. Britain does not pretend any more to a global reach; America is deeply in debt; and Australia and New Zealand — both of them isolated, under-populated, and flagging in the economic race — are minor actors on the regional stage.

Meanwhile, the security challenges are themselves changing. Malaysia's proposed ZOPFAN, a 'zone of peace, freedom and neutrality', creates tensions within ASEAN, as does the related Indonesian enthusiasm for a zone free from nuclear weapons (since it would, as with New Zealand, prevent American warships from entering the area). Peace in Cambodia or the reunification of the Korean peninsula should calm the atmosphere, but it could just as easily be disturbed once more by conflict in the Himalayas, revolution in China, a Chinese invasion of Taiwan to forestall independence and force instant reunification with the mainland, insurrection in Burma, separatism in Indonesia, a resurgence of militarism in the Soviet Union — or by some accident of history that no one can yet foresee. As the US Department of Defense noted in its Strategic Framework for the Pacific Rim:

> The 1990s will be a decade of transition in the Asia-Pacific region. Political volatility and turbulence will characterise key countries — China, the Soviet Union, North Korea, Cambodia and the Philippines to name a few. Political uncertainties are exacerbated by the major changes in generational leadership that will occur, such as in China, North Korea,

Singapore, Vietnam and Indonesia. Intensified economic competition within the region and with the United States will increasingly complicate security relationships . . .

In which case, as the Singaporeans are particularly willing to admit, it is just as well that the American policeman will still be around, patrolling the area in the ships of the Seventh Fleet. What would help, of course, would be good behaviour — in human rights, foreign relations, economic policy — even when the policeman is not around.

Nine

External Appearances

Jealousy and spite cling to the wheels of the prosperous wagon' — Chinese proverb

*T*he Philippines says it can no longer cope with the influx of Chinese boat people . . . Australia denies discriminating against Asian immigrants . . . Hong Kong's satellite television company signs a new contract with Pakistan . . . African students demonstrate in Beijing's Tiananmen Square . . .

(international possibilities for Asia 2000)

Lee Kuan Yew, whose powers of political analysis have never been in doubt, once noted that Chinese emperors 'have not governed by counting heads — they have governed by chopping heads'. Why, then, was the West so surprised, as well as outraged, when the Chinese army used tanks and machine-guns in the bloody pre-dawn hours of 4 June 1989 to clear student democrats from Beijing's Tiananmen Square? After all, whatever the death toll (believable estimates range from around 300 to over a thousand), it was clearly less than many others elsewhere that the West had chosen to ignore. Yet the United States, with Congress egging on a reluctant President Bush, led the world in imposing sanctions: no soft loans, no high level contacts, no military assistance, no transfer of technology.

There is no single, simple reason for this sense of outrage. But what it betrays is the gulf of understanding (or rather misunderstanding) that separates Asia from the West — and the West from Asia. Just as young Westerners cling to their naive belief in some form of quintessentially Asian 'inner wisdom', so do most Asians naively measure with awe the technology, military might, and consumer comfort of the West. Many millions of Asians dream of leaving their homelands for a life in the West or perhaps in another Asian country. Each year, hundreds of thousands succeed, braving all the uncertainties that face migrants and refugees. What impels them are not just the basic forces of poverty and repression, but also the more subtle influences of exaggerated hearsay, of the idealised image that puts out of focus anything that spoils the dream. And the influences work both ways. Just as Asians want to think well of the West, so do Westerners of Asia.

All too often, however, it is a case of 'same bed, different dreams', as the Chinese adage wryly comments, and all too ironically it is the spread of information — especially by television — that encourages the dreams to be different. The misperceptions of reality thread their way through seemingly separate phenomena: the demonstrations of Asia's students; the flight of its refugees; the plight of Hong Kong's Chinese; the repression of human rights; even the trendy language of Asia's teenagers.

To return to the example of Tiananmen. Part of the West's reaction to the violence in Beijing was sheer disappointment: after the xenophobic madnesses of the Mao Zedong era, the 'open door' policy of Deng Xiaoping had seemed to promise real liberalism. It seemed inevitable that economic freedoms would lead to political freedoms of the kind the West takes for granted as the right of all people — hence that quintessentially Western expression 'human rights'. For the Americans, this disappointment was deepened by their own historical fascination with China. That fascination, bordering on the obsessive, began more than a century ago with the dispatch across the Pacific of missionaries to convert the heathen 'Middle Kingdom' to Christianity; it continued with the political and military support given to Chiang Kai-shek and his Kuomintang government after their ignominious flight to Taiwan from Mao's victorious communist guerrillas (not to mention the lobbying on Chiang's behalf of Henry Luce, publisher of *Time* magazine and once a schoolboy in pre-revolutionary China); and it exists now in the thousands of American students who study Chinese, and the hundreds of American businessmen who invest in China (and seldom see any profit).

But another part of the answer is that the students whose lives were so wastefully crushed around Tiananmen Square had become intimates of the West. Courtesy of Western television crews, they had appeared for weeks on end in living rooms from Los Angeles to London. The TV people, and hundreds of print journalists such as myself, were there by one of those accidental ironies of history — not originally for the students, who had been demonstrating since early April, but to prepare for the arrival in Beijing of Russia's Mikhail Gorbachev, on May 15th, for the first Sino-Soviet summit in thirty years. Instead, we witnessed a tragic progress from euphoria to inevitable disaster. The idealism of hundreds of thousands of young Chinese camped out in Tiananmen Square, the symbolic heart of modern China, was compelling, infectious, and almost tangible. They wanted 'democracy', 'dialogue', and an end to corruption — simple slogans which they would have been hard put to define in detail, but which nonetheless struck a sympathetic chord throughout China. After martial law was declared on May 20th, one old man in the Summer Palace said openly to me: 'We all support the students.' Two weeks later, the Chinese did not talk to foreigners; they rode by stony-faced on their bicycles or walked past without eye contact. The spirit of Tiananmen had been silenced — for how long, no one could tell.

All this, from elation through to violence and on to despair, filled the world's television screens — and for much of the time did so with the immediacy of live television. American television reporters strolled through Tiananmen Square giving live reports through their cellular telephones; for several weeks Ted Turner's Cable News Network was able to satellite its transmission non-stop, watched by everyone from President Bush in the White House to the dwindling number of guests in Beijing's Palace Hotel. Just as with the fall of Marcos in the Philippines, three years earlier, here was a convulsion of history that, while it happened, was witnessed by the whole world.

Contrast that instant gratification of man's curiosity with the convulsions of earlier decades — the Arab-Israeli wars of 1967 and 1973, the Indian-Pakistan war of the early 1970s, the student riots of Paris in 1968. Those shifts of history never commanded the rapt attention of a world-wide audience. In those days of old technology, news cameras used film, not videotape, and the film had to be shipped and processed. Most of the world did not have television sets. For those who did, their opinions could not be instant; they had to wait on complicated flight schedules and scarce satellite stations. Only since the 1980s has the world become a 'global village' of instant, ubiquitous information.

The question is how the neighbours will behave in this crowded village. Veteran China-watchers — such as Lee Kuan Yew — always feared the Beijing crack-down was bound to come. As one American diplomat observed at the time, Deng Xiaoping had been hardened in revolutionary chaos: he was thus 'allergic' to any hint of instability, which would surely follow if China's workers joined with China's students. Henry Kissinger suggested later that the Chinese leaders had actually been remarkably patient — would America's have tolerated such behaviour for so long in the heart of Washington?

But ordinary Western television viewers know nothing of China's history: they simply react to the images before them, and influence their political leaders accordingly. (Arguably, it was the television reporting of the Vietnam war which led to America's defeat by constraining the military and undermining support for the war at home — in which case, logic dictates that modern television technology would have helped everyone by bringing defeat sooner.) For America, in the Tiananmen aftermath, the popular reaction transposed to the political level meant a determined effort by many in Congress to deny China the Most Favoured Nation status that allows China to export to the United States without discrimination. For Australia, it meant an amnesty for illegal Chinese immigrants and extended visas for Chinese students. A generation of television viewers around the world will forever carry in their minds' eye the image of a young student defiantly standing alone in Beijing's Changan Avenue to halt a column of tanks.

Doubtless, the 1990s will bring other images. China is only one part of the Asian neighbourhood. Television pictures will colour attitudes, in Asia and beyond Asia, to Japan's industrial advance, conflict in Cambodia, Hong

Kong's countdown to 1997, AIDS in Thailand — and to a dozen other issues as yet unrevealed to a world that quickly grows complacent. The more dramatic the visual information, the less predictable (or at least controllable) its consequence.

The reason is that television 'fosters contextless and placeless experiences', in the words of Joshua Meyrowitz, of the University of New Hampshire. 'Television,' he explained in *No Sense of Place*, 'breaks the age-old connections between the places we are in and what we can experience and see with our own eyes.' So what, you might well ask. The same is true of the cinema, of theatre, and of radio. The answer is that we all instinctively recognise that television's power reaches millions more than other media — and does it effortlessly, while its viewers are eating breakfast and performing all the other humdrum activities of their daily lives. When Lee spoke at the Hong Kong Foreign Correspondents' Club in October 1990 (he sardonically claimed to be entering 'the lions' den'), he referred to Meyrowitz and added:

> I believe it is this contextless television experience that led to the tragedy of Tiananmen on June 4th. Students in China had been watching on Chinese television for several years the almost nightly demonstrations of 'People Power'. People Power in 1986 won in the Philippines when President Marcos fled from Manila. Violent demonstrations by South Korean students and workers in 1986–87 forced changes in the political system, including direct elections for President. For many years, Chinese students watched South African policemen beating black demonstrators and firing tear gas. They also watched Israeli police firing rubber bullets, tear gas . . . But although there was the occasional death, no demonstrator was ever shown being shot and killed on television . . . Because their television viewing was contextless, China's students forgot that China was a very different country from either the Philippines or South Korea, two countries with close links to the United States, where the media and Congress wield immense influence . . .

In other words, Lee argued, the students of Tiananmen lost touch with the reality of their position, which was close to that of the students in un-televised Burma. Instead, they believed 'the feedback from Chinese students abroad' (who, of course, were watching the televised events of Tiananmen) and 'pressed on hoping to achieve something as dramatic as the changes in the Philippines and South Korea.'

Actually, Lee exaggerates. The students began their protests in early April, when there were no foreign TV crews roaming through Beijing. They were commemorating the spontaneous demonstrations that broke out on the death of Zhou Enlai – and that was in 1976, when most of the students of the time had never seen television. It is simplistic to see the Tiananmen protests as copy-cats of Manila and Seoul; they had an originality and momentum of their own.

But there is clearly something in Lee's argument. How, for example, could Gorbachev have become a hero to China's students except through the electronic media — BBC short-wave radio, the Voice of America, China's own radio and television? By the late 1980s, there were at least 100 million radios in China, and a television in every third household; in richer countries, from Japan to Malaysia, the devices of the electronic media were in virtually every household — sometimes in virtually every room. As Asia's population continues to grow, so obviously will its material possessions. In the process, the television set will become one of Asia's modern icons and its power to inform and delude will become ever more pervasive.

Take the idea of 'contextless experience' a little bit further. Asian countries are littered with foreign symbols whose meanings are trivial, obscure, or simply non-existent. Teenagers in Tokyo, Hong Kong, and Singapore wear clothes embellished with misspelt gobbledegook English graffiti — 'MUSTANG this pants was once loved by an American hero, and makes you now a good sensitive' or similar nonsense. Borneo tribesmen wear T-shirts with Coca-Cola logos. Middle-class Indians parade the streets of Bombay and Delhi pretending not to flaunt the Harrods shopping bags left by visitors from England. I remember visiting the local army chief in Davao City, in the southern Philippine island of Mindanao, and being distracted from his commentary on the security situation by the huge poster behind his desk of Sylvester Stallone as Rambo.

The symbols are not exclusively visual. China's young no longer want the outdated language of 'class struggle' and similar pap; instead, they mark their trendiness with a new set of words and slogans. 'TDK' is a brand name for Western cassette tapes — but among China's teenagers it is the 'in' acronym for their fascination with the glamorous West. It stands for TOEFL, the Test of English as a Foreign Language, which is a prerequisite for studying abroad; Dancing; and Kissing. Similarly, the Chinese phrase for goodbye is being replaced by 'bye bye', which has long held sway in Hong Kong. Obviously, a Chinese youth cannot pass for an American — and probably would not want to — but he can certainly pretend to the sophistication and cosmopolitan airs of his compatriots in Hong Kong.

All this, of course, is natural. Teenagers everywhere develop their own symbols and slang; they help affirm a separate identity simply because they are so unintelligible to others. The question is whether what is natural is also healthy. The fascination of modern Asia for the West is not so much a curious interest in the unknown as a sometimes obsessive envy. Hundreds of millions of Chinese, Vietnamese, Indians, Pakistanis, and others assume the world beyond Asia is superior — if not in culture (the Chinese bow to no one) then certainly in education, defence, medicine, science, technology, and, of course, standards of living. They watch the occasional cheap American television series or low-budget movie; they see Western tourists casually spending in five minutes what it would take them a whole year to earn (in 1990, the Saigon Floating Hotel was charging over $120 a night and was full — whereas the average salary for a Vietnamese civil servant was about $8 a month); they listen to the tall tales of friends who have been abroad to work. What they conclude is that the West is rich and easy, offering a life-style for Westerners that they themselves will never enjoy at home. The only Asians free from this envy are those with standards comparable to the West's — the Japanese, for example, and perhaps the Hong Kongers and Singaporeans — and those who are remote from the insidious influences of the outside world.

This second group will have virtually disappeared by the end of the century, not just with every upward notch of economic growth but with the continuous advance of technology. Consider the launching, for example, of AsiaSat I, a satellite owned by companies from China, Hong Kong, and Britain, to its geostationary orbit above Singapore on 7 April 1990. AsiaSat I has the ability to beam telephone calls, computer data, and television signals in two giant 'footprints' that reach from Iraq to Malaysia and Burma almost to the Arctic. Those television signals in theory could mean all kinds of television programming; in practice, most programmes will be the pop music and entertainment shows churned out by the dream factories of America — they are the only ones able to provide the volume the AsiaSat channels will need. The effect will be to reinforce the illusions, and hence the envy.

But what will Asians do to assuage their envy? In a general sense, they will make ever greater demands on their governments: to provide better housing, education, health care, and entertainment — all the elements that define the quality of their lives. In a particular sense, the impatient and the adventurous will simply leave: the tide of Asia's refugees will continue to flow out to the promised lands of the United States, Canada, Australia, and Europe — and thousands will find themselves marooned at various points on their way, in Hong Kong, for example, or Malaysia, Thailand, and the Philippines.

Purists, of course, will protest that most are not 'real' refugees, fleeing their countries, according to the 1951 United Nations definition, because of a well-founded fear of persecution on the grounds of 'race, religion, nationality, membership of a particular social group or political opinion'. They may also protest that few will be the displaced victims of war. If history is any guide, the protesters will be only half right. It is true that most of the thousands leaving Vietnam in the 1980s were 'economic migrants', seeking a sanctuary not from persecution and war but from poverty. But they were more than balanced by the thousands who were fleeing religious and ethnic persecution in Tibet and Burma, or civil war in Sri Lanka and Afghanistan. At the end of the 1980s, India, for example, was host to some 300,000 refugees and displaced persons; Pakistan was host to an astounding 3.6 million. Even if peace breaks out everywhere, such problems will linger for years — and, unhappily, wars are just as likely to break out as peace. Whatever the individual spur to flee, the tide of humanity flowing around Asia and out of Asia is a collective tragedy.

But the purists have a point. People displaced by war normally want to return to their homes; so, probably, do most refugees (in the UN sense of the word). By contrast, economic migrants do not. They are abandoning their countries, their homes, their friends because they despair of their future if they do not. Instead, they are willing to exhaust their savings — and often risk their lives — in a voyage to Western countries they know of only by 'contextless experience'. It is a terrible indictment of their homelands that so many Asians believe the voyage worth making.

Just how many manage the whole voyage is another matter, since escape is one thing — finding a sanctuary another. The saddest example is the plight of the Vietnamese. Ever since Saigon, the capital of South Vietnam, fell to the communist North in 1975 (it was promptly re-named Ho Chi Minh City, after the communist leader), there has been a continuous flood of people leaving Vietnam. The Southerners leave because they hate the privations and repression of the new regime; the Northerners leave because they hate the grind of a poverty that never seems to ease. There are often additional reasons: discrimination against those who had served in the armed forces of South Vietnam, or who had helped the American allies of the South; discrimination against those Vietnamese citizens who happen to be ethnically Chinese. Whatever the reasons, whether Southerners or Northerners, ethnic Vietnamese or ethnic Chinese, the dream since 1975 has always been to escape to America — although Canada, Australia, Norway, indeed anywhere in the West, would do. The result is that there are now well over one and a half million Vietnamese settled abroad, half of them in America. They send back money, and letters that boast (however inaccurately) of their new lives. Since 1987 they have been allowed to make visits to the motherland they illegally left (the government craves the foreign exchange they bring with them). When they arrive, with their gleaming wristwatches, portable stereos, and flashy clothes, they are proof that the grass is indeed greener on the other side of the Pacific. And so a new collection of poor and restless Vietnamese decide to take the risk.

That risk used to be extremely high. Over the years, scores of boats have been lost in the storms of the South China Sea; hundreds of 'boat people' have been killed or maimed by pirates, who have raped the women and left the children to drown. Now, the risk is minimal. The intending 'boat person', whether from South or North, simply goes by bus to the border with China and then along the Chinese coast to the Pearl River Delta — where he and his colleagues buy an old boat to make the short trip by sea to refuge in Hong Kong, a 'port of first asylum' in UN jargon. The British colony used to be third choice for the boat people, behind Malaysia and Thailand — by the end of the 1980s, helped by tales of boats being pushed back to sea by Malaysian and Thai police, it was very much the first choice.

But what then? The sad truth is that the port of first asylum becomes a prison. At the start of the 1990s there were some 56,000 Vietnamese boat people cooped up in camps in Hong Kong. Around 3,000 of them had been in the camps for three years; over 2,000 had been there for more than five years; over a thousand had been there for eight years — and more than 2,000 had been born in the camps. Some of the camps are 'open', their residents free to go out to work or shop; others are simply gaols, with high, barbed-wire tipped fences. None of them is an ideal place for long-term inmates, who usually live in what are little more than cages set three tiers high, one on top of the other. Theoretically, under an agreement between Britain and China, their stay cannot be indefinite. Because China, which has taken from Vietnam a quarter of a million ethnic Chinese, has no wish to inherit any more Vietnamese, Hong Kong's boat people are all supposed to be gone by 1997, when the colony reverts to China's sovereignty.

It will take a political miracle to turn theory into practice. First asylum is meant to be followed by resettlement, but the resettlement countries show increasing signs of 'compassion fatigue'. In 1980, they accepted 37,468 Vietnamese refugees from Hong Kong — but in 1990, they were willing to take just 7,656. This was by far the highest total since 1982, but was almost matched by the numbers still arriving in Hong Kong. Since compassion fatigue is unlikely to be quickly banished, how can Hong Kong get rid of its Vietnamese? One answer (understandable, but in retrospect probably mistaken) was implemented on 16 June 1988. All Vietnamese who arrived before that date were automatically considered 'refugees' in the UN meaning of the term. Anyone arriving on or after this crucial date was to be screened by the immigration department to determine whether he is indeed a refugee, or simply an 'economic migrant' masquerading as a refugee. Out of those so far screened, only one in every eight has been screened in as a refugee, with a guaranteed right of resettlement abroad. This obviously means that the process is alleviating by seven-eighths the demands on the resettlement countries. But what about those screened out as economic migrants? They have no right of resettlement and are therefore eligible only for repatriation to Vietnam. Under a 'Comprehensive Plan of Action' adopted in Geneva in June 1989, Vietnam promises not to prosecute those boat people who volunteer to return, nor to discriminate against them for their illegal departure from Vietnam in the first place.

Real life, however, is not so pat. Relatively few boat people in Hong Kong have volunteered to return (less than 7,000 in the first two and a half years, compared with a government target of 1,000 a month). The calculation of those who stay is both pragmatic and emotional: pragmatic in that staying on in camp may eventually blackmail the resettlement countries into accepting them — and in the meantime they will receive food, clothing, shelter, and health care, mostly of a higher standard than they would get back in Vietnam. The emotional part of the calculation is that to return home would bring the shame of failing to find a place in the West. Tragically, this shame preys particularly on unaccompanied minors in the camps — they have been sent off by their families to be 'anchors' in America, so that their parents and siblings can later migrate under family-reunification schemes.

If the economic migrants will not volunteer to return, then the alternative is to force them to. But how? At 3 a.m. on 12 December 1989, some two hundred men from Hong Kong's Correctional Services Department, dressed in full riot gear, swarmed into a holding centre for boat people and bundled 51 bewildered inmates (42 of them women and children) onto a plane to Hanoi. This was the first attempt at 'mandatory repatriation' — and it was disastrous: it horrified the Western world in general and America, which has yet to resolve its feelings over the Vietnam war, in particular. It also gave the government of Vietnam a useful card to play in its negotiations with both America and Hong Kong, along the lines of 'We will not sanction the use of force against our citizens . . . We will accept those who return of their own free will, but only if all expenses for their trip and their rehabilitation into our society are paid for by you or others . . . We cannot be held responsible for the flow of migrants while the American trade embargo keeps our economy in penury' . . . and so on. They are arguments to be used as and when they are useful, and in the meantime Hong Kong's decision to initiate the screening process means that it, rather than the resettlement countries, is *de facto* and *de jure* responsible for the unwanted guests who have been screened out — hence the judgement of Hong Kong's best-known liberal, Martin Lee Chu-ming, that screening was an avoidable and costly mistake.

But one cannot blame the Hong Kong government for trying. Since 1975 and the arrival in Hong Kong waters of the Clara Maersk ship with 3,743 Vietnamese refugees, more than 170,000 boat people have landed in Hong Kong and been given shelter — and all the while the same Hong Kong government has been summarily returning across the border illegal immigrants from China's Guangdong province at the rate of 20,000 a year. It is a double standard that enrages the Hong Kong people, who are 98 per cent Cantonese: why should their Cantonese kith and kin from Guangdong be expelled (often after being put in prison), while the Vietnamese are not? Moreover, the exodus of boat people mocks normal logic. Ever since 1980, with an interruption in 1986 and '87, there has been an Orderly Departure Programme to allow Vietnamese to leave their country legally. Yet in the late 1980s, when the ODP became bigger, when the Vietnamese economy became more liberal and its political regime less harsh, and when Hong Kong introduced its screening process as a deterrent to would-be boat people, the exodus of illegal departures to Hong Kong paradoxically accelerated, from 3,291 boat people aboard 165 ramshackle boats in 1987 to 18,101 in 590 boats in 1988 and 34,114 in 797 boats in 1989. Over time, perhaps the armada will be reduced to insignifance, as the hopelessness of seeking refuge in the West becomes accepted in the villages of Vietnam or as the Vietnamese economy, with international financial assistance, begins to flourish like neighbouring Thailand before it. But neither possibility looks imminent. In the meantime, the Hong Kong Chinese, for whom charity most definitely begins (and often stays) at home, have much more immediate remedies. When asked in a government-run survey in early 1991 whether Hong Kong should abandon its policy of first asylum, 88 per cent said 'yes'. When asked, 'Given that the boat people may be drowned, do you still think that the port of first asylum policy should be abolished?' some 70 per cent still said 'yes'.

Yet these Hong Kongers, apparently so ready to let the wretched Vietnamese drown, are the same people claiming sanctuary in the West from the potential disaster of China's takeover in 1997. Because they fear the worst they queue at Hong Kong's foreign consulates in the hope of an immigrant's visa; they invest millions abroad to secure the status of a business migrant; they send a wife or child to live abroad to qualify for residence (while the husband commutes across the Pacific as an 'astronaut', in the slang of the moment); they buy counterfeit visas or fake passports. When General Noriega still ruled the roost in Panama, one consular official in Hong Kong sold dozens of

Panamanian passports to eager Hong Kong businessmen. Passports from the Pacific kingdom of Tonga could be bought in the late 1980s for up to $35,000. It is quite common for affluent Hong Kong mothers-to-be to fly to America as tourists, and then to give birth there, so ensuring American citizenship for their 'passport babies' (and a near-guaranteed right of entry to the United States for themselves). One of the publishing successes of Hong Kong at the start of the 1990s was a bi-lingual monthly magazine called *Emigrant*. All this smacks of an underlying desperation just as intense as that of the Vietnamese — and yet precious few Hong Kong Chinese see the parallel. If their worst fears are confirmed — by which most people mean the Shanghai-style confiscation of property and loss of personal freedoms — then their comparative wealth may well make them 'yacht people' rather than 'boat people', but they will still depend on the mercy of foreign countries. It is foolish to erode those countries's sympathy ahead of time by being so contemptuous of the unwanted Vietnamese.

Whether Hong Kong's fears are justified is an open question. The promise of the Joint Declaration, signed by Margaret Thatcher and Zhou Ziyang, the then prime ministers of Britain and China, on 19 December 1984, is that when Hong Kong on 1 July 1997 becomes a Special Administrative Region of the People's Republic of China, 'the socialist system and socialist policies shall not be practised in the Hong Kong Special Administrative Region' . . . and 'Hong Kong's previous capitalist system and life-style shall remain unchanged for 50 years'.

Fair enough, it was thought by many, even most, at the time. But that was before the tragedy of Tiananmen Square reminded Hong Kongers of the unpleasant side of Chinese communism. Forget the signatures on a document lodged with the United Nations as an international treaty; remember, instead, the communists' broken promises that allowed the plundering of rich Shanghai after 1949, and the depredations of the Red Guards in the Cultural Revolution of 1967–76. Since almost everyone in Hong Kong is either an immigrant from China or the child of an immigrant, they have a right to be nervous — which is why in the years since the Tiananmen bloodshed Hong Kongers have been emigrating at the rate of 1,000 or more a week. Unlike Asia's other migrants, they do not envy Western wealth and living standards. Indeed, most of the Hong Kong emigrants are materially happy in Hong Kong, and many will lose money and comfort by emigrating. What they do envy is the Western freedoms of speech, travel, and association — the very ones they enjoy under the British but suspect they may lose under the Chinese.

The result is an alarming, and rapid, depletion of what makes Hong Kong tick: its most resourceful and skilled people. Optimists (who, on this particular issue, are dwindling in number) argue that there has often been a sizeable emigration from Hong Kong. In the 1970s, for example, the net outflow averaged 30,000 a year. Why worry, when those leaving can be replaced so easily — and so cheaply — with immigrants from across the border? In any case, a lot of emigrants will soon return, clutching their foreign passports as an insurance policy against the worst, to resume their work in Hong Kong.

The optimists should not be dismissed out of hand, but it is a lot easier to be a moderate pessimist. In the 'old days', before successive British immigration acts deprived Hong Kongers of their right of abode in the imperial motherland, and before the question of 1997 loomed in anyone's consciousness, it was the poor and unskilled who tended to migrate. Now it is the highly educated and technically qualified. Surveys conducted in the aftermath of the Tiananmen bloodshed found that two-thirds of Hong Kong's accountants had already applied to emigrate, and of the remainder some 80 per cent intended to apply. Three-quarters of the colony's lawyers said they planned to leave by 1997, and 70 per cent of the doctors in government hospitals. The same story applies to computer programmers, bank managers, nurses, pharmacists, and social workers. It applies also to secretaries: the *taipan* ('big boss') of Jardine Matheson, Hong Kong's most famous *hong*, or trading group, related to me once how his huge organisation once nearly ground to a halt — long before Tiananmen — when almost all the executive secretaries suddenly left for Canada, which in the mid-'80s was giving high points on the immigration scale for secretarial skills. Even the Church is not immune: by 1990 a tenth of the colony's Protestant clergymen had already left, and more will follow.

All this is happening at a pace which will defy the quick replacement of the emigrants. By the government's reckoning, the outflow will average over 60,000 a year in the run-up to 1997 and beyond, draining a tenth of the territory's population away in just one decade. Obviously, many of the emigrants will be children and other dependants, but a good guess would say that one in every four is leaving a professional, administrative, or managerial post in Hong Kong. It is simply impossible to fill their places overnight with newcomers of the same quality. How, for example, can China provide English-speaking lawyers qualified in British law, the system of Hong Kong? Or doctors and nurses qualified and competent in Western medicine? The answer is that it cannot — and any suitably qualified replacements brought in from the United Kingdom or from the rest of Britain's Commonwealth will be grossly handicapped by their ignorance of the Cantonese dialect.

As for the argument that many of the emigrants will return, it seems fundamentally unlikely that they will do so in significant numbers. True, tales abound of Hong Kongers finding only unhappiness abroad — having to take inferior jobs in Canada and Australia and so adjust to a lower standard of living in an alien environment. One friend of mine, with good English, a degree from a British university, and five years' experience working for a British company in Hong Kong, spent six months looking for what she regarded as appropriate work in Canada before finally reconciling herself to helping out in a Chinatown restaurant. But with the passing months the misery will fade: the immigrants will adjust to their new countries, get better jobs, take on mortgages, and so on. Their children will make friends at school and be on course for future examination qualifications. When all this is happening, and when they have spent three years acquiring their new citizenship, will they then want to uproot their families and return to Hong Kong? Surely not.

The inescapable conclusion is that if Hong Kong is to maintain its standards, it has to stop its best and brightest from leaving. Since Hong Kong under the British is not a police state, this cannot be done by compulsion, only by persuasion — which is why after Tiananmen Square Mrs Thatcher's government pushed a bill through the House of Commons which will give full British passports to 50,000 heads of households as an inducement for them to stay in Hong Kong. This lucky élite, deemed vital to Hong Kong's continued prosperity and selected through a points system of eye-glazing complexity, will consist of 36,200 professionals in the private sector, 13,300 government employees, and 500 key entrepreneurs. Take in their immediate relatives, and Britain is offering her citizenship to a maximum of 225,000 Hong Kongers — in the profound hope that they will never arrive in Britain. (Whether they will or not remains to be seen. What seems clear is that few Hong Kongers want to move to Britain — the demand for the British package was only a smidgen more than the passports offered.)

The offer, of course, is one of expedience rather than honour. After all, if Britain were being truly honourable she would have offered full passports to all 3.3 million of her subjects born in Hong Kong — just as Portugal gave full passports to her subjects born in Macao (an easily manageable 100,000). But if honour is ignored, what of expedience? The criticism of the British nationality package is that it is too little and too late: it will fail to anchor enough people in Hong Kong to make a difference — which means that those who do take up the British passports will quite possibly use them not to stay in Hong Kong but to leave it. On the other hand, the British offer should be added to the escape routes proffered by other countries should the worst come to the worst: France, Belgium, Denmark, Germany, Italy, America, and Singapore all have schemes which give Hong Kongers visas whose use can be delayed until a time of need. Their motives, of course, are not entirely altruistic: France promised visas to about 1,000 Hong Kongers so that the Banque Nationale de Paris could continue to staff its operations in Hong Kong; and Singapore has offered to take up to 25,000 Hong Kong heads of family at least in part to transfuse more Chinese blood into the ethnic mix of the nation, which is suffering a brain drain of its own — and one which at the end of the 1980s was proportionately as severe as Hong Kong's.

Yet this anchor of foreign visas, impressive though it may appear on paper, cannot on its own hold Hong Kong's most talented to their homes. One reason is that China, both before and after 1997, will consider all Hong Kong Chinese, including those awarded full British passports, as Chinese citizens, ineligible for protection by a foreign power. In that case, if you have a foreign passport or visa, perhaps you should use it before China takes over. A second reason is the herd mentality: the more people who leave, the more who will decide to follow them. At one time, would-be emigrants kept their plans a secret, not wanting to be accused of cowardice or betrayal; after Tiananmen Square, there was no longer any shame — emigration became a topic of open conversation, and the restaurants were full of leaving parties. A third reason is Hong Kong's intrinsic 'refugee mentality': because most Hong Kongers are either refugees from China or the children of those refugees, they have not had time to develop the commitment to their homes that characterises people who have lived in the same place for generations, even centuries. This lack of commitment helps explain that oddity of British imperial history — a colony that has never agitated for democracy, self-rule, or independence. Instead, the Hong Konger's attitude is to make money while he can — and move on when threatened. But move to what?

All the great European powers of the last three centuries had their colonial outposts in Asia: Britain coloured the map from the Middle East, through the Indian subcontinent, and across to Burma and Malaya; the Dutch and Germans colonised the Indonesian archipelago and the giant island of New Guinea; the French held sway in Cambodia, Laos, and Vietnam, the trio of countries they called 'Indochine'; the Spanish held the Philippines; the Portuguese stretched Lisbon's arm past Goa and as far as Macao. Even where the Europeans did not claim sovereign power, they wielded the influence that comes with military might and trading dominance. Shanghai had its 'International Settlement', where the European powers ruled the roost immune to Chinese law; in China's north-east, the port of Qingdao was ceded to Germany for 99 years. Surely such a history must leave unbreakable ties of culture, trade, investment — the same colonial legacy that binds North Africa's economic migrants to France and many of the West Indies' to Britain.

Perhaps so. Yet the three favourite destinations for Asia's people in flight — whether from persecution or poverty — are, and will remain, the United States, Canada, and Australia. True, America, with its half-century in the Philippines, has a colonial past, but it has little of the sense of empire that permeates the history of Europe — and Australia and Canada have no sense of it at all. Something else must explain the modern ties that are so much stronger than those of Asia's colonial past.

The answer has three parts. The first is the 'geographical magnetism' that runs around the Pacific Rim and, more than a century ago, attracted Chinese coolies to build America's railroads and dig Australia's gold mines. The second is the economic opportunity that comes with large spaces and small populations. The United States may have 250 million people — but they are spread across an area bigger than Western Europe, which has around 400 million people. The statistical quirk is that the average American has six times more space than the average Briton and is a third richer. The quirk becomes an absurdity when applied to Canada, with 26 million people living in a country bigger than the United States, or to Australia, whose 17 million inhabit an island almost as big as America. And the third reason is the corollary of the second: all three nations advertise for immigrants to help them exploit their resources and create new wealth. Not for them the anti-immigration legislation of Britain and other European countries. Instead, America has its annual quota system to attract fresh blood from countries around the globe. Those quotas are based on all sorts of factors — especially the lobbying powers of America's various ethnic groups and the concern they can arouse over human rights in their nations of origin. By contrast, Canada gives points based on how valuable the putative immigrant will be to Canada's needs. So, too, does Australia, giving substance to its assertion that the 'White Australia' policy was indeed abandoned in 1973. After all, a Singaporean graduate — be he Chinese, Indian, or Malay — is bound to score more points than an Irish labourer who left school at the age of fifteen. Even insular New Zealand, with 3.3 million people dotted around an area bigger than Britain, is beginning to see the attractions of immigration: by the end of this century there will be more and more non-white faces to join the Maoris in adding colour to the Kiwis' Caucasian blandness.

Whatever the demand and wherever it arises, Asia can provide the supply. In the five years from 1981 to 1986, America welcomed 1.6 million Asian immigrants — as many as in the whole of the previous decade. In Canada, Asians accounted for 44 per cent of the one million who settled in the country between 1980 and 1988. Two out of every three migrants entering Australia in 1990 were Asians, compared with one out of every three in 1988. The trend may be slowed through the 1990s, but it will not be reversed: more and more Asians will adopt the citizenship of Pacific Rim nations first settled by Europeans.

They will come from nervous Hong Kong and from the impoverished countries of Indochina (in 1990 a group of Cambodian boat people managed an incredibly long voyage to make landfall on the north coast of Australia). They will include Singaporeans who find their country of birth either too stifling or too competitive (why should a middle-class Singaporean risk his child failing in his homeland's exam-based élitist system of schooling when a move to Australia will virtually guarantee smooth, stress-free progress to a university degree?). And they will include many thousands of Chinese.

Some of the Chinese will obtain student visas, especially to take language courses in Australia, but will have every intention of making their sojourn away from China permanent. Others will simply be illegal immigrants. New York City officials estimated at the start of 1991 that in the city's Chinese population of 300,000 there were about 30,000 with either false papers or no papers, having paid anything up to $50,000 to reach America. Since that is an enormous fortune in China, it has to be borrowed from overseas Chinese gangs — which then force the immigrant into virtual slave labour to pay off the debt. On a lesser scale, the same is true for Chinese students in Australia: they borrow hard currency on China's black market to send off for their school fees, and then pay off the debt (quite easily) by taking jobs in the hotels and restaurants of Melbourne and Sydney. It all works wonderfully — until things go awry. In 1990, for example, Australia started rejecting many student applications as a first step to reducing the abuse of the system (many of the Australian language schools were simply money-grabbing shams). As an immediate consequence, the Australian consulates in China were besieged by angry students protesting that their fees were being returned to China's State banks — which were converting the Australian dollars back into local renminbi at the official rate, leaving the would-be students hopelessly in debt.

But whether the migrants come from China, Vietnam, India, or Singapore, how will they be received? There is no answer that fits all the thousands flying the Pacific each year to sow new roots in alien countries. The trite view of many Asians is that America is the world's melting pot, happily absorbing its new immigrants from Asia just as in earlier decades it accepted its Irish, Germans, Poles, and other impoverished or persecuted Europeans. By contrast, Canada and especially Australia are supposed to be homogeneous societies (Canadian 'native people' and Australian aborigines are too few, it seems, to be counted), perennially suspicious of different colours and different cultures. The newspapers of migration-conscious Hong Kong have frequent letters and articles complaining of racial prejudice in Sydney and Melbourne or Vancouver and Toronto. The chairman of

Prudential Asia Investment, Hong Kong businessman Dr Victor Fung, bluntly told the 1991 session of the World Economic Forum in Davos, Switzerland: 'Australians regard themselves as part of Asia and as making inroads into Asia. But Asians regard Australia as a Western country, as very distant cousins. Asians still perceive Australia very much as having a White Australia policy. It will take more than one per cent Asian immigration a year to change that. It will have to be increased several times that.'

As soon as Dr Fung's remarks were reported in the Hong Kong press, the furious Australian consul general, Geoff Bentley, fired off a reply: nearly 42 per cent of the previous financial year's immigrants to Australia were Asian; more than 12 per cent were from Hong Kong alone (making some 17,589 in the calendar year 1990); and, 'on a per capita basis, Australia resettles more immigrants on humanitarian grounds than any other nation in the world . . . In Australia it is illegal to discriminate against people on grounds of race, gender or religion. The overwhelming majority of Australians welcome new arrivals. If this were not the case, it would have hardly been possible for nearly five million migrants from 120 countries to have settled in Australia since World War II.'

Game, set, and match, one would think, to the consul general. But if Dr Fung was mistaken in his figures, he was nonetheless accurately reflecting what many, perhaps most, Asians — especially Chinese — feel. And the feelings are not groundless. Whenever there is a large influx of foreigners into any community, there is bound to be resentment. In Vancouver, environmentally conscious Canadians are enraged when rich Hong Kongers buy handsome properties and then, for reasons of *fung shui* superstition, chop down the century-old trees in their new gardens. In Sydney, the suburb of Cabramatta is known as Vietnammatta; its commercial bustle makes white Australians envious and resentful — and apt to criticise the financial help and special schooling given to incoming Vietnamese refugees when so many white Australians are unemployed or going bankrupt. Because they resent the Vietnamese, they also resent anyone who looks like them — including Hong Kong and Singaporean Chinese who will be net contributors to Australia's economy from day one. In the same way, Chinese, Japanese, and Koreans all look alike to Australian bigots. Why should they bother to distinguish between them? Bruce Ruxton, leader in the state of Victoria of the Returned Services League, a veterans' organisation, and self-appointed spokesman for the common man, agrees with Dr Fung. Ruxton, an amiable man for all his forceful views on life, once told me: 'What I say, 80 out of 100 Australians think . . . This country remains basically European . . . The basis of immigration should be from Britain, Ireland and Europe in that order . . . We're not culturally, legally, geologically, geographically or racially tied with Asia.'

And what of the United States? The truth is that it is not so much a melting pot as a mozaic, with ethnic communities — from Hispanics to Croatians — determined to preserve their individual heritages. Like other immigrants before them, the various Asian newcomers work hard, save hard, and help each other. The result, again, is resentment. Universities are under pressure to limit their intake of Asian-Americans lest they keep out other groups who score lower on high-school tests. By the end of the 1980s, Asian-Americans accounted for one in four of the students at Berkeley and for one in every five of the students at the University of California in Los Angeles. In his Doonesbury comic strip, Gary Trudeau brilliantly satirised the attitude that Asian students were being 'un-American' by studying so hard. In New York, where Korean immigrants run more than 90 per cent of the small fruit and grocery stores, angry blacks in 1990 led a much publicised boycott of one such Korean store after a scuffle between the store's Korean employees and a Haitian woman they suspected of stealing. While the boycott was running, a Vietnamese who happened to be near the store was beaten up by some blacks — all Asians, after all, look alike . . .

All this is reported in newspapers right around the Pacific Rim, until it becomes a kind of received wisdom that Asia's migrants will be the victims of racism. But the wisdom is of the 'contextless experience' kind, unable to put images in perspective. Of course there will be incidents of discrimination, but they have been relatively few in the past and will probably be relatively few in the future. The fact is that America has a welcoming culture which rewards talent and hard work with material and social success. The fact, too, is that the Canadian west coast has been absorbing Japanese, Koreans, and Chinese for generations — and can easily embrace a few more thousand a year from Hong Kong. As for the Australians, they have a down-to-earth humour and friendliness that no others can match. Finally, there is one other aspect that should encourage Asians to think well of America, Canada, Australia, and other Western destinations. These countries all care about Asia's human rights in a way that puts most Asian governments to shame.

The United States of America has a government officer known as the Assistant Secretary of State for Human Rights and Humanitarian Affairs. In 1990, this officer — one Richard Schifter — wrote:

For our part, the United States remains committed to the worldwide promotion and consolidation of human rights and democracy. We see these goals as principal foreign policy challenges. We actively champion them abroad because they reflect the best that is in ourselves. And we do so because we have found that in those countries where human rights and democratic values have taken hold, we find friends — not enemies. These are the world's most stable governments, the most dynamic societies, the bulwarks of freedom, respectful of the rights of their citizens and of their neighbors, and the most responsible contributors to the well-being of the world community.

To cynical Europeans, such a statement may seem an amusing conceit of the superpower. To Asian governments — China's is a good example — it denotes the arrogant American tendency to 'unwarranted intrusions in our internal affairs'. But what do 'ordinary' Asians think? I suspect that most, if asked, would be quite impressed by Mr Schifter's words — including those Asians, be they radical students in Seoul or extremist Muslims in Aceh, Indonesia, who believe America is the fount of practically all evil in the world. Whatever the misconceptions gained from their 'contextless' experience of America, Asians are right about one thing: they recognise the freedom enjoyed by Americans as their birthright — and very often they envy it.

The reason is obvious from the mammoth report on global human rights presented each year to Congress by Mr Schifter and his colleagues in the Department of State. It is obvious, too, in the reports from independent agencies such as Amnesty International and AsiaWatch. Finally, it is obvious in the visa queues at Western consulates in countries from the Philippines to Pakistan. The truth is that most Asians have precious little of the freedom taken for granted in the West. Instead, they suffer from a whole list of ailments: arbitrary arrest, detention without trial, torture, religious discrimination, restrictions on travel, and so on. Sometimes, these ills are enshrined by law: in China, for example, a worker needs official permission and the consent of his work unit before he can move to another part of the country. Sometimes, the ills are in defiance of the law: the same Chinese worker, for example, can legally be held for a maximum of ten days before formal charges — and yet often detainees in China are held for months without charge. And sometimes, there is no law at all: in Burma, for example, forced labour is not against the law because there is no law to prohibit it — and so no embarrassment for the army when it forces local men to act as porters in areas of insurgency.

But whatever the ills, they will remain depressingly common. The rule of thumb is that rich Asians enjoy more human rights than poor Asians — and the poor very much outnumber the rich. Apologists for this situation may argue that the Western definition of human rights is inappropriate for Asia: how can the 'rights' that are defined by and for individuals in the adversarial societies of the West be applied to the consensual, Confucian societies of the East? From childhood, Westerners are told to 'stand up for your rights'; Orientals are told to 'respect authority and obey your elders'. But the apologists are wrong. Mr Schifter's definition of human rights, contained in America's Foreign Assistance Act, is applicable universally, whatever the culture. Confucius would surely not have objected to

> freedom from torture or other cruel, inhuman, or degrading treatment or punishment; prolonged detention without charges; disappearance due to abduction or clandestine detention; and other flagrant denial of the rights to life, liberty, and the security of the person. Internationally recognised worker rights, as defined in Section 502(a) of the Trade Act, include (A) the right of association; (B) the right to organise and bargain collectively; (C) prohibition on the use of any form of forced or compulsory labour; (D) a minimum age for the employment of children; and (E) acceptable conditions of work with respect to minimum wages, hours of work, and occupational safety and health.

By that definition, few countries in Asia meet acceptable standards. Japan, Hong Kong, Singapore, Malaysia, and perhaps Thailand would pass highest — with black marks in Thailand for the sale of women into prostitution, and the legal employment of children as young as twelve years old; and black marks, too, for Singapore's restrictions on the media and for the occasional use by both Singapore and Malaysia of an Internal Security Act which allows indefinite detention without trial. Taiwan and South Korea are on the way to joining this élite — but will need first to sweep away the remaining vestiges of their martial-law pasts. A Taiwanese must be able to advocate independence and not be guilty of sedition; a South Korean must be confident that he will not be arrested and tortured for possessing books about North Korea.

There are other countries which have excellent protection for human rights in theory, but which in practice fall short. The Philippines, for example, has had a genuine commitment to democracy and human rights ever since the overthrow of the corrupt and dictatorial Ferdinand Marcos in 1986 — but the police and armed forces, struggling to cope with the communist insurgency and the labyrinthine complexities of the country's judicial system, are prone to resort to the shortcuts of torture and extrajudicial killings (which, of course, the insurgents use too). Another example is India, where poverty and tradition combine to mock the law and constitution — and the mockery is flagrant: a quarter of India's children between the ages of five and fifteen are working (which means India is responsible for a quarter of the world's child labour); each year hundreds, even thousands, of young women are burned to death by their husbands' families on the grounds that the brides brought insufficient dowry to their new homes; and low-caste and tribal women are constantly at risk of rape by the police.

But then there are the totalitarian nations where no citizen can be sure of any rights. There are no free elections in North Korea, nor any free trade unions. Instead, the ordinary worker in Pyongyang is forced to vote for an approved list of Korean Workers' Party candidates. Only athletes and selected officials are allowed to travel abroad — and if they defect, the State will retaliate against their relatives. Otherwise, contact with the outside world is virtually impossible: the only radios and televisions North Koreans can buy are doctored so that they can receive only the State's transmissions. According to some defectors, there are at least 100,000 political prisoners and their relatives held in special concentration camps. But if North Korea is possibly the most daunting example of the totalitarian state, it is not without its rivals. China, for example, has thousands of prisoners whose only crime is to have criticised the State, and some two million people, according to China's own account, were sent to 'labour education camps' in the 1980s for offences against public security. While the Chinese constitution guarantees all sorts of rights of expression and association (although not of religious belief), these rights are then restricted by the assertion that the interests of workers, Party, and State are identical — which means that workers do not have the right to set up their own unions, or go on strike or campaign to change their government. In Tibet, which still dreams of gaining its independence, China's behaviour to the local people is brutally, sometimes fatally, repressive. And so, too, in Burma: in 1988 troops of the ruling State Law and Order Restoration Council killed thousands of unarmed student demonstrators in Rangoon and other cities; the following year, this ugly-named SLORC allowed general elections — and reacted to overwhelming electoral triumph of the opposition by simply retaining power and putting the opposition's leaders in detention.

But examine any of Asia's, indeed the world's, authoritarian regimes and the abuses will soon be evident. There are arbitary arrests and beatings in Nepal, the world's only Hindu kingdom; Pakistani police are just as corrupt and prone to violence as their counterparts in India; Vietnam, even as it liberalises its economy, remains a police state with constant surveillance of its citizens, who risk 're-education' camps if they dare to criticise the government and party.

The question is how to stop the abuses. Mr Schifter would doubtless invoke the power of America's foreign policy — the tying of aid to democratic reforms, or the blocking of trade with those who refuse reforms. This power is not to be derided: America's trade embargoes have crippled Cuba and Vietnam; its economic arm-twisting has helped open up Eastern

Europe. But those who control the power will use it selectively. The embargo imposed on Vietnam lasted through the 1980s mainly because it costs America nothing, and because there was no strong lobby in Washington to repeal it. Compare, by contrast, the relatively light American sanctions imposed on China after the Tiananmen tragedy of 1989: they were never likely to force reform out of China's gerontocrats (China, after all, kept its Most Favoured Nation status, the loss of which would have deeply hurt China). Moreover, the sanctions were quietly dropped the following year when China's vote in the United Nations Security Council became important to an America facing the prospect of war with Iraq. The difference between China and Vietnam is not in their human rights' records, but in the weight they command in the world. America can afford to snub Vietnam; China, with a fifth of the world's people and a border next to the Soviet Union, is another matter.

The real solution to the abuse of their rights lies with Asians themselves. It cannot be an accident that the countries that protect the rights of their citizens are also the ones with the highest standards of living. Whether one must come before the other may well be the futile debate of the chicken and the egg. The challenge for the poor countries of Asia is to emulate their richer neighbours. If they fail, they should not be surprised if their people continue to flee for a better life in the West. The 'contextless experience' of the world beyond may be a distortion, but it is not a lie.

Ten

The Challenge Ahead

'Rich men think of the future, poor men of the present' — Chinese proverb

*J*apan and Germany, taking their seats as Permanent Members of the UN
Security Council, pledge themselves to the pursuit of world peace . . . An
Indonesian conglomerate bids for control of the Ritz Hotel in London . . .
The Singapore government announces the creation of an annual prize for
'Creative Thought' . . . India's new prime minister says the privatisation of
inefficient state corporations is essential for the nation's economic survival
. . . Representatives of Taiwan's ruling Kuomintang take their places
alongside delegates from Hong Kong and Macao in the first United China
Congress . . . The World Bank predicts that South America's economies will
be more dynamic than Asia's over the next decade . . .

(feasible, but uncertain, thoughts for Asia 2000)

P rediction is a risky business — and
it is always easier to be wrong than right (how else would bookmakers
become rich?). One spectacular misjudgement was the comment by the
American journalist, Lincoln Steffens, on his return from the Soviet Union
in 1919: 'I have seen the future, and it works.' Will this book's vision of Asia
turn out to be just as myopic and distorted?

In some aspects, I fear so. Pundits cannot tell which straw will actually
break the camel's back — and so they fail to foresee history's more fateful
moments: in 1973, Sadat's visit to Jerusalem; in 1989, the collapse of
communism in Eastern Europe and the dismantling of the Berlin Wall; or in
1991, the crushing defeat of Iraq in the Gulf. Who foretold the fall of Marcos
in 1986, or of South Korea's Chun Doo Hwan in 1987? A legion of China-
watchers failed to predict both the sustained liberalisation of Taiwan in the
late 1980s and the 1989 tragedy of Tiananmen Square, when euphoric
liberalism was followed by State repression.

The reason, of course, is that we are all — some more, some less —
trapped by conventional wisdom, which describes the future by extrapolating
from the past. It is why, thirty years ago, few people recognised the
potential of Asia's dragon economies, bereft of every resource except
people; it was easier to concentrate on the known potential, with their
agricultural and mineral wealth, of Burma, the Philippines, and Vietnam. In
a world dominated by Ford and General Motors, it seemed impossible that
Nissan, Toyota, and Honda would ever make a car worth buying in the
West. Chase Manhattan and Citibank never imagined they would ever play
second fiddle to Dai-Ichi Kangyo and other Japanese banks the West had
never even heard of.

Are we to remain the prisoners of conventional wisdom? If so, we must
assume that we are entering the 'Pacific Century', in which the balance of
the world's power — first economic, and later political, cultural, and

military — shifts from America to Asia, just as in this century it shifted to America from Europe. In particular, we must assume that Japan will build political and military muscles to match its economic and financial ones, and that lesser Asian nations will follow its lead, like the formation of geese described in Chapter Six. Because East Asia saves more than it invests, and South Asia invests more than it saves, we will conclude that China will pull ahead of India — and that the developing nations of Latin America, the Caribbean, and Sub-Saharan Africa will continue to lag because, by the figures of the 1980s, they invest so little of their economic output. But will we be right? Marc Faber, a Hong Kong investment adviser whose contrarian views have earned him the nickname 'Dr Doom', wrote in 1990:

> One of the problems of investments is that whenever a trend or theme has been around long enough, it is perceived as permanent . . . While there is little doubt that global economic activity tends to expand, economic growth can be asymmetrical. In the 1980s, economic growth bypassed Latin America. In the 1990s, we could see a shift in economic activity away from Tokyo, Taipei, Seoul, Hong Kong and Singapore. Real estate in Xiamen, Shanghai, Ho Chi Minh City, Rangoon and Vladivostok may yield superior returns than the shares of Nomura Securities, Hong Kong Land and Singapore Airlines . . .

The warning is worth listening to (although, of course, even small improvements in places such as Rangoon could bring high yields). But it is a caveat, not a prohibition. Conventional wisdom may on occasion be wrong, but what choice do we have? As Confucius sagely advised: 'Study the past, if you would divine the future.'

It is precisely because Asia's past, and present, are so mixed, that its future cannot be confined to a neat prescription of the 'Pacific Century', or some similar phrase of the moment. Such terms usually refer to a selection from the Far East of Asia — prospering Japan; the dragon economies of South Korea, Hong Kong, Taiwan, and Singapore; baby dragons such as Thailand and Malaysia; embryo dragons such as Indonesia and the Philippines; and, because it is so enormous in population and area, China. But 'Asia', properly defined, spreads west from the Pacific to touch Europe along the Ural Mountains. It takes in Siberia, the southern republics of the Soviet Union, all of Turkey (save a few square European miles of Istanbul across the Bosphorus), the Arabian peninsula, and the rest of the Middle East, from Lebanon to Iran. This book has used a definition of Asia — from Afghanistan eastwards to Japan; from China southwards to Indonesia — that lies between the modern abbreviation and the larger version of geography. To have included the Arab Middle East and Iran would have meant a focus on Islam, the Arab-Israeli conflict, the price of oil; to have included the southern, often Muslim, republics of the USSR would have meant a focus on the potential (even actual) disintegration of the Soviet Union. All those issues will have their impact on the rest of Asia — and yet the rest of Asia feels separate from them. Only occasionally, in the Muslim fringe of Asia that runs from Afghanistan down to Indonesia, do the problems of the Middle East make a political and popular impact. As for the Soviet Union, my feeling is that the Asian ambitions of Gorbachev's Vladivostok speech cannot be achieved within the decade or so of this book's horizon; instead, the problems of economic collapse and political dislocation will keep Moscow's mind on Euro-centred matters. The overtures to South Korea and Japan will be welcomed — but they will not produce an instant remedy for the economic ills that affect the Soviet body.

If the Middle East and Soviet Asia are excluded, why not also India and its subcontinental neighbours? Why not simply concentrate on the modern, abbreviated Asia of the Far East? The answer is that India can never be separated from the calculations of the Far East: its huge population, growing fast enough to overtake China's within a couple of generations; its nuclear capability; its increasingly interventionist instincts and military ambitions; its abrasive geographical contact with China. All these are factors that will affect the rest of Asia, especially the vibrant but militarily vulnerable economies of South-east Asia.

By contrast, I have excluded Australasia, despite the fervent belief of modern governments in Canberra that Australia's destiny lies in Asia. That is true, and yet Australia does not 'feel' part of Asia and will not while most of its people — albeit not as vociferously as Bruce Ruxton in Chapter Nine — still identify with a British heritage. Australia's destiny lies in Asia because it needs Asia's markets, and Asian capital to help upgrade Australian skills. But Asia does not need distant, sparsely populated Australia — and until Asian immigration slowly changes Australia's sense of a European past, Asia will continue to see Australia as a Western transplant, to be exploited for its beaches and minerals but not yet to be considered part of Asia proper.

Whatever the exclusions, the Asia described in this book still cannot pretend to cohesion or homogeneity. In personal wealth, it ranges from the comfort of Japan to the struggle even to scratch a living in Laos, Nepal, and Bangladesh. In political culture, it ranges from the fractious democracy of India to the dictatorial personality cult and *juche* 'self-reliance' of North Korea. In social terms, it encompasses the caste system of India, the feudalism of the Philippines, and the middle-class egalitarianism of Taiwan. Whatever the surprises that will confound us over the next decade, one certainty is that Asians will remain divided among themselves by the differences of economics, politics, and culture. The Pacific Rim, integral to the concept of the Pacific Century, will have numerous chips along its edge: Japanese yuppies will trade billions in foreign exchange with their counterparts in Singapore and San Francisco — and have no inkling of the tribes of Irian Jaya or the rice farmers of Vietnam. Yet within the confusion, there will be some signposts to Asia's future: the discipline of Confucianism, the influence of the Chinese diaspora, and the infusion of Asian capital, accumulated from years of East Asian trade surpluses, into the spread of industrialisation. Assume no catastrophe of nature or mankind — an earthquake that levels Tokyo or a war that lays waste Korea or South-east Asia — and that future will, for most Asians, be better than their present. What will shape this future will be the fortunes of three countries in particular: China, India, and Japan.

The importance of China and India to Asia's future is fundamental: two billion people, one third of them still children, are too many ever to be ignored — their behaviour, good or bad, is bound to affect the nations around them for generations without limit. The expansionist tendencies of Indian foreign policy have already been described in Chapter Eight — but those tendencies will not necessarily be pernicious. A confident and assertive India could well be a force for regional stability, but that will mean an India whose domestic policy concentrates on sound and liberal economics — not on the political infighting that has characterised Indian politics ever since independence and especially after the deaths of Indira Gandhi and her favourite son, Sanjay, in the early 1980s. As the 1990s get underway, the signs do not look good: to have three prime ministers — Rajiv Gandhi, V.P. Singh, and Chandra Shekhar — within a year is hardly evidence of democratic maturity. Nor is the assassination of Rajiv Gandhi in May 1991, and the deliberate painting of the political landscape of the 1990s with racial and religious hues.

But India could yet surprise us. The success of its overseas businessmen is convincing proof of a vast entrepreneurial reservoir at home that could be tapped if only a future Indian government would have the courage (as Rajiv Gandhi briefly did in the mid-1980s) to jettison the protectionist and socialist baggage it picked up with independence. If China could grow so dramatically in the 1980s, once it had thrown off the shackles of the Cultural Revolution, why not India in the 1990s, once it decides to throw off the ties of its red tape? After all, India starts from a much sounder platform: a broad industrial base, extremely cheap skilled and unskilled labour, a vast supply of engineers and computer experts, a political system resilient enough to cope with all manner of stress and strain. These are assets that could catapault India ahead of China, if only the political will and imagination exist to use them.

That calculation, of course, supposes that China will not accelerate again in the 1990s as it did in the 1980s. The supposition seems reasonable, if only because the challenge of political transition, from the era of Deng Xiaoping to that of his successors, will divert the government from the need to complete the market freedoms begun in the 1980s. The probability, therefore, is that the economy will move patchily onwards, much better than in the days of Maoism but achieving only a fraction of China's real potential. If so, the rest of Asia will hardly notice this giant under-achiever.

But what if things go wrong in China, a possibility that no Chinese leader, least of all Deng Xiaoping, would exclude in the aftermath of Tiananmen Square? The collapse of communism in Eastern Europe happened with, in Chinese eyes, frightening speed. The same collapse is unlikely in China: first, because the Chinese Communist Party came to power in 1949 not through outside intervention (as its counterparts did, with Soviet help, in Europe) but through an indigenous revolution against a corrupt and economically disastrous Kuomintang government; second, because Chinese communism has been adapted to the passive Confucian tradition; and third, because 'socialism with Chinese characteristics', to use Deng's phrase, has succeeded — unlike Soviet communism — in feeding the people and filling the shops with goods that they both can buy and want to buy (in March 1991, China condescendingly gave the Soviet Union 'soft loans' of food, textiles, and consumer goods worth $733 million). The problem for the 1990s is that China's communism, for all its achievements in the 1980s, has gone as far as it can, which means it has outlived its usefulness. But that argues not for sudden collapse but gradual erosion and disintegration. Conceivably, by the end of this century, this will bring some political pluralism, enabling Taiwan to reach a *modus vivendi* in union with the mainland. That must involve some form of genuine representation in Beijing for Taiwan's KMT — something more than the subservience implied in the 'one country, two systems' formula under which Hong Kong will return to China's fold in 1997 and Macao in 1999.

The question is whether this pluralism can happen smoothly. When foreign analysts look at China they often conclude that only a federal system can bring such a huge population and land mass across the threshold from reasonable subsistence to comfortable luxury. But how does China get from here to there? Chinese analysts look at the idea and conclude that the journey would stall in 'warlordism', pitting province against province and local army against local army. And what then? One scenario is a collapse of the Chinese state and the exodus of scores of millions across China's southern frontiers, or in small boats out to sea. That would be a nightmare not just for the authorities in Beijing — but for every reluctant host to the fleeing Chinese, from Japan to Thailand and Malaysia.

Most countries in Asia, however, discount that particular nightmare. They have confidence that China's basic Confucianist discipline will preserve stability, or at least that its introspection will keep any repercussions of instability confined within its own borders. Instead, they fear the future role of Japan. Their worries are founded in an instinctive logic: economic power cannot be separated from political power, and political power cannot be separated from military power — ergo, Japan, its bloodthirsty imperialism still fresh in Asian memories, will again impose a cruel tyranny over countries as near as South Korea and coastal China and as far away as Malaysia, Singapore, and Indonesia.

The logic is a mix of the compelling and the alarmist. What seems clear is that by the end of this century the fig leaf of General MacArthur's 'peace constitution' will be far too small to cover Japan's process of re-arming. One reason is that Japan will, quite naturally, want to protect the assets it has accumulated overseas. Would a Japanese government sit idly by if — unlikely though it may be — a revolutionary government in Indonesia nationalised Japanese subsidiaries without compensation, or put Japanese citizens on trial for 'crimes against the revolution'? At the moment, the answer is 'yes' (Japan would, instead, appeal to the Americans for help, or would try to bribe a new government with the provision — or withdrawal — of development assistance); in a decade or so, the answer could be very different. Another reason for the fig leaf's inadequacy is that in the age of the microchip the border between civilian and military technology is becoming increasingly blurred (witness Shintaro Ishihara's warning, in *The Japan That Can Say No*, that the whole military balance would change if Japan sold its microchips to the Russians instead of the Americans). A third reason is that, as this border blurs, so Japan's corporate sector will covet the high, cost-plus margins that conventionally come with defence contracts. One sign of this was the argument in the late 1980s over the FSX aircraft to renew Japan's air-force fleet: America, determined both to safeguard its technology and to reduce its trade deficit, argued that Japan should buy American planes, virtually 'off the shelf'; Mitsubishi Heavy Industries (which makes its own corporate jets and, under licence, McDonnell-Douglas F-15 fighters) wanted to build to its own design. The compromise will be a Japanese-built version of the General Dynamics' F-16 — but with a lot of its technology developed in Japan. In the short term, this will mean delving deeper into the pockets of the Japanese taxpayer; in the long term, it will give Japan's aerospace industry a product to sell abroad — and so an incentive to end the post-war ban on foreign arms sales.

But perhaps the most convincing reason to believe that Japan will want to spread political, as well as economic, influence abroad is that the Japanese themselves, ever more confident and assertive, are seeking broader horizons. The word they use is *kokusaika*, or internationalisation, and it involves everything from taking holidays in Hawaii to studying political science at Berkeley. That, of course, is the benign definition of the word: the assumption that a less insular Japan will be a friendly and helpful Japan. Sceptics offer an alternative, malign, interpretation: Japan's foreign trade, overseas investments, and foreign aid — over $50 billion to be disbursed in the five years to 1992, and much of it tightly tied to Japanese interests — add up, they say, to a creeping imperialism, a new form of the old Greater East Asia Co-Prosperity Sphere. America's dominance after World War II was based on export surpluses, excess capital, and industrial and technological superiority — precisely the qualities that Japan had as the 1990s began. True, Japan does not have the military power that characterised post-war America — but perhaps the lack is only temporary.

My personal feeling is that the sceptics are overly pessimistic: Japan's past militarism is rooted in its cultural chauvinism and *bushido* obsessions. How can such externally anti-social qualities survive the pressure of *kokusaika*, when young people travel and work abroad (there are almost 300,000 Japanese — businessmen and their families, students, government employees — stationed overseas) and realise the complexities of the world beyond Japan? Or when NHK, the state's broadcasting giant, relays foreign newscasts to Japan's television screens? Or when Japan's newspapers send educated, multilingual journalists scouring the world with a passion that now puts many of their Western counterparts to shame? Meanwhile, the economic dominance upon which the sceptics base their pessimism is starting to weaken. The capital surplus is declining, savings rates are falling, imports are rising, consumerism is everywhere — in short, the Japanese are responding to the laws of economics just like everyone else.

There is one other point that should give the fearful and the doomsayers cause to suspend judgement: for the moment, Japan clearly has no idea of what political role to play on the global stage. The forces demanding it play a constructive part are inexorable: the distribution of more development assistance than any other country; the investment of capital overseas; the bailing out of indebted America — all demand that Japan 'take a view' on the way the world should be run. But of Japan's leading politicians, only Yasuhiro Nakasone, in the second half of the 1980s, has had the vision to look beyond the myopic horizon of Japan's post-war foreign policy. It was Nakasone who committed Japan to recycling its trade surpluses in aid to developing nations rather than just in buying more of America's treasury bills; it was Nakasone who cleverly thought up the idea of diverting $2 billion specifically to encourage private sector investment (much of it, of course, with Japanese partners) in ASEAN; and most of all it was Nakasone who identified Japan as a member of 'the Western alliance' — an idea that under his predecessors would have seemed both incongruous and impossible. No wonder President Ronald Reagan called him 'Yasu' — the Japanese prime minister had become, like Margaret Thatcher, almost an honorary American.

Yet for all his high reputation abroad, Nakasone did not manage to move the LDP very far from its traditional insularity. The proof came in Japan's non-plussed reaction to the Iraqi invasion of Kuwait in August 1990. While Japan's Western allies immediately emphasised the threat to world oil supplies (especially Japan's) posed by Saddam Hussein's adventurism, most Japanese politicians viewed the invasion as something odd happening far away that could be easily ignored. China exploited the Gulf crisis as an opportunity to get post-Tiananmen concessions from America, while simultaneously posing as a champion of Third World non-alignment (hence China's abstention, but not veto, in the UN Security Council resolution authorising the use of force against Iraq). Japan, by contrast, reacted with ostrich-like indecision — its first tangible commitment to the allied effort was to send Walkman personal stereos to the troops — and so ducked the challenge to shoulder its political responsibility as the economic powerhouse of the Western alliance.

This is not to argue that Japan will never undertake the burdens of political and military responsibility — they are an inheritance of Japanese economic strength and American financial weakness that cannot be avoided. But the failure of Japanese imagination over the Gulf crisis has surely delayed that inheritance. The rest of Asia had grown used to seeing America as a spent force and Japan as the new power to be placated, and even feared. Now, America's military will-power and technological bravura has compelled a re-assessment: perhaps Uncle Sam is stronger than he looks, and perhaps Japan is weaker than anyone ever imagined.

In which case, what happens to the idea of a Japanese-dominated Asian trading group, a 'Yen Bloc'? The answer is that Japan's perceived unsureness in geo-politics will have little impact one way or the other. It will be the underlying forces of economics that create such a grouping — but those forces will work in contrary ways. The immediate impulse for such a bloc is 'defensive'. Asia looks at the free trade pact signed by the United States and Canada in 1987 (which will become an enormous North American free trade zone when Mexico joins), and it looks at the European Community's pledge to dismantle all its internal bars to trade by the end of 1992. What it sees in its more alarmist moments is the imminence of a protectionist North America and a 'Fortress Europe'. Since Asia has trade surpluses with both North America and Europe, and since the United States is the single biggest market for almost every Asian country, the alarm is natural. The European Community's anti-dumping laws and American trade weapons such as 'Super 301' could wreak havoc among Asia's exporters — and even if such weapons are not used, European and American manufacturers will doubtless lobby hard to raise hurdles to the free entry of Asian competitors into their new 'free trade' zones.

In such circumstances, an Asian bloc would be only natural — but it would be, in the trade-strategists' jargon, a 'negative sum game' in which everyone ends up a loser. The whole world has prospered because of the multilateral trade freedoms developed since the General Agreement on Tariffs and Trade was signed just after the second world war: in the quarter century between 1950 and 1975, world output rose by 220 per cent — and world trade rose by 500 per cent, which meant that more people were getting extra tastes of the growing cake of world output. It is true that the growth of both output and trade has slowed down since 1975 — but often because new restraints have been placed on trade, from 'voluntary' agreements to limit the exports of Japanese cars and microchips to complex quotas for T-shirts from Thailand and China. The underlying fact remains: free trade benefits everyone — not just the efficient producers but even the inefficient (because the 'law of comparative advantage', formulated in 1817 by the perceptive David Ricardo, gives them the chance to produce low-value products while the efficient concentrate on more valuable output).

The proof is in Asia, where the economies of Japan and the four dragons have risen from the ashes of war to be dazzling testaments to Ricardo and his predecessor, Adam Smith. Japan, China, Hong Kong, South Korea, Singapore, Taiwan: all have managed, in the years since 1945, to double their output within a single decade, and all have done it more than once. By contrast, no country — not even America and Australia in their boom periods last century — ever managed to double its output in any decade before the second world war.

It will, then, be economic folly if the world does split into an isolationist North America, Fortress Europe, and aloof Asia. Yet it is all too possible while the United States suffers annual trade deficits of over $100 billion — of which in 1990 two-fifths was caused by Japan and another fifth by Taiwan and China — and while the European Community suffers a deficit with Asia of around $25 billion a year. The need for East Asia to shed its mercantilist instincts, open up its market — including its financial markets — and rely less on exports to America is urgent.

Fortunately, the need is being met as a Yen Bloc forms for positive rather than defensive motives. The cause is the spread of Japanese investment described in Chapter Six, and the carefully structured collaboration with developing Asian nations — ASEAN in particular, but also China and India

— by which aid-bearing Japanese civil servants apportion various industries to various areas. What they have in mind is a giant master plan giving practical expression to Ricardo's law of comparative advantage: highish technology investments for Singapore; petroleum investment in Indonesia; automobile factories in Malaysia and Thailand — and all will export part of their output to Japan. The result has been so dramatic an increase in trade within Asia that very soon it will surpass trade across the Pacific. According to the Nomura Research Institute, intra-regional trade by the countries that border the western Pacific will rise from two-fifths of their total trade in 1988 to over half by the year 2000. Putting the equation another way, this means that the dragon economies of South Korea, Singapore, Hong Kong, and Taiwan will lessen their dependence on the United States from 31 per cent of their total exports to around 24 per cent — while their export dependence on Japan will rise from 12 per cent to 18 per cent.

Tomoharu Washio, of the Japan External Trade Organisation (JETRO) makes a different, but complementary, calculation: that trade will fill an 'Opportunity Triangle', with Japan, Korea, and Taiwan at its western point, the USA and Canada at its eastern point, and the ASEAN states at its southern point. He points out that while total world trade from 1980 to 1988 grew by 42.8 per cent, from $1.9 trillion to $2.7 trillion, trade within the Opportunity Triangle more than doubled, from $281 billion to $585 billion. That sort of growth implies the efficiency that comes with the free movement of goods and capital — and the implication is correct: in the second half of the 1980s, prodded by America's complaints about East Asia's 'unlevel playing fields', Japan, South Korea, and Taiwan all reduced their barriers to foreign capital and foreign goods. With luck, the fear of a Fortress Europe and a protectionist America will induce Asia not to 'get its retaliation in first' but to liberalise its economies still more.

Meanwhile, because so much trade and aid is flowing from Japan, the yen will increasingly be the obvious alternative to the American dollar. One problem for Indonesia, for example, is that much of its $53 billion or so of foreign debt is denominated in yen and will have to be repaid in yen — but its petroleum exports are tied to the American dollar. When the dollar weakens, the burden of debt servicing will obviously rise — not to mention the rise that comes when the world oil price falls. It is obviously possible, with luck and skill, to switch currencies or arrange interest-rate swaps in order to smooth out the fluctuations, but the simple solution is to use the same currency for revenues and spending. No wonder, therefore, that between 1980 and 1987 the use of the yen rose tenfold for Japan's imports (to just over a tenth of the total), and double for its exports (to just over a third of them). And no wonder that Asian central banks now hold up to a third of their reserves in yen.

But is this a 'Yen Bloc'? It depends on definition. Japan certainly leads East Asia's economies; it finances them; and, with varying degrees of subtlety, it directs them. But a true Yen Bloc would mean the use of the yen as an international reserve currency, with Japan's central bank willing to adjust its supply of yen according to the interests of its trading partners, as well as of Japan itself. That would mean exposing the value of Japan's currency — and so the interest rates and money supply policy of Japan's domestic economy — to the economic fortunes or misfortunes of other countries. The reverse side of the coin is that it would tie other Asian governments to the monetary policy of Japan, so restricting their ability to manage their economies by tinkering with interest rates and the money supply. Considering Japan's consistently low rates of inflation, that might not be a bad thing — but it is hard to see other countries readily surrendering their economic sovereignty to their war-time oppressors. Meanwhile, America's attitude is ambivalent: although the internationalisation of the yen would reduce the pressures on the dollar and be a sign that Japan was shouldering its responsibilities to the rest of the world, America would hardly like the dollar to fade from prominence. The simple truth is that while people trade in dollars they will still want dollars — which means they will still lend to America for repayment in dollars. The attendant logic of this is that America can always repay its creditors — because, if necessary, it can simply print more money.

The most likely outcome is not that an Asian bloc will form in opposition to America and Europe, but that Asia will form a set of blocs that overlap both within Asia and with the rest of the world. One reason is that the dependence on the American and European markets is permanent (and is being strengthened as the web of direct investment spreads around the globe): what is at issue in the 1990s is the reduction in the dependence to levels acceptable to all trading partners.

A second reason is that most of these blocs already exist: the ASEAN declaration was signed in Bangkok by Indonesia, Thailand, Malaysia, the Philippines, and Singapore as long ago as 8 August 1967 (Brunei joined on its independence in January, 1984); there is the UN's Economic and Social Commission for Asia and the Pacific (ESCAP), which, with 38 countries, is too unwieldly to have real force; the Indian subcontinent has its SAARC; there is the non-governmental Pacific Economic Co-operation Council, set up in 1982 to link businessmen, academics, and government officials from both the industrialised and developing nations of the Pacific; Australia dominates the South Pacific Forum and also the Cairns Group of 14 unsubsidised agricultural exporters; and Australia, anxious not be excluded from Asia and the world economy, was also the moving spirit in 1989 in forming APEC, or Asia Pacific Economic Cooperation. This group links a dozen nations circling the Pacific Rim — the ASEAN states, Australia, New Zealand, South Korea, Japan, America, and Canada. Early in 1991, Malaysia's prime minister Dr Mahathir Mohamad started arguing for yet another bloc: the East Asian Economic Group — which would be ASEAN plus China, the countries of Indochina, and South Korea.

All these combinations have their defects. ASEAN, for example, has been united only in fear of Vietnam; its members' economies are competing, not complementary. Thailand, Malaysia, Indonesia, and the Philippines all grow rubber; Indonesia and Malaysia produce petroleum; Thailand, Malaysia, and Indonesia produce tin. The result is that they all compete for outside markets and have little to sell to each other (ASEAN's preferential trading arrangements cover almost 16,000 items — but they account for less than 1 per cent of ASEAN's trade, and famously include snowploughs). The Cairns Group is an important lobby against agricultural subsidies, but has no other excuse for including Hungary along with countries such as Malaysia and Chile. APEC's flaw is that it was founded without China, Taiwan, and Hong Kong — the diplomatic challenge of reconciling the three Chinas was judged too difficult to attempt, yet their absence at APEC's birth meant the exclusion of two dragon economies and the region's biggest country. As for Dr Mahathir's idea, it smacks of a protectionist anti-Europe and anti-America sentiment — despite the good doctor's insistence that it involves merely the establishment of an Asian consensus. Certainly, it would undermine the role of APEC, which is valuable in that APEC links Asia with the Anglo-Saxon nations of the Pacific.

But if Asia's organisations all have their weaknesses, their saving grace is in the Churchillian maxim that 'jaw jaw' is better than 'war war': the more that Asians talk with each other and with the trading partners beyond Asia's borders, the less the chance that their differences will escalate into conflict. As Gorbachev pointed out in his Vladivostok speech, Asia has suffered enough since the second world war. He was referring to armed conflict — but trade conflict, as the American embargo on Vietnam has shown, can be just as damaging.

Fortunately, most of Asia's leaders realise as much (which is why they have not warmed to the Mahathir proposal, with its protectionist tinge). Economically, Asia is certain to grow stronger in the 1990s. It has a wealth of advantages: the high technology of Japan; the cheap labour of China and the Indian subcontinent; the entrepreneurial talents of the Chinese and Indian diasporas; the natural resources, from rubber and rice to oil and gas, of South-east Asia; the dynamism which comes from having young populations and growing internal markets. With good judgement and a dash of good fortune, there is no need for this collective and increasing strength to be dissipated in the 1990s by foolish trade conflicts with America and Europe.

Instead, there will be a more subtle challenge for Asia: how to adapt its personality to its changing circumstances. The countries of this book's Asia divide culturally into two: the Confucian and the non-Confucian — and the Confucian are without doubt the more successful. Japan has emerged from the nuclear clouds over Hiroshima and Nagasaki to become a civilised first among its equals in the developed world. Its literacy rate is total; it has more telephones per head of population than Britain; and its infant mortality rate (just five deaths for every thousand live births) is lower than those of France, Germany, Canada, and America; the citizens of Tokyo and Osaka enjoy a level of personal safety that New Yorkers and Washingtonians can no longer imagine, let alone remember.

Almost as advanced as Japan are Hong Kong, Singapore, Taiwan, and South Korea. Within just two generations these dragons have achieved almost full maturity; within just one generation they will be matched by Thailand, Malaysia, and perhaps even Indonesia and the Philippines, all of them countries where tinges of Confucianism help colour other social values. True, constant war, economically obtuse leaders, and the American trade embargo (which cannot be permanent), have kept Indochina in poverty. But by the end of this century, Vietnam will probably be the new favourite for direct investment from Japan, and Cambodia and Laos — now as poor as anywhere in the world — will benefit from the overspill. Even China, huge and unwieldly, can be reasonably proud of its record and of its prospects. No longer can Russia, as in the days of Stalin and Khrushchev, be a condescending older brother. Now, the average citizen of Beijing has a better living in real terms than the average Muscovite — and, barring an economic miracle in Russia, the gap will widen over the next decade.

By contrast, what can one say for the non-Confucian nations of the subcontinent? Afghanistan, Bhutan, India, Nepal, Bangladesh, and Pakistan show depressingly few signs of escaping the curses of under-development. In Bhutan, ten thousand people must share the services of just one doctor; in Nepal, each doctor serves twenty thousand; in India, out of every dozen babies one will die in infancy. Probably the best placed nation is Sri Lanka, where people are as literate as in the Philippines and Thailand, and where 'only' 20 or so babies in every thousand die in infancy — as good a rate as China's and much better than in Indonesia or the Philippines. But what chance will Sri Lanka have of giving its people true prosperity when it is so predisposed to racial violence?

There is, of course, no secret to the success of the Confucian nations. Hard work, discipline, thrift, a respect for authority, and — perhaps most of all — the instinct to put the group above the individual: these are qualities that when combined are awesome in their economic force. The obvious course for Asia's other, poorer, nations is to adopt some of these Confucian traits. India's energies would be formidable if they were not constantly dissipated in selfish, ultimately fruitless, political bickering; Filipinos, who culturally inherit many Confucian attributes, would flourish if only they could add the sense of social discipline that characterises more fundamentally Confucian societies.

But if the course is so obvious, why has it not been taken? The answer is that countries cannot simply switch their personalities at will. Indians value argument too much ever to tolerate a Lee Kuan Yew; Filipinos will not suppress their Malay sense of relaxation and their Latin love of show in order to beaver away with the relentless purpose of the Hong Kong Chinese. The better course for Asia's non-Confucians is not simply to 'Look East', as Dr Mahathir once advised his country's Malays, but to look West as well: Germany and Switzerland are proof positive that discipline and thrift are not purely Confucian characteristics; America, with the world's highest standard of living, is similar proof that material well-being is not at odds with individualism.

Meanwhile, 'Confucianism' is too simple a slogan to guarantee Asia's future well-being. China, 'a civilisation pretending to be a state' in the words of Professor Lucian Pye, is proof — for all its economic advance in the 1980s — that Confucianism is no panacea for economic and social ills. Confucian discipline and respect for authority can all too easily lead to brainwashed enthusiasm, as in China's Great Leap Forward (into famine and chaos) and Cultural Revolution, or to the collective inertia that today afflicts China's State enterprises.

Arguably, such Confucian ills occur only in nations with wrong-headed dictators — the China of Mao Zedong or the North Korea of Kim Il Sung. Japan and the dragons are surely different: their brand of Confucianism is dynamic, not lethargic. But will it be enough to secure their future beyond this century? In comparison with the successful economies of East Asia, Western nations are demonstrably lazy and ill-disciplined: their workers go on strike; their children play truant from school. In October 1990, a Toyota official in Nagoya told visiting American component makers that the parts they and their European competitors supplied to Toyota had 100 times more defects than the parts supplied by Japanese suppliers.

And yet, despite all, America and Western Europe have managed to sustain high living standards and profligate life-styles well beyond the zeniths of their power. Perhaps they are defying gravity, and are doomed eventually to fall, but in the mean time the achievement is impressive. Its explanation is only partly the accumulation of debt (that is an especially American phenomenon, is relatively recent, and, anyway, is a sign that the debtor is worth lending to). More important is the well of invention and creativity that seems to flow without pause in the Hellenistic and Judaeo-Christian cultures of the West. Families in the slums of Harlem have refrigerators and colour televisions — because others in America are somehow so inventive and dynamic that the wealth they create trickles down to even the lowest levels of America's chaotic and bloodthirsty society. A Dutch psychologist, Geert Hofstede, used IBM's work-force around the world to rank forty different cultures according to their individualism. The top five were America, Australia, Britain, Canada, and Holland, all of them sustaining high living standards despite industrial mayhem and falling educational standards; predictably, East Asia's nations were way down the ranking.

That should worry them. It will take more than consensus and discipline, the great strengths of East Asia, to solve problems such as population growth and pollution. It will take also the individualism and enterprise that led Marco Polo, Magellan, and Cook to explore the Orient, and which has been relatively so absent in the countries of Confucianism. Just as the West needs to adopt the practices of the East, so Asia will have to absorb some of the essence of the argumentative, aggressive, individually motivated West. Without that individualism, Asia will stumble under the burden of global leadership which, some day, it must assume from a tiring America; it will fail to create the wealth that makes solutions possible for complex economic problems or unforeseen political emergencies. That would be a sad outcome for an area which has just produced half a century of the most explosive economic growth the world has ever experienced.

But why should it happen? As their nation grows richer, so young Japanese are becoming more like their Western counterparts, and less like their elders. So, too, are the young in Singapore and Hong Kong. Later, other nations will breed similar generations, more inquiring and more adventurous than their elders. Travel through Asia and its difficulties soon become apparent, but so does its potential — and, most importantly, so does its confidence. Asia's flying geese still have the wind beneath their wings and clear skies ahead.

Index